MW01293038

Thug Mentality Exposed

Ephesians 5:11

California Gang Members
Speak Out From Prison

Essays and Photos
from a Correctional Counselor
Rayford L. Johnson

THUGEXPOSED.ORG PUBLISHING

Copyright © 2007 by Npaphoto.com

Thug Mentality Exposed
Out of Darkness Into the Light
by Rayford L. Johnson

Printed in the United States of America

All rights reserved solely by the author. The author guarantees all contents are original and do not infringe upon the legal rights of any other person or work. No part of this book may be reproduced in any form without the permission of the author. The views expressed in this book are not necessarily those of the publisher.

Unless otherwise indicated, Bible quotations are taken from the New International version. Copyright © 1995-2007 Gospel Communications International by Zondervan Christian Publishing

TABLE OF CONTENTS

Author's Note

In summary, this book's mission is to bring awareness of how eastern Babylonian paganism has integrated and reinvented itself in the various cultures of today. Again, I just utilized the thug culture as a platform, due to that being my field of expertise, and where God revealed to me a lot of the information contained in this book.

Once spiritual awareness is obtained, then hopefully people will become aware that in order to be delivered from this addictive culture, they must first obtain some deep-rooted knowledge about it. After knowledge is acquired, Godly wisdom is required in order to correctly apply it. Then once knowledge and wisdom have brought forth salvation and deliverance through the spiritual truth of Jesus Christ, an individual has then been commissioned by God to take up the mission of rescuing the prisoners of war (p.o.w.) who are captive to sin and heading into eternal damnation. Many Christians believe this is an option. It is not; it is a commandment by God!

Matthew 28:19

19 Therefore go and make disciples of all nations, baptizing them in the name of the Father and of the Son and of the Holy Spirit,

My prayer for you who are reading this, is that you apply the principals contained in this book to strengthen your spirit in Jesus Christ so that your life will be blessed and anointed. Prayer, reading God's Word and Obedience is key in order to clearly understand and accomplish God's mission for your life. The Christian life, when lived out in obedience to God's Word is an exciting, adventurous and rewarding life. There is no better time than right now to get started with your mission.

The author would also like to express that the testimonials from the wards have also been kept as closely written to their original manuscripts.

Both the following versions of the bible, The King James and New International, were referred to during the writing of this book.

Dedication

This book is dedicated to the memory of my father, Campbell C. Johnson Jr., who taught me by example, by role modeling what it means to be a real Christian man- by illustrating what he taught.   He demonstrated, to me, how to walk in unselfish and true "agape" love and how to have a joyful, positive outlook on life, regardless of life's challenges. He was a man who put God first then his wife – my beautiful loving mother – and family and he always had a loving word of encouragement for us. He was a man of great compassion, with the gift of sacrificial giving at the drop of a hat. When I strayed away from God in my younger years, God used his example to stir my conscience and make me feel accountable, which eventually led me back in fellowship with my Lord and Savior Jesus Christ. I am forever thankful and blessed to have had the father I had, and this book is a token of that appreciation.

I would also like to thank my entire family, my wife Kay, daughter, mother, all of my sisters and my brother and two brother in-laws who gave me Godly advice in order to keep me on the path which God had intended for me.

Also my pastor, Dr. Darnell Thomas of Showers of Blessings and my church family, who have mentored me, and taught me practical ways in living a victorious Christian life. I also would like to thank my former pastor, Phillip G. Goudeaux of Calvary Christian Center and the church family there, who trained me up in Godly values at a critical time in my youth. Goudeaux also taught me the meaning of faith.

I would like to thank Dr. William H. Lee, publisher of the Observer Newspaper and the whole Observer family. I thank Dr. Lee for giving me my first opportunity as a photojournalist and for believing in me and his words of wisdom and encouragement throughout the years.

I would also like to thank the following people for their contributions: Samuel Iniguez (Editor), Robert J. Maryland (Author Portrait), Ebers Garcia (Graphics), Genoa Barrow (Editor) and ThugExposed.Org.

Introduction:

I started writing this book more than seven years ago, while working at N.A Chaderjian, Youth Correction Facility, where thug mentality is alive and well and violence was a regular daily occurrence. Being a thug behind these barbwire fences for many is not a badge of shame, it's a badge of honor.

Why? Because thug mentality is a mental weapon they used on the streets, to intimidate others, and to obtain the nerve to carry out some of the most heinous and vicious crimes imaginable upon their street rivals and the innocent victims within their community, with little or no conscience at all. This book will discuss how this mentality is cultivated and why it continues to be embraced.

Thug mentality has crept its way into society's households because it's not easily identified as some might think. It is often masked as "just a fad," and it has a trendy, cool face to it. One can go to most malls and at the athletic and youthful clothing stores they'll find playing on multiple television sets: gangster rap or hard-core rock videos. Fortune 500 corporations are cashing in on the gangster image, which is spreading this thug mentality like wild fire around this nation and world.

This mentality is not just associated with rap and rock music, but with many styles of music. It's a mentality that is programming new values and beliefs in our society, which in turn is creating new destructive behaviors and cultures. In the thug culture, rebellious and criminal behavior is not only tolerable, but also encouraged. Individuals who commit crimes such as assault, robbery, rape and even murder are often looked upon as heroic.

Getting locked-up is now a 'badge of honor'. Going to prison is like getting a scholarship to a prestigious university in the thug culture. An example of this is infamous gangsta rapper, X-Raided. His album sales and popularity have soared nationwide since he was locked up over 10 years ago for murder. To date, he has made over 10 albums utilizing prison phones for a recording studio and has sold more than 400,000 copies.

What do these astronomical sales figures say? It shows this is a widely supported and thriving culture. "Gangsta" music is now outselling every other type of music. What does that say about the overall values of our society when the "gangsta" entertainment industry, has risen to be one of the most profitable?

Meanwhile, society wonders why gang membership is soaring in our communities; it's because thug mentality makes gangs look attractive, because those who embrace thug mentality often want to legitimize their "thug", by "keeping it real." Gangs offer that perfect avenue for those individuals, in that they offer an exciting role that is perfectly "gangsta," Hollywood scripted, to live out a thug's fantasy. Thug Mentality is not bias to just the lower income "hoods" or ghettos, it is thriving in every economic class from city to city.

Growing up in my community, many of my close friends and peers had extensive criminal records, joined gangs, and a number of them were shot and even killed. Two very close friends of mine were murdered growing up: one in a gang-related drive-by shooting, another was killed right in front of the house I grew up in. The latter was murdered after an on-going verbal feud with a hardened x-con from down the street erupted in gunfire in the early morning hours, which left my childhood best friend with a fatal gun blast wound to the abdomen. The shooter was a career criminal with a long prison record. I hear more tragic stories from time to time about the peers I grew up with. Recently, I found out one was killed in a shoot out with police, and another was killed in a gang-related home invasion, in which he was the invader. One was stabbed to death in a dispute in front of a pizza parlor. Another who has been in and out of correctional facilities all his life is now a nationally known millionaire gangsta rapper, and a few of my former peers are now pursuing their gangsta rap careers. Also another childhood friend is in prison with a life sentence for a gang-related killing. Another is using a cane after he was sprayed by gunfire. An extreme situation is also a peer that has to urinate using a plastic bag after he was shot in the groin area in a gang-related incident.

The area I grew up in was a nice mixed ethnic middle class neighborhood in South Sacramento. We played little league; some of us were in the scouts and some of our families went to church on a regular basis. What happened in this nice middle class neighborhood? Thug Mentality happened. It planted its poisonous seeds through its music. I was there to see it grow for years, as I saw the hearts of fairly innocent, good hearted kids, grow cold and hardened during the gangsta rap era in the mid and late 1980's.

Gangster rap was the manual and doctrine for what was "cool." The artists gradually became our role models. It was simple: they had money, fame, women and respect, and we wanted it too. My conscience without me realizing it, started gradually becoming desensitized to the immoral messages being preached to me through the music, and after a period of time, I became tolerant of it, even craving to hear it.

It was very liberating music, listening to someone put out the message that they didn't care and didn't have to listen to anyone but themselves and have people admire them for it. As I was getting older, life was becoming more stressful, due to all the rules and responsibilities that were being loaded on me in the process of preparing for adulthood. The thug life appeared simple, exciting and carefree to all of us.

Did I become a hardened criminal? No. Were all my friends corrupted by gangsta rap? No, as a matter of fact, some of them went on to be very successful and are now giving back to their community in various ways. I didn't do drugs based on talks with my mom, who would on a regular basis point out to me two individuals on our street who had done marijuana laced with a foreign substance, which made them insane and gave them permanent brain damage. I still thank my mother for those talks, because that was the most powerful deterrent for me, to never do drugs. It wasn't because I was so good; because I wasn't. It was truly because I was too scared to try them. My late father was also a solid deterrent for me, in that he was great role model, who I will always have deep respect for. My parents lived-out God's Word in our house all the time; it was virtually impossible for me to develop a hard-core mentality no matter how hard I might have tried, because it was the Word of God being preached and lived in my home, keeping my conscience alive. Thanks to Godly parents, the Word of God eventually won the battle for my heart, not thug mentality. I'm also grateful for my sisters and brother and brother-in laws who believed in me, and helped me back on the right track when I was starting to fall off.

I was compelled by the Holy Spirit to write this book for the ones who are going through life aimlessly, to help them find God's mission for their life. The Bible states *"where there is no vision the people perish"* (Proverbs 29:18). I wanted to put everything in this book that I wish I would have known or applied while I was growing up. I did not write this book to be judgmental, because I know I'm far from perfect, but to challenge the destructive beliefs that are shaping and molding the mentalities and cultures within our world.

The lessons I have learned from the wards that I counseled over the years have been priceless. A little over 7 years ago I told the wards at the correctional facility where I worked that I was going to write a book and that I would need their input. I conducted countless anonymous interviews and received quotes and stories that would help society and my self better understand their views about life. I also let them know that their stories could possibly help many youth who were heading toward the same road they went down. Contrary to popular belief, there is a great amount of pain behind the masks, mixed with some remorse and empathy. Many volunteered enthusiastically, feeling that their story was an offering or atonement for their past sins. Their interviews, you will read, and you will hear a lot of hurt, anger, malice and lack of remorse for the sins they've committed. However, the majority, I believe, deep down inside, know that their stories might reach and deter a hurting or naïve youth from heading down a destructive path full of painful regrets, prison time, or death.

From the numerous interviews, many which are not contained in this book, I have learned to be more effective in relating to them as well as to countless others. I have discovered that true wisdom and knowledge can come from just humbling yourself and listening to others. Many intellectuals and texts claim they know the thug mentality, but I have learned that every individual has their own unique story about why they have come to embrace the thug culture.

I will be forever grateful to the youth within the California Youth Authority(CYA) who have shared their stories with me. For their protection, privacy and per legal counsel, the wards will remain anonymous and I have edited out certain specifics within their quotes and stories, along with blocking out recognizable faces in the photographs.

4

Is Education the Key?

As a photojournalist for over 20 years, I have attended countless forums on youth issues revolving around gangs, crime, drugs, teen pregnancy, unemployment and the escalating high school drop out rate (30% and growing). "Education is the key!" I've heard over and over. "Knowledge is power!" I agree, but I also know that power given into the wrong hands can be very dangerous. For example, when I look at the music moguls who have been heading up the thug mentality culture such as Russell Simmons, Ice Cube, Snoop Dogg, P-Diddy, Master P, Jay Z and others, these are not only Hip Hop artists, they are shrewd intelligent business men. They are educated and full of knowledge, which has given them the power to influence millions to embrace the thug culture at the same time allowing them to profit beyond most people's wildest dreams. They are not just investing in music, but numerous other profitable industries. They have inspired countless youth to obtain knowledge in owning their own businesses. Though owning a business is a good thing, their message can inspire youth to obtain knowledge for the purpose to achieve the power to obtain and operate their own "gangsta dynasty" to be idolized and feared by others for their "mafia-type" mannerisms. Speaking of using knowledge and creating business ventures, the Thug Movement has gained so much mainstream popularity that they even have named a number of energy drinks in honor of the culture. One is named "Hyphy Juice" which is named after the Hyphy Movement, which will be discussed later on in this book. This drink is endorsed by gangsta rapper Too Short. Then there's"Crunk Juice"(East Coast version of Hyphy) introduced by the Crunk Movement's founder, gangsta rapper, Lil Jon.

The other energy drink is called "Pimp Juice" which is promoted by gangsta rapper Nelly. A pimp is like a decorated war hero in the thug culture. Many of the music industry's songs pay homage to pimps. Ice-T even has a CD, which is a step-by-step manual on how to be a pimp, with real legendary pimps narrating throughout the recording. I mentioned this drink to a church youth group, and to my surprise, the majority were familiar with it. A few gave me their opinion on the taste of it. Notorious Gangsta Rapper 50 Cent even has his own mineral water called Formula 50, which has global distribution.

The entrepreneur message is clearly present in many of these artists' songs, movies and music videos. I often hear it from the wards on our unit. Many talk about how they want to make or produce a rap album, own a record label, invest in real-estate and other businesses to build their own "gangsta empire". Though I am an advocate of entrepreneurship, absent is the foundation of morality in the way it is promoted in the thug culture. Is this the type of power we want our youth to have? Power which will lead them and others down a path of self-destruction? Think about all those who are in prison and are buried in graveyards that were inspired and manipulated by the knowledge of these elite gangsta artists to live out the thug culture to the fullest.

Make no mistake, I am a strong advocate for education and vocational training. Do I feel it is a cure all for the Thug Mentality epidemic? No. Let me tell you why! Thug Mentality is truly a spiritual issue. This issue has to be dealt with spiritually, before it can be dealt with in the natural state. It is the spiritual realm which controls the natural realm, not the other way around. God has the antidote in His Word, as I will go on to explain in this book. In order to do so, this Book is presented in four parts:

The first segment-_Awareness_: will explain the social issues and impact of Thug Mentality and its core beliefs. How it's been hidden as just a "trend" and the horrific consequences, both natural and spiritual, it will have on those whom embrace it.

The second segment –_Knowledge:_ will discuss the ancient history behind thug mentality and its deep spiritual roots. I will discuss an awareness on how this mentality is being propagated through its music and culture, and the spiritual purpose behind it.

The third segment-_Wisdom:_ will discuss the only answer to this deadly epidemic, and how to know God's perfect will and purpose for your life.

The fourth segment-_Mission:_ will discuss how to discern and utilize your God given gifts and talents. This, along with the previous three principles will allow you to take action on the deadly thug mentality epidemic.

I.

"Prison Thug Culture"

Prison Culture

When people ask me about my career as a correctional counselor, many believe that I sit behind a desk in a nice office and summon a guard for my next counseling appointment. My duties as a correctional counselor have a much wider scope than that. To illustrate, let me explain what happened just two days ago. I was conducting a routine room search looking for weapons and gang related contraband for our gang intelligence unit, when suddenly I heard a commotion. I quickly exited the cell, and observed a ward who just picked his handcuffs and evaded a correctional officer's grasp come racing down the stairs from the second tier. He comes down yelling his gang name, pumped up in a rage, swinging his cuffs as a weapon. He attacks a worker (fellow ward) before being maced by another officer. I then push him off the worker, but he runs under the stairwell. I take chase after him, catching up to him and restraining him to the ground, before we are both fogged by a powerful chemical agent called Z505, released by another officer. Nearly two hours later, after I have finally washed the intense burning from my eyes and face, I have to physically push back another ward that attempts to barge out of a secured recreation cage. A few cages down, another ward refuses to give back his cuffs, angry that he has been denied a cage recreation mate. The ward has recently been placed on independent status and is a sure target for his former fellow gang members. We perceive he wants to set up a fight, to get some of his respect back for being dropped from his gang or, as they say in Y.A., being placed on "leva" status, or "out the car." As I walk back inside the unit, both my fellow officers and I are being verbally abused by angry inmates on both the top and bottom tier, who are demanding to get into the one shaving cage, which also serves as a phone booth, to either shave or use the phone for their monthly phone call. We have incident reports to write, and there are still many who need a shower, along with one more meal that still needs to be delivered through the tray slot in their door. As I'm looking for wards that still need their shower, other wards are demanding a one-on-one counseling session with me. Moments later, I hear what sounds like Niagara Falls. The ward that I restrained earlier has just flooded his room with water by clogging his toilet. Water is flowing down from the second tier to the first tiers and into the cells of other inmates, and down the hallway on the top tier. The wards on the unit are now yelling and demanding to have their cell decontaminated, yelling for their food and others are still yelling for a shave, a telephone call or a shower. I glance upstairs at Niagara Falls, make eye contact with one of my fellow officers and just laugh under my breath, as I often do to relieve stress – trying to find the humorous side of every issue in order to keep my sanity. But as I stand there trying to laugh off the stress, we also have other wards holding their cell tray slots open, in protest of one thing or another. There are only 3 officers on the floor, including myself and one is outside on the caged recreation yard, still negotiating with that inmate to give up his cuffs.

Meanwhile, the Lieutenant has been called, and they send back-up security to help us start pulling out wards in order to have the cells cleaned and disinfected. These wards are the most violent in the institution, with an extensive history of assaulting other wards and peace officers. As we escort one inmate in full restraints to the phone and shaving cage, who just the day before had rushed out his room to attack a worker, he begins to demand another cell. There are not many cells available, due to the fact that many of the fixtures or toilets have been broken by angry inmates. After his room is cleaned and disinfected by inmate workers from another unit, he states, "fu*# that, I'm posting up (Refusing to move), I want a clean room." The duty Lt. then warns the ward that they will deploy the pepper ball launcher on him(which contains hard plastic balls filled with pepper ball gas) if he fails to comply. He screams a mouthful of obscenities towards the Lt. and security and then indicates he's ready for whatever they have for him. For many of these inmates, getting pepper ball scars is a way to obtain status for themselves and their gang. There is word on the unit that an Asian ward took 20 pepper ball shots. Attempting to compete, this inmate tears his shirt, then makes a turban and a mask and begins to hit his chest like King Kong, yelling out his gang name, as other wards from his gang cheer him on by banging on the door – some advising him "don't go out!", while rival gang members advise him to "break your life down." When it's all over, he walks proudly to the MTA (medical technician) for medical attention before being taken back to his cell, having taken 7 pepper ball shots – 13 short of the record.

After a very long hour, we are finally able to secure him in his cell. I turn to my right and notice that a third of the dayroom floor is under water, including our Youth Correctional Counselor's office. I turn again to my fellow officer and laughingly smile in an attempt to lighten the mood. When I turn back around, security is shaking their heads, wondering what issue to attack next: the ward who had busted out of his cuffs or the ward who took the pepper ball rounds. The other wards become even more frustrated and angry, still demanding what they want. Meanwhile, it's institutional count time. However, we are unable to clear count, due to the wards refusing to take the towels down from their cell windows. Others are plastering paper to their windows, so we are unable to see inside.

Finally, their meal is served, leading to more tray slots being held hostage, more hails of verbal abuse coming from the unit, and new demands - now we have a group demanding that the radio be turned on. A verbal battle between numerous wards commences, some demanding the oldie's station; while the opposition is R & B. The radio will not be turned on due to the chaos. The refusal escalates the already frustrated wards who are now even more angry because all the water has been turned off due to the flooding: the whole dorm is on water management program, which mandates only one flush and one drink of water every half hour. Meanwhile, we have a program (recreational period), or group of inmates to retrieve from outside, and we have word that the two gang members associated, along with the two who caused the earlier incident, are refusing to take it down to their cell. The reason is because one of them has refused to have his cuffs checked, so we can assure that they are double cuffed. Just two days ago, we had to restrain this ward in shackles after he exhibited hostile and aggressive behavior towards staff. A cell extraction is about to proceed, so the video camera comes out, and the wards begin yelling their monikers and gang names to the camera, excited about being taped. In the interim, we are escorting other wards into the unit, attempting to avoid the terrain of floodwater. Many of them are becoming angry, believing that someone else's "piss water" has saturated their cell. The dorm's volume has escalated a couple of notches, because the wards now realize the lateness of the hour, and know many will now be unable to shower, shave or use the phone. A half hour passes; the two-gang members in cage #2 finally comply before the pepper ball launcher is deployed again. They are taken in the shower to be held temporarily until their room has been disinfected. To this point, I have been on the unit for roughly 15 hours and 30 minutes, which is not unusual. Many times we are forced to stay due to staff shortage, but today I'm working a 16-hour shift because of a shift swap. We have made a little dent in the floodwaters: numerous officers are on the unit assisting and supervising the wards on the clean-up team. At 2210 hours, the Lt. tells me that I'm released to go home, since by law I can't go on to work the 17th hour. My co-workers look and smile at me in envy, knowing that they're being held over for an under determined amount of hours. Tomorrow at 0600 hours, less than 8 hours away, I will report back to the unit again, working off of less than 6 hours of sleep due to my hour commute, with reports to write, and individual counseling sessions to attend to. Days like these are not uncommon: sometimes they include riots, gassings (feces and urine thrown on staff), attempted suicides, and staff assaults.

You ask, "Do I like my job?" To be honest, I love my job. Days like this are not every day, and there are many inmates that have a true desire to change. They just need the right tools, and it is my job as a counselor to provide them. I believe that this is my God-given purpose. Therefore, it brings me joy and satisfaction, even in the heart of the trials and tribulations that occur.

Ward stories:

<u>"My Crazy Life"</u>

As I was growing up as a young teenager it was very hard for me to understand what was right from wrong. But as I was becoming a young man, I started to realize my mistakes were very wrong. As I was growing up, my mom and dad use to tell me to do good and stay in school and do something good with my life. But during that time I started to get more involved into gangs and going to parties so I didn't care what my parents told me. Every time my parents told me to do good or was telling me not to go out at nights with my homeboys to parties. I would ignore their wishes and whenever they told me these things I would sit there and listen to them give me their advice but it would go through one ear and out the other. I was being very ignorant and didn't want to listen to no one's advice but one day I started to realize and regret everything I was doing and knew I was in the wrong. I wasn't thinking about the consequences of my actions I was doing. I didn't really care because I use to tell myself I would never get caught up and go to jail or anything.

I wanted to do what I wanted to do when ever I did it, I didn't care. I use to love going to parties when ever there was one popping off some where. I would go with my homeboys a lot and things turn out to be fun and I thought all parties were going to be fun for me. My parents didn't like me leaving the house at night and going to parties, but I didn't care. I still went anyway. One day my homegirl called me up on the phone and asked me if I wanted to go to a party with her. She also told me there is going to be a lot of girls there so that caught my attention so I said yes, but not knowing who is going to be there and who is throwing the party. I didn't think of it. So my homegirl came and picked me up and we both left together. When we got there it looked to me like it was going to be a fun party. We both went into the house and right away I started talking to the girls because that was my type of thing. I started to dance with some girls when this guy came up to me. I didn't know who he was.

I was trying to figure who he was because he looked like someone I knew from my past. Then all of a sudden he started introducing me to some other guys that were there at the party. Then he took me to the other side of the living room where there was not much people dancing and he hit me in the face. I kinda fell back a little bit then I caught my balance and I started to fight back. Then I noticed that he was an enemy from a different gang.

A lot of the girls and people that was there started to get scared and left. I was trying my hardest to self defend myself until other guys jump in on me then I started to tell myself I wasn't going to win. I was getting jumped so bad I blacked out. All I remember is waking up the next day in the hospital. I had to stay the night in the hospital for three days until they let me go home. I was hurt very bad. My face and my head looked like a smashed pumpkin. When I went home my homegirl paid me a visit to tell me how sorry she was but I told her it wasn't her fault. She sat there and told me all about that night and details about what happened to me that night. She told me she thought I was going to die and she was very scared. I didn't blame her for nothing because I wanted to go.

The following week I had a lot of time to think about my actions. I sat there at home and started to realize a lot of the bad choices I was making. Me getting jumped at that party had a big impact on my life and made me think twice. I finally realized I was in the wrong for going to the party and I should of took my parents advice and stayed home. Being ignorant didn't get me anywhere. I know that there are a lot of teenagers out there that don't like to listen to their parents, but what does it have to take to open up their eyes to see how dangerous things can get. How come something bad has to happen to get your attention and find out the hard way while you can stop now and think twice about your life and what you're doing? You don't need a wake up call because next time it might be too late.

"Why I stay in this crip life."

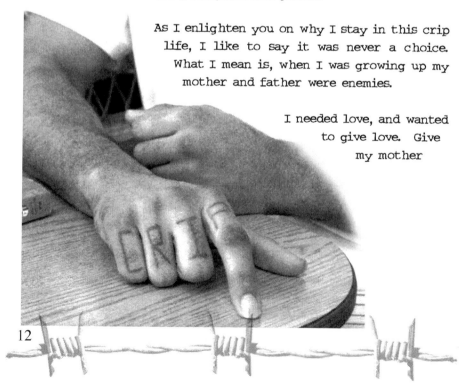

As I enlighten you on why I stay in this crip life, I like to say it was never a choice. What I mean is, when I was growing up my mother and father were enemies.

I needed love, and wanted to give love. Give my mother

love, my father will hate me. Give father love, mother will hate me. That is what I thought. So I gave the homies love and that gave me love.

I led a lot of kids into negative behaviors cause I knew they looked up to me and that I could get them to do the things I wanted, because they seen me as an idol.

"I don't feel that hurting people is right but I don't think that it is wrong."

No one understands me. How could they when I don't even understand myself.

I am afraid of the unknown, a lot of other people should feel the same if they knew not only what I am capable of doing, but what I plan to do. If they did know they would have me put to death. After I am deceased they would take my brain and examine it to try to understand what God has created. As sad as that fact may be, I am not sad. In fact I hope that after I pass away there is someone to examine my brain. Then people would come to understand that maybe this is not my fault. Maybe God has made another mistake. God created Satan once, could it be that he made the same mistake or a similar one? I hope so. Why? We'll then my actions would be justified that I was not given the freedom of will. My fate was preordained. If that is the case then I can commit any deed that my heart may desire and know that no matter what I do, I will be damned to hell.

The signs of a monster were present from day one, but nobody took the time to look, but like I said before I am not like any other. I wasn't molested as a child, I never tortured any animals, I wasn't an abused child. All of the signs were still there. The hallucinations, the hearing of voices, being placed in mental institutions numerous times for a variety of reasons, all have something to do with the other some how.

I like seeing people in pain, in a lot or in a little, it really doesn't matter to me. It doesn't matter if I am the one inflicting the pain or not, just as long as you are in pain. Age is of no importance nor is race, religion, or what the situation.

13

You might be wondering what the person has gone through to make him into what he is not. I can answer that question with one word, nothing. But I know it is hard for the brain to assimilate that, so lets take it into further detail. Why do I like seeing people in pain and when was the first time that I realized that I do? I like seeing people in pain because it is exciting. To see, read or hear somebody being tortured ignites something inside of me that captures my attention. I don't feel that hurting people is right, but I don't think that it is wrong. I think that it is just part of life.

I first realized that I was different five years ago but it goes back further than that. Five years ago was just the point where I was like I am not like any of those around me.
As I began to read a lot of fictional books that were suspenseful, horrific and things of that nature about five years ago. I read about people being tortured, mutilated, raped, molested, kidnapped, shot down, and I began to think that I would like to do some of these things. I've already hurt people in the past, but the books were talking about taking it to a new level. Within time I began to fantasize about some of the things that I wanted to do. It almost became an obsession.

People ask me about my spiritual aspects concerning the things that I plan to do. I believe there is only one god. I believe in heaven and hell. I believe everyone will be held accountable for their actions. But like I said before, my destiny might have already have been written and there is nothing that I can do to change that. I kind of feel the earth is preparing some of us for hell. In a sense earth is hell. We now live in a place where kids are killed by the one that brought them into this earth. We have best friends murdering one another. We have mother and father having sexual relations with their own children. All of that and that is barely the tip of the iceberg. I feel that hell can't be too much more worse than earth already is.

I also practice hedonism; I pursue this belief as a way of life. I am infatuated with worldly possessions, big houses, fancy cars, women, jewelry, name brand clothes, yachts and foreign places drive me. I want all of the finer things in life. One only has one life to live while on this earth, so why not make the best of it? There is always hell. To think about it, I am not afraid to go to hell. Don't get me wrong. I don't want to go but these worldly possessions have too much of a hold on me. I feel that hell may be my final destination anyway so why not indulge. Unlike why I like seeing people in pain, my wanting all of the finer things in life has reasons. The most prominent reason being that as a child I came from the slums, surrounded by bums. Even though my mom did the best that she could do, it was still bad. Wearing third generation hand me downs, eating cereal with sugar water, sharing our apartment with roaches and mice. Even though I got used to living that way, I could never accept the fact that I would one day raise my family the same way. As I began to grow older, I slowly but surely began to think there was a way for me to live in luxury but I had to be willing to take risks. At first it started off with little petty things, but it soon escalated to bigger and better things. And as the prizes began to get bigger, so did the risks. I have committed robberies, burglaries, g.t.a's, assaults and batteries. I sold drugs; I got to the point where I wanted money by all means necessary. On numerous occasions I had to put my body through pain in order to obtain what I desired. I not only had to hurt myself, but I had to hurt others. It didn't and still doesn't matter. It's a must that I survive at any cost. As of now we live in a world where it is survival of the fittest it is a must that you must be fit to survive. I proved that I can survive and I will continue to do so until I no longer breathe. When I die, that is when I will stop doing what I feel I must do. And it is then and only then I will stop doing what I want to do and plan to do.

"I put my family in danger."

I joined the barrio because it runs in the family. That's all I know, the gang lifestyle was no problem for me. I breathe it and lived it. The only thing I don't like about gangs is homeboys passing away, so soon, yes, by me joining the gang I put my family in danger, but they already done that before my time. I just added a little piece to the cake, my pro was excitement and the power. The cons, are early death, and return to jail or prison.

"I have about 2 female relatives that are real killers."

I am a known member of the most ruthless blood street gang in Compton, California. My whole family are gang members from the same gang I represent. My uncles, aunties, my dad and a few blood cousins are deeply involved in blood gang activity.

I have about 2 female relatives that are real killers and will take the life of a person without any remorse. The 2 of them are from the --Street -- blood street gang.-which is on --th---th --------Street and -------Street. I myself witnessed these two relatives in a drive by shooting trying to get ------- a rival gang of -------. The oldest out my two relatives got shot to death in ----------, California on ----- Avenue and ---th between --------- and ------------. She was being chased by some rival ------- and they started shooting at the car and my relative took two in the back and they came straight out her heart and now she's dead and her lil sister is following her footsteps killing people, robbing, stealing and the bad thing is she has a 1 year old baby girl. She takes good care of her daughter but her daughter can easily be killed as an innocent bystander and in a walk up or a drive by shooting and she has about 25 murders under her belt and I'm not just talking, I swear it's the truth. But it's not a right choice to keep bang'in the only reward is death or prison time, but it's up to you to make that choice as for me I can't stop, won't stop, I'm gonna bang till my heart stop beating. I don't believe in nothing but this street life and if you really a dedicated crip or blood keep bangin, I'm out.

"What am I thinking about the fact that I'm getting out?"

Well as you know I've been incarcerated going on ten years coming the 24th of this month(November) 200,. I got arrested at the age of 14 for a gang related shooting and am currently 6 months away from my release back to society. What am I thinking? To be honest I have been thinking of the many circumstances I can be placed in that will result in criminal prosecution and interfere with my release. Beyond that, I'm thinking about how I should conduct myself out there. I have good adaptability skills, but in my mind it's like "well in order to adapt I have to observe the conduct of others". I think this observational period might affect how others view me and also if I just go out there being myself then people might think", Damn being locked up fu**ed this guy up. Other things that are on my mind about being released are-1. jobs 2. housing 3. schooling 4. family/friend relationships. First of all, I've never held a real job so I don't have any job skills. CYA hasn't been able to provide me the skills on how to acquire a job, maintain it, nor did they train me in any trade. So knowing that I'm going out there with absolutely no job skills whatsoever has me thinking, "fu*&%, I got to sell drugs or rob people to make some money to get by in life." Believe me, I don't want to resort to this and I will exhaust all avenues before I do resort to it, but this is my reality here. This is what I know how to do by nature. Now, housing, I know where I'll be staying in Fresno. I plan to stay there with my sister. The reason I'm choosing to move there is to remove myself from the criminal and gang activity which is present there in -------. I know a lot of people there who I'll feel obligated to kick it with if they're around. This is going to end up getting me back into the same activities I engaged in before I got arrested, so to minimize my chances, I'll stay out in Fresno where I can meet new people with better interests in life. Now what I am worried about is me having to be dependent on my sister for housing. I do not want to be a burden on her in any way. I know her doors are open and I'm welcomed to stay at her house but I'll be 25 years old I need a house of my own. Now schooling since my incarceration I haven't been able to so much as obtain a G.E.D. or High School Diploma so that is one of my priorities to receive either one. I understand that any educational level can and will affect what kind of jobs I'll be available for so I'm wanting to work on my schooling and go to college if possible. I'm thinking of trying to earn a degree in business management and theology, but I'm open to change. What ever grabs my interest and has an opportunity for me I'll jump on that first. It's all stepping stones in my eyes. I love to learn so even If I don't end up going to college believe me it is not going to stop me from learning at all. Now family and friend relationships, this is like the biggest damn thing I think about. I don't really have any affection for none of my family members, they are some what strangers we have never been real close to my remembrance. And since I've been locked up they haven't been here for me in respects to emotional or financial support so I always think about how it is going to be to socialize with them, are we going to get along? Are we going to be at each others throats? See the thing is I can get along with anyone but there's these miserable people that I just can't stand to be around they're so lousy that they want you to be lousy with them and some of my family and friends are like that. Friends, since I'm moving out to Fresno I really won't have too many of them back, but I think about how what they do may affect me. If they use drugs am I going to end up using (I don't have a drug problem) If they run into problems with other gang members am I going to back them up? The thing is, I know I'll back up my friends, family at the expense of my life and since I want to live a long life I worry about this type of stuff. What else? Well I think about all the food I want to eat, places I want to visit, women I want to marry, things I want to learn (languages, histories, religions, etc..) All in all I just think about striving to live a happy successful and prosperous life without disruptions, but since this is life on earth, I face reality, life is going to have a lot of bitterness. Well brother Ray, this is all I have for you.

"I was raised in the church"

I was raised in the church and on a daily basis my family preached to me, but I was so infatuated and drawn to that impure lifestyle: I ceased to listen to anything my loved ones said. Now through my journey of incarceration has not only made me wake up to the realization of the world, but has given me a chance to unfold and break these negative flaws, that seems to bound me. I came a long ways, but still have so far to go.

Say you have a daughter right, you believe in being strict. You don't let her talk to boys on the phone, and when she's about to go out you be all overprotective, making her feel that you don't trust her. 9 times out of ten she's going to feel like she can't come to talk to you whether it's about boys, sex, gangs, and peer pressure. Naturally she is going to be curious, wanting to explore these things and probably end up caught up having a baby, joining a gang or having some type of STD. All because her parents wanted to hide things like there's no such things as boys, sex, STD's, thinking they could protect their little girl from all this corruption of today. What a parent should have done was taken her to a library, read about diseases, show her them pictures of what can happen when you have unprotected sex. She might get the idea that you low key letting her have permission to have sex. So what you do is let her know you're against it from the start, but also let her know you can't be there 24 7 to watch her every move, but it's her body and her decision. Explain as much about it as you can. Let her know the ball is in her court now. After you have that heart to heart talk no matter the situation she will always have trust to come talk to ya'll.

"I lost my freedom for them."

I could see that being in the gang made my mom and dad start to care and I saw it as a way to get the attention I wanted. But the bad part to being in the gang was I had to watch my back and sacrifice a lot of things. I would do bad things to win their acceptance. I lost my freedom for them and my life is always in danger, even now, I'm in danger and I quit. It follows you for the rest of your life. I also learned quick that once you tell your own homies you don't want to gang bang anymore they think your weak or they may respect it. I don't want to show my kids the wrong thing. I am their role model and if I ain't got values, they won't either. You need to have values and goals and your kids learn from their parents. I know the only thing a gang is going to get me is dead or in prison, and believe me - I don't want that. I have goals and plans.

"My life is not the way it's supposed to be."

I'm not sure how to put this. My life is not the way it's supposed to be. I've suffered trials and tribulations of an unprohibited thug. I thought that life on the streets of Stockton was such a beauty. Never and forever will I ever want to leave them, but at the age of 18, I understand much of what life has to offer.

My mother is not in the picture and hates the way I lead my life. I can't blame her. I don't even know if my pops is alive, but I really don't care. If I understand nothing more than I do now, I will survive, unless I realize there is something much more, something much different, that I can take and get on a smoother road.

To keep it real, I don't want that road. I've chosen this life over

19

that. The gangsterism of my vicious ways resembles some of my past life. Something I will never forget. To the rest of the world or the "norm society", I and the rest of my street family shall forever be outcasts. We shall never fit in.

My time has been spent in the "Y" (Youth Authority) because of crimes that I did commit and I am very proud of them. You say I am crazy, but am I? I just keep it real. I'm not gonna lie, I love what I do and what I'm about. Beatings, slanging, bangin: it is all a part of something so beautiful in my eyes, which to y'all is filthy.

To people that know me, they shall always love me. To people who hate me, they shall always hate me. But the weak will always feel my wrath. Not weak physically, but in your mind. To play you like chess is what I thrive on. To play you is to gain my life, but I'm the most loyal person out there. This is me, this is my life.

You're stepping into something that might seem shallow, but it isn't. Gangsterism and thugism is a whole different thing. I'm ruthless in all activities because of this. The system and streets made me. At least they made me slowly over time. I would have to laugh if I said they didn't help me on my way to uncaringness. It is like drunken debauchery.

I'm not insane, but it is funny. What is sane? What people understand hurts them, do them harm or it can do the exact opposite and they can thrive from it. For all you that don't understand, you're safe.

Look in my eyes one time please, pleasure runs quite frequently in them, but it is the pleasure that I want. When I started this "thug life," it was because I was poor and now it's because I've grown to love this. I still ain't got it all and probably will never be hella rich, "but I still love this sh#%."!

Can you handle this? Maybe. Can you handle time? Maybe. I know I can. I ain't never gonna change. Like I said, "I love this sh*t! The penitentiary is just the down fall. Are you ready motha fuc*as?!! Cause I am. So lets do this and see who stands last. Cause I ain't going out. I keep it gangsta.

Mr. Soldier.

"Getting out the Gang"

Well I started wanting to gang bang because when I was younger, I say about 11 or 12, I seen the respect and money ,well, all the good parts of the lifestyle my cousin lived. And being that me and my cousin shared a room together, I looked up to him; I wanted to be like him. He was my role model. So I started off by always wearing the color red and smoking mari-juana, running the streets with my cousin and the fellas who were older than me so my mentality started changing. I started breaking the law first, it started small stuff like stealing cans to stealing cars and carrying handguns. Well at the age of 14 I was put into the system, group homes, etc. I never stayed in the places they sent me to, because I would rather be on the streets with my boys for the hood, Lokos. I was getting bad, I started smoking crank and robbing people. My own family was scared of me: they didn't want anything to do with me. Well finally the law caught up to me and sentenced me to the Youth Authority for a burglary, well when I came here to YA I found out the reason why I started banging was not the right reason. But the real reason is something I agreed on and fully dedicated myself to the (gang). I sacrificed my PCD's (parole consideration date) and my family for a cause that I believe in. We'll after 2 years of sacrificing my eyes were finally opened and seen these guys in here don't function the way the teachings are said to function. So I decided to step away from the fake and look forward to the future with my family and try to be something in life. This gang banging life ain't what people think it is. I still believe the reason why it started was for a good reason , but that reason is long gone and people need to start realizing that and get on with their life. Because these people who call you their homie really ain't your homie.

Because when you are not a part of them they want to start talking crap about you and to you. But when you are right there putting it down with these guys you're their bro and all that stuff. But as soon as you separate yourself all that changes. I seen that before I stepped back and that helped me make my decision because I don't want to be apart of nothing fake and that is going to keep me from being someone in life. I would rather have no respect and no money then to be fake with all that. Those are my reasons why

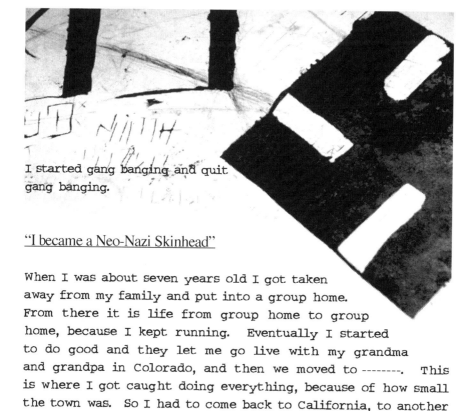

I started gang banging and quit gang banging.

"I became a Neo-Nazi Skinhead"

When I was about seven years old I got taken away from my family and put into a group home. From there it is life from group home to group home, because I kept running. Eventually I started to do good and they let me go live with my grandma and grandpa in Colorado, and then we moved to --------. This is where I got caught doing everything, because of how small the town was. So I had to come back to California, to another group home. I ran and came up north to stay with my mom in Modesto, where I was born.

This is where I became a Neo-Nazi Skinhead. It started when one of my uncles got out of prison and seen me walking down the road. He pulled over and asked why I'm acting something I'm not. "Be white, be yourself," well I got involved in robbing houses and I was going out with a woman that was 12 years older then I was. I was 13 at the time. I got another chance, but then I screwed that up, I then got committed to the Youth Authority on January 1-, 200- and this is where it mostly all happened at me being White Power. I got labeled as SWP, so I said hell with it and followed through with it. I was at OH (O.H. Youth Correctional Facility) and everybody looked up to me, because I acted a lot older and so I thought I had to act the macho look, and that got me to Chad, were I was influenced even more. I was reading nonstop about our cause and stuff about our ancestors, the stuff that they have accomplished for us and how we were letting it get taken away from us so easily.

To wrap this up, I am still known and involved with White Power Movements. I am a Neo Nazi Skinhead known as "--------". I follow the name too, but I'm changing slowly but surely. I still have my beliefs, but I carry them out in a different way.

II.

The Thug Culture & it's Ancient Pagan Roots?
The Spiritual Ingredients of a Thug

People sometimes ask me when I'm teaching on this topic, why do you have to bring religion into it? Through my research over the years I have discovered, that every component of Thug Mentality is religious, even the name "thug" itself. Believe it or not, all of it has its roots in Bible history. It is impossible to deal with this subject effectively, without dealing with it from a spiritual level. To do otherwise, would be just plucking the fruit and leaving the root.

I do not ask my caseloads any more when they plan to get out of their gang. I now ask them "when are you going to come out of that religious cult?"

Thug Culture a Cult?

After researching the history of the dark Babylonian arts, it is evident that street gangs possess and practice everything a typical pagan cult does.

Let me explain: The definition of an occult is: *relating to, involving, or typical of the supposed supernatural, magic, or witch craft.*

Lets first look at some of the cultic practices that were done in ancient Babylon:

* Drugs
* Human Sacrifices
* Tattooing
* Sexual Perversion
* Cursing
* Musical Worship

* Dancing (a form of worship)
* Chanting
* Painting Symbols (graffiti)

How many similarities do you see between these acts of the occult and those of the street gang? The music industry has become the street cult's supreme guru and church. This music has created a cult of millions of thug "wannabes."

What is a Cult and where do Cults come from?

The question I'm often asked is where did all these religions and gods come from and how do I know which one is the true one? Well if you believe the Holy Bible, (*which later on in this book I will present to you undeniable proof why the Bible is the most supernatural and accurate book ever created.*) and do your research, you will discover that you can trace all the foreign gods such as Tao (*Taoism-Yin and Yang, associated with martial arts, Yoga, Feng Shui and Tai Chi*), the numerous Hindu gods such as Kali, Shiva, Greek gods such as Zeus, Amitra, and even the Muslim god Allah, back to ancient pagan worship, dating to Babylon B.C. as described in the book of Genesis of the Old Testament.

Bruce Lee, the deceased legendary martial artist writes (*Bruce Lee's Wisdom for Daily Living*):
On unity with Tao-A personal experience: "I lay on the boat and felt that I had united with Tao; I had become one with nature."

In his book, *Tao of Jeet Kune Do*: He writes:
"The spirit is no doubt the controlling agent of our existence. This invisible seat controls every moment in whatever situation arises. It is thus, to be extremely freedom never "stopping" in any place at any moment, preserve this state of spiritual freedom and non attachment as soon as you assure the fighting stance. Be 'master of the house.'"

Entertainment is one of the biggest catalysts of the occult, because entertainment molds the culture within our communities. We have Harry Potter, which has inspired countless youth to experiment and engage in witchcraft and the occult. Why? Because the youth are eagerly looking for something powerful, real and supernatural to solve life's problems and bring excitement and purpose into their lives.

The Disney series *"That's so Raven"* is a show about a young hip girl with psychic abilities, which she utilizes to navigate herself and others magically out of life's problems. The Bible defines this as witchcraft. Jesus' disciples casted out a fortune telling demon out of a girl in the New Testament book of Acts.

Criss Angel, a modern day warlock, who dresses and looks like a rock star, has his own show on the Discovery Channel, where he demonstrates his black magic every week. In one episode he walks on water, in another he walks straight through glass.

But where did this cultic worship start? The Holy Bible brings light on this in the Book of Genesis, in the Garden of Eden. Believe it or not, but many of the cult legends and beliefs validate accounts of the Garden of Eden and the Tower of Babel.

My brother-in law who is a missionary trainer told me of a friend he had who went to do mission work in a primitive village in Africa. When he began to tell the tribe about the biblical story of Babylon, how the people had begun to build the Tower of Babel, he noticed the tribal members became very attentive. Once he had finished telling the story, one of the elders of the tribe (through a translator), told him that the story of Babel had been passed down to their tribe for centuries, and that his ancestors where involved in that monumental construction project. This tribe was so primitive that they had no written language, and had never heard or been told about the Holy Bible until the missionary spoke of it.

In many of these occults throughout the world, they pay homage to the snake or serpent as a sign of wisdom. Let me give you a little background on the serpent from a cultic perspective. One of the Babylonian gods named Asherah, in which the Israelites of the Old Testament in their disobedience built Altars to called "high places"(where perverted sexual rituals were performed under) believed that it was Asherah's snake that enlightened Eve to eat the fruit of the Tree of Knowledge so she could be empowered and be like God. A satanist on my unit told me he believed likewise. Many religions such as the ancient Mayans and voodoo tribes also paid homage to the serpent.

It was Satan, the serpent, which first isolated and convinced Eve to eat from the forbidden fruit. Satan tempted her by making her believe that he would reveal to her a powerful secret. A secret that he said would empower her to be like God. The temptation was so great for Eve, that she disobeyed God's divine order of Adam as headship over the home, and asserted herself to make this tragic decision herself, which Adam followed. This was the first recorded act of feminism (1 Timothy 2:14).

Satan's great secret was "sin", and steadily through out the years he cleverly crafted sin within man-made religion. Once Eve took part of the fruit of the Tree of Knowledge and gave it to her husband Adam, Satan's secret would be revealed for all mankind. Satan had a diabolical plan to get man to meet their fate in the eternal lake of fire, just like he and his demons would. Satan had been ejected out of Heaven, for the treason he committed against Almighty God as the head angel. Lucifer, which he was known at the time as, was found with the sin of pride in his heart. He desired to place his throne over God. He wanted to be like God. The Holy Bible makes it very clear that Satan's main objective and mission is to be worshiped, whether directly or indirectly. We see this in scripture when Satan attempted to get Jesus to worship him in the desert during the 40-day fast. The Bible describes how Satan set up temples so people would sacrifice to his demons which indirectly gave him worship, because he is the king of the demonic under world. All false gods and religions are creations of Satan, therefore the worship of them, is the worship of Satan.

1 Corinthians 10:20 *No, but the sacrifices of pagans are offered to demons, not to God, and I do not want you to be participants with demons.*

1 Corinthians 10:21 Y*ou cannot drink the cup of the Lord and the cup of demons too; you cannot have a part in both the Lord's table and the table of demons.*

1 Timothy 4:1 [Instructions to Timothy] *The Spirit clearly says that in later times some will abandon the faith and follow deceiving spirits and things taught by demons.*

Revelation 9:20 *The rest of mankind that were not killed by these plagues still did not repent of the work of their hands; they did not stop worshiping demons, and idols of gold, silver, bronze, stone and wood—idols that cannot see or hear or walk.*

Revelation 16:14 *They are spirits of demons performing miraculous signs, and they go out to the kings of the whole world, to gather them for the battle on the great day of God Almighty.*

This is the culture of thug mentality. The music these artists create is all about worship and glorification unto themselves. Through their talents, they have obtained followers who worship and idolize them, known as fans. Hip Hop artists Jay Z and 50 Cent are now doing Reebok commercials, in which the slogan is "I Am, What I Am", a quote from God in Exodus 3:14. This is what the Hip Hop culture is teaching, to be your own god. The Hip Hop culture and the thug culture are synonymous in that they are one in the same.

Kimora Lee Simmons, the wife of Hip Hop Mogul Russell Simmons writes in her new book:

"I am a goddess and my body is my temple."

Back to the story, Satan in his bitterness for being casted out of heaven wanted revenge, knowing he was no match for his creator. Satan and his demons planned to attack God indirectly, by deceiving man, because they hated God, and anything that resembled his image and man was made in God's own image, so Satan's goal is to deceive mankind to qualify them for eternal damnation.

Genesis 1:27

27 So God created man in his own image, in the image of God he created him; male and female he created them.

So what was Satan's secret? After Adam and Eve broke God's commandment, they were evicted out of the Garden of Eden. The Tree of Life, which was beside the Tree of Knowledge, was protected so they could not eat it and live forever. The consequence of their sin was death both physical and spiritual (eternal damnation which meant total separation from God for eternity) along with the curses of life (sickness, famine, toiling of the land, etc...). After the eviction from the Garden of Eden, man was sent into a cursed world, full of famine, disease, danger and excruciating hard labor. Man needed help. God still stretched out his hand to man with sacrificial rituals, however man was looking for something easy, which would tantalize the flesh and give them supernatural power (magic, witchcraft, divination, sorcery) over their problems and over others, along with giving them pride and the belief that they were too divine and in control (like a god or goddess).

Satan offered quick spiritual solutions to man, in that he introduced new substitute gods to man. Knowing man had the innate desire to worship God, Satan fabricated a host of counterfeit gods to be worshiped, through rituals which catered to man's sinful natures of pride, sexual perversion, drug use(sorcery) among others, and in return he promised to bless them, by relieving some of the curse put on them by God. Satan gave them hope that through the rituals to those gods, that they too could promote to become a god or goddess status (common belief of cults).

To be successful at this plan, Satan carefully crafted cultures which met man's fleshly desires. The acts of all the rituals to the gods had to be sinful. That's how Satan finally got what he wanted. And what was that? He finally obtained worship by getting man to perform sinful rituals to the false gods he created which were dedicated to himself. In doing this, Satan was also able to hurt God's heart. He knew that God's Word stated that the price of sin was death, not just natural, but spiritual death in the spiritual is hell first, than the lake of fire. What better way to get back at God, than to deceive and send the very ones that God sent His Son Jesus to die for, to eternal damnation?

These religious cultures created by Satan became known as the occult. The next segment will enlighten you on how these very pagan rituals from Babylon are blatantly and covertly embedded not only in thug mentality, but many of the cultures in America and have been since this country's infancy.

Satan has covertly infiltrated our society with cultic elements since the birth of this country, but that's a whole other book I'm currently working on. But to give you a little preview, for starters, the woman portrayed on the Statue of Liberty is the pagan goddess Ishtar and the woman on the California Seal is the pagan goddess Minerva. The Washington Monument is modeled after a pagan obelisk (used in sexual perverted rituals which included homosexuality to the gods and goddesses). It was and is still used in pagan societies to worship the pagan gods of Baal. Pagan symbols such as the pyramid, and the "all seeing eye"on our one-dollar bill, are all elements of witchcraft. January, March, Saturday, Sunday, Jupiter, Mercury are not just days, months, planets and cars, these are the names of ancient pagan gods and goddesses which have covertly crept into our society and have embedded themselves into our culture. The Statue of Liberty is the great harlot talked about in Revelations (Chapter 17). It is a replica of the goddess Ishtar- a consort or companion of Ashera, the goddess that King Solomon was guilty of offering sacrifices to in the Old Testament.

In the medical field, we have the ancient physician Hippocrates(460 BC-380 BC), the Greek physician known as the father of medicine, who instructed his students in astrology, saying, "He who does not understand astrology is not a doctor but a fool." Each of the astrological signs (along with the Sun, Moon, and planets) are associated with different parts of the human body. Also, many natural herbals are referred to as being under the influence of a planet.

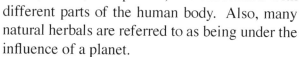

The common "medical" symbol used by organizations is of a short rod entwined by two snakes and capped by a pair of wings, which represents the caduceus or magic wand of the Greek god Hermes (Roman Mercury), messenger of the gods, originator of incantations (magic), conductor of the dead and guardian of thieves and merchants. This is a segment of one of the versions of the Hippocratic Oath which medical doctors take in this country even up today:

"I swear by Apollo Physician, by Asclepius, by Health, by Heal-all, and by all the gods and goddesses, making them witnesses, that I will carry out, according to my ability and judgment, this oath and this indenture."

So does this mean we shouldn't respect America and its government? Of course not, in the gospels, Jesus paid taxes to the pagan government in his day and even instructed others to do like wise. He stated; *"give Caesar what's Caesar's and to God what's God's"* (Matthew 22:21). In the book of Romans, God's Word tells us to respect the governing authorities.

Romans 13:1

1 Everyone must submit himself to the governing authorities, for there is no authority except that which God has established. The authorities that exist have been established by God.

Does this mean these pagan symbols and cultures are okay with God? By no means, there is a spiritual consequence to everything done in the natural world. That is the reason why the crime and immorality are at an all time high. The seeds of these sins were planted at this country's infancy.   Yes, this country was founded on Christian principles, however the truth is it was also founded on many pagan ones too. Some of the founding "Christian fathers," were Free Masons, which mixed Christianity with paganism. The Masons if you do your research are a modern day extension from Cabalism.

Cabalism was one of the dark arts, learned and practiced by the Israelites when they were held captive in Egypt. When the Catholic Church was being formed in the 3rd Century, there were secret groups that held on to the dark secrets of Cabalism at the same time attempting to hold on to some elements of Christianity. This doctrine evolved into the Gnostic gospels, which mixed sexual ritual, goddess worship and elements of the Bible's New Testament together. They rejected the God of the Old Testament, because they blamed him from trying to keep back the knowledge in the Garden of Eden. The Gnostic gospels are the whole foundation in which the Da Vinci Code is based on. The Gnostic gospels were not admitted into the Holy Bible, because of their blasphemous doctrine and the fact they were written 150 to 300 years after the events they were testifying of. The writers of the New Testament were there at the time of the events and there were many witnesses to testify for them, such as the Roman historian Josephus.

Although America is known as a Christian nation, the fact remains it was also built upon many pagan beliefs. Think about it? How else do you think a nation could cultivate and condone such sinful acts such as: slavery, racism, abortion, and homosexuality among others. Though America is not alone, the paganism epidemic has spread like a cancer through governments through out the world, starting from the first structure of government in Mesopotamia B.C.

Know your Enemy

God tells us not to be unaware of Satan's schemes (2 Corinthians 2:11). We all have the same enemy; his name is Satan or the devil. Any war general will tell you, that in order to effectively fight your enemy you must know his schemes. Many are indulging in pagan cultures and worship to these false gods unknowingly, yet because of the spiritual laws in place; some are reaping the same consequences of those who do it knowingly. The Bible says my people perish for a lack of knowledge (Hosea 4:6) Satan is continuously looking for willing vessels (bodies) which will open themselves up to worshipping his many false gods and their cultures directly or indirectly. This is all designed to plant sinful desires within, in order to do his (Satan) will. Again, his goal is to direct you down a path of self-destruction to eternal damnation.

Hyphy Movement Culture

I was talking to two wards a couple of weeks ago from the Bay Area, and they informed me about a new cultural movement that with the help modern satellite technology is spreading world-wide fast. It's a movement called the Hyphy Movement. When I asked the wards what the movement was about, they all gave me similar answers such as: "You Go stupid, dumb, retarded." Then they told me about a ritual of the movement called Thizz'n, which is about taking "E-Pills"(Ecstasy drug/along with misc. drugs capsulated within). I'll let them tell it to you in their own words:

"Sometimes I thizz, Sometime I shroom, But whatever I do. I stay a tycoon!"

The hyphy movement is basically us niggaz from the ghetto throughout the Bay Area really dancing and functioning in the streetz, mostly hanging out of cans while the doors are open. Sometimes it gets out of hand due to katz coming from other cities and towns not knowing about the movement and trying to fit in and fall victim in this movement.

Going hyphy: Is not ever said, going dumm! Going dumm is shaking your dreads, hair period. If you aint got none, shaking your head wil do while hitting your turf dance. While going 18, which is another word used for getting hyphy in the Bay Area, we worship the music we listen to because most of the sh** we done did, or listen to because of the beat or simply cause the rapper's from our "stable" which means our town city or block. We go dumm mostly off a thizzle, which is also called Stunnaz, E Thaz and Ex. The pill for most , gets us comfortable enough to dance, even sometimes for some it helps them drive better. This is the movement in the bay area that every child, teenager and adults is in some (way) affiliated with. We get drunk, not really pissy drunk, but enough to know whats going on around you, but enough to hang out our scraper'z and yell out our blacks that were in to each other. A scraper is a car by the name of a Buick in the year of the middle 80s to the late 90s. These cars are called scrappers because the dubz we put on them rub and scrape up against the fender and (make) a scrape like sound. We have side shows which is where niggaz from everywhere, mostly Oakland, come together on a strip in the town and start swanging and scraping our cars in circles. The cleanest cars, trucks, wagons, even vans on dubz profiling in front of hella niggaz.
We even got this hyphy movement with cars called the hyphy train. That's all cars from the side show and cars that was just watching form a long line and paint the town from like 9:00 p.m. to 5:00 p.m. Painting the town is going from the east to the west and from the west to the north. Remember going dumm, going crazy, and aint listening is the same. Dancin drunk hella high off grapes which is purple weed that is the best weed out since "lite." This is truly a movement in the Bay.

All day, everyday, you'll find someone in any kind of car profiling in and out of lanes "gassin" and or "braken." We

highspeed from the police 'cause most of us aint got licenses and we call that "taking them on one," basically a long drive without giving up to the law. You learn more from listening to these rappers .keak da sneak, e 40, Mac Dre, The Team, Federation and yes the famous youngster from North Oakland FxAxBx.
Use this information to build this hyphy movement we got going not knock our foundation we're creating. Thizz nation! Go Dumm, Go Stupid. S.T.U.P.I.D.

"FUNCTIONS"

A function is a social affair. A function is a place where a bunch of niggas as well as females go to have a good time. I would say the bigger percent of people that go to these functions are young black males from the ages 13 to 32 and usually are in some way or the other involved in the fast life, you know pimping, murder, dope game type sh@% and at the end of a lot of functions, things tend to get ugly. So my advice is if you are scared, then go to church. But yeah, there are all types of functions; for example, a rave is a sort of function. This is more of a middle class type of affair, where anything's goes sex, drugs whatever. White people usually throw raves but in the Bay us dudes don't discriminate, if its poppin' then we are there and at most of the raves I've been to, you had to pay to get in but you got free e pills (ecstasy), as much as you can take and its open sex, you see people fu%#ing a little bit of everywhere. But that is a sort of function. But the functions I tend to go to, with me being in the dope game lifestyle, are a little different. In Oakland that's all we do is get money, fu%# and have fun. The type of functions we go to are side shows, concerts, and block parties. Me and my niggas have even turned high school basketball or football events into a function. Me and my rowdy as# partners would just get on the side line and get real loud and hyphy and pump the crowd up until everyone is going dumb. Here is a quote from a Bay Area rapper Mac Dre:

"'We go S.T.U.P.I.D. when we go to the club we don't need I.D. everywhere we go it's a party y'all and we go get it crackin like the mardi gras we go stupid...''

That's real as fu%#, that's all we do, and everyday of my life when I was free was action packed but yeah, a side show is a function where a bunch of guys come together at a known rendezvous point with clean, fast cars and start hittin' donuts, then other cars come and join in and onlookers comes to look and pretty soon you have a function with a bunch of hyphy dudes and gangs of females and music. These side shows go on for hours and word spreads quick that one is going on so pretty soon it's a lot of different people from different turfs, cities or spots and that's why it gets ugly toward the end. The lil' function usually gets broken up by gunfire, but hey, who am I to complain. probably one of the dudes doing the shooting. But yeah, like I said a function is a social affair where dudes get hyphy, go dumb and thizz all at the same time, so the functions I attend, with me being from the Bay are an everyday thing.

Quote: "We thizz super sick with it we is super sick with it Hey scrapa scrapa filled up with the ripper's purple purple gone off that liquor."

And if you want to know more about the functions, then go to one.

Let me give you a little background on the spiritual origin of this movement. The movement is based on the worship of the Greek god Dionysus. The followers of Dionysus believed that he was the presence that possessed a craving within man that desires to "let itself go" and to "give itself over" to their lusts and passions, in other words "anything goes". Dionysus was known as the spirit of unbridled passion which meant they appeased this god by giving into the most sinful desires, with no willful restraint. Dionysus's companion was Pan the demon god of sexuality and lust, also of music (there are numerous Hollywood Artists who pay homage to Pan for the spiritual gift of music).

The most celebrated guru of this Pan movement was Aleister Crowley (1875-1947). Crowley was a faithful worshiper of Pan. He had his "Hymn to Pan" read at his funeral: " I rave and I rape and I rip and I rend Everlasting world without end!" Crowley had a significant impact on the music industry, especially rock & roll, which later evolved into heavy metal.

Ozzy Osbourne called Crowley "a phenomenon of his time"

35

(Circus, Aug. 26, 1980, p. 26). Ozzy even had a song called "Mr. Crowley." "You fooled all the people with magic, You waited on Satan's call Mr. Crowley, won't you ride my white horse"

Iron Maiden lead singer Bruce Dickinson said: "we've referred to things like the tarot and ideas of people like Aleister Crowley" (Circus, Aug. 31, 1984). Their song "The Number of the Beast" said, "666, the number of the beast 666, the one for you and me."

Marilyn Manson has a song entitled: "Misery Machine" the lyrics say, "We're gonna ride to the abbey of Thelema." The Abbey of Thelema was the temple of Satanist Aleister Crowley.

Crowley, who was also a Freemason, died a heroin addict. His last words were "I am perplexed (confused)."

This demon Pan was known to rival up other demons on earth to cause chaos, which came to be known as pandemonium. There are many cultic tribes throughout the world who worship Dionysus. Just like in going "Hyphy", which the movement states means going "dumb and stupid", the worshipers of Dionysus are no different. The Greeks "going dumb" rituals escalated from getting drunk and "high", to orgies, rape, incest, murder and even cannibalism to the point to where they ate their victims alive, both human and animals, all for the purpose of giving praise and worship to Dionysus. Think these horrific behaviors are foreign to the Hip Hop thug industry? Think again, there is now a song by a very popular gangsta rap artist named "Brotha Lynch Hung" who has a song about cannibalism entitled, "The Return of the Baby Killa", the song is about his fetish for eating babies. A ward on our unit had the rapper's lyrics written down on paper in his cell. I discovered it during a cell search. "When I questioned him and his peers about the song", they all gave the artist and the song high ratings. One of the individuals stated that it made him fantasize about doing cannibalism. These are the seeds that are being planted in this generation. Think music doesn't have this power? Listen to one of the artist's from Bone Thugs and Harmony boast about their influence on this nation:

Quote from the website: (www.bonethugsnharmony.com)
"It's basically what we've been trying to organize ever since

we came out," Krayzie says of the mission for the group's new album. "We wanted to have a following of a whole lot of thugs and if you listen to what is going on in the industry today, that's all people are talking about and claiming to be, thugs. You haven't heard nothing about gangsters. We were trying to create a Thug World Order that we'd be running. We aren't finished with it yet."

This group has sold more than 15 million albums and has won a Grammy.

Tattooing

Tattooing is quickly becoming a fast growing ritual in the thug culture. Many get them to show society their allegiance to the thug life. There was a time when a person would usually have to take off their shirt or roll up their sleeves to show off their tattoos, but now the growing trend is to have tattoos printed on blatant parts of the body, such as the hands, wrist, neck and even face. This has become a harmful and even deadly trap magnet for many, especially gang members who tattoo their gang or disrespectful slogans about their rivals on these areas of their body.

This week I was talking with a ward who just recently placed "Fu@# It" on his eye lids, he also had "666" (mark of the beast) on the back of his shaved head. Another had "Fu%# the World" on the front of his neck. When I asked the first one why he did it, he stated, "because, I don't give a fu#%", and then smiled in a deviant manner.

These gangs and thug-related tattoos build up major obstacles for these incarcerated individuals when they attempt to break back into the job market after they are released. Often after they experience the rejection from the appearance of their bold tattoos, many violators have conveyed to me that

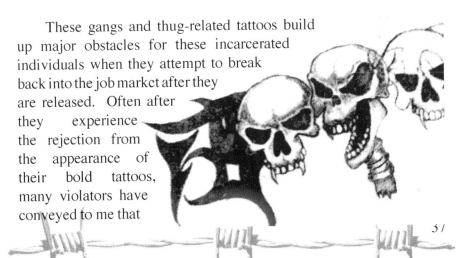

they felt justified to turn back into a life of crime, which often led them into a state of hopelessness and depression, which opened the door to walk back into the thug life where they felt loved and accepted.

As I have stated earlier, thug mentality is all about intimidation, because the culture's belief is that intimidation is power and power creates respect. What better way to put intimidation in others than putting obscene, bold artwork and scary words all over your body for others to see? Putting their gang name on them is to convey that they have no fear and that they are willing to take on any challenge placed before them. Tattooing evil pictures and words such as snakes, demons, skeletons and guns is often a defense mechanism, to convey to others that they have an evil nature within so beware it's the same concept as of a "Beware of Dog" sign.

The person that tattoos their body like this also knows that people know that this is not normal behavior and that they will appear to look crazy or insane to the public which is their objective. Why? The majority of people in society fear crazy people, because they can be violent and unpredictable. They know insane and crazy people intimidate those in society, so if they appear that way, than in their eyes they obtain immediate power and respect from others. Criminals believe it makes it a lot easier when committing crimes on their victims because fear and intimidation is present by the mere appearance of their tattoos.

Intimidation is the philosophy which is consistent in all aspects of the thug culture such as the thug attire (gang-related, sagging pants), jeweled teeth grills, excessive piercings, bizarre hairstyles or shaved heads along with the playing of loud and obscene music. It's all about "shock value", because the belief is, that shock presents automatic fear and intimidation.

History of Tattooing

Again, we can look back into the past and see that tattooing was a spiritual art form, which derived from eastern religions in pagan societies such as Babylon. Many people ignorantly are rushing to tattoo parlors selecting any piece of artwork that looks "cool" or "cute", not knowing the spiritual background and harmful consequence that the artwork or words might have on their life. God said, *"Ye shall not make any cuttings in your flesh for the dead, nor print any marks upon you: I am the LORD"* (Leviticus 19:28). God said this because tattooing was a spiritual ritual of worship to the many false gods in the pagan culture. In the 10 Commandments, God said, *"Thou shalt have no other gods before me"* (Exodus 20:3). For not following these commandments, the consequence would be curses. A spiritual ritual to pagan gods is witchcraft also known as sorcery. This is detestable to God. Listen to God's thoughts on this practice:

"Let no one be found among you who sacrifices his son or daughter in the fire, who practices divination or sorcery, interprets omens, engages in witchcraft, or casts spells, or who is a medium or spiritist or who consults the dead. Anyone who does these things is detestable to the LORD, and because of these detestable practices the LORD your God will drive out those nations before you" (Deuteronomy 18:10-12).

This is God's spiritual law, tattooing is a direct violation of His commandment. He didn't just make this commandment to be controlling, he made it because he loves us, and wants to protect us from the evil spirits (demons).

In the occult, tattoos were utilized as a way to open the portal of the soul to channel in spirits (which were demonic). In other words, a tattoo is a door to the soul. Specific tattoos were utilized for various purposes. Such as if a cult member wanted protection, he would get a tattoo of a warrior god or would get a tattoo put on them of a wild animal to channel the nature and fighting skills of the creature. If they were sick, they would get a tattoo of a healing god, believing they would be healed. In some cults, it is a common belief that after an individual dies, tattoos will help them be recognized in the after life. Believing that the spiritual guides can lead them to their divine destination without tattoos, they believe you will be lost in the after life wandering around restlessly.

In Hawaii, they even have tattoo priests and temples that assist individuals in obtaining what they believe to be the appropriate tattoos for the person's needs and spiritual development.

The occult also believes that the pain they endure from the tattooing and piercings are taken up as a sacrifice to the gods, in which they will be rewarded for enduring it. Much of the drawings, symbols and line-design patterns in these tattoo shops are of the occult, they are utilized to summon spirits. This means the original creator of the artwork received the inspiration through sorcery and divination for spiritual purposes. It is impossible to separate the artwork from the curse, because they are one in the same. Many people have the Yin and Yang (black and white symbol) tattoo which is associated with yoga, tai chi and martial arts. This is a symbol of the pagan god Tao, which its believers say split into Yin and Yang and controls the earth with the five elements of nature. They believe that success and harmony in life comes from controlling the energy from the elements called "Chi". This is done through breathing techniques, crystals and yoga exercises among other things. Some satanists will get a pentagram print. Later ,in this book, I will tell the story of two wards who were in a cell of former satanists which had sketched a pentagram into the cell floor. At night, these two wards stated that demons would come out of the pentagram and torment them with fear. Take notice that though these wards did not make the pentagram, they were still tormented by being in the midst of its presence, because the artwork was satanically ordained as a door to the demonic spirit world. How many individuals have been duped into getting tattoo prints on them which have opened a demonic spiritual door into their soul? Tattoos are a form of sorcery (communication with evil spirits) which gives worship whether intentional or unintentional to pagan gods, which is giving glory to Satan.

Recently, I was viewing a documentary on television on the various cultural practices of tattooing. It had footage of monks in Thailand conducting a massive religious ceremony for the intent to ignite and recharge the spiritual tattoos of the cult members. During the ceremony, over 200 tattooed individuals became spiritually possessed by the spirit of the images tattooed on them, which they referred to as deities. I watched in amazement as these grown men went ballistic running uncontrollably in an unorthodox manner like wild beasts. Those who had animal tattoos on them were acting out in the nature of the animal. A cult member with a snake tattoo on him fell to the ground violently and started slithering on the ground, one with a tiger tattoo begin roaring like a lion with his hands in the air like claws and then started to run and jump like the beast.

When a member of the documentary team interviewed the cult members, they reported that they had been taken over by a spirit against their will. This tattoo ritual practice is not just practiced in Thailand. It is widely practiced throughout the world and has been for thousands of years, having its origin in cultic witchcraft and slavery. Just as slave owners in ancient times marked their slaves, tattooing has been a way Satan has marked individuals as slaves to his sin, the demons being their under-masters.

What to do if you have Tattoos:

- Ask God for deliverance from any curses and evil spirits associated with your tattoos. A prayer of deliverance is on page:262
- Get them removed. There are non-profit organizations which offer grants for individuals to get gang-related tattoos removed for free. I heard one minister state that he was believing for God to supernaturally remove tattoos for those who wanted to be delivered from them. I believe this too. I myself have been supernaturally healed so I am a true believer of miracles. The Holy Bible says: "Nothing is impossible with God" (Luke 1:37).

Profanity/Cursing

Ever wonder why we have a desire at times to curse, to say sinful things that are out of context or literally don't make sense grammatically in what we are attempting to communicate at the time? Cursing is a sinful act, which Satan uses to curse the curser. Cursing is an old witchcraft art form. It was used for the intent to speak out destruction and spells overs someone. However, throughout the years, Satan has slickly embedded cursing into many individuals day to day vocabulary. People curse for different reasons; such as to fit in, to emphasis their argument, to intimidate or to be merely comical. The Holy Bible says: *"life and death are in the power of the tongue"* (Proverbs 18:21).

As I said, individuals curse for different reasons; however, the curse words associated with their statements don't make grammatical sense. Cursing is a desire which Satan attempts to place in an individual to spew out sinful taboo words, which are fecal, sexual, malicious or sacrilegious in nature. For spewing out these abominations, there are real spiritual consequences. God says in His word that we will be held accountable for every idle word on Judgement Day we say (Matthew 12:36). Bottom line, cursing is sin, and God's Word says that the price of sin is death. The Word also says that God will not be mocked; a man will reap what he sows. When a person recklessly speaks forth curse words whether in anger or in their daily conversation, in the spirit realm, they're being held accountable for every word they say. Those words are seeds of curses and death, because they are sin, and remember the price of sin is death. A person's words are planting death seeds in their life which will grow harmful curses. This is a spiritual law, just like gravity in the natural. That individual is literally cursing their life on a daily basis and not even knowing it, and that's the way Satan has purposed it. He attempts to manipulate us through embedding sin in society's custom and cultures so individuals can curse their lives away.

The Empowerment of a Street Name

At the prison, you can often learn something about an individual's character and past by simply knowing their "street name" or the terminology we use at the institution, "moniker". For example, a ward nicknamed, "Do Dirty" most likely is known for his dirty or sinful deeds. "Skitzo" acts like Dr. Jeckle and Mr. Hyde, and probably displays a bipolar condition. "Cocaine" tells others his drug of choice and "Weasel" is usually small, sneaky and always up to something mischievous. "Crazy", well, that needs no further definition. The music industry encourages street names. Here are just a few of the names of some main stream gangsta rappers:"X-Raided, Mack 10, Ghost Face Killa, the ideology is that the more deviant the name, the more their respected in the thug culture, because evil is equated to power. This is because evil creates fear by intimidation and intimidation is perceived as respect in the thug culture.

How Can a Street Name Be Harmful?

The Bible states that life and death are in the power of the tongue

(Prov.18:21). Something that comes from the tongue is our names. Names are very sacred to God. If we look in the scriptures, we see how God gave specific names to his servants. For example, he changed Abram's name, because of his faith and obedience to Abraham which means "father of a multitude"(he was given the birth seed of Israel). His wife Sarai's name God changed to "Sarah" which means "Princess". God changed Jacob's name who was the father of the twelve Israeli tribes to Israel, which means "God's strong one". Any time God named or renamed someone there was always a spiritual meaning and intended purpose behind it.

When we use this frame of reference and look at a name like "criminal" or "Do Dirty", what is the meaning of such a name? Just like there is the law of gravity in the earthly hemisphere, there are also spiritual laws such as the one I presented earlier. "Life and Death" are in the power of the tongue (Prov.18:21). God prophetically named his servants based on what he planned for them to accomplish in their lives. When we look at Satan's name, the name Satan literally means slander. It has been his mission to slander God's name since his eviction from heaven. Satan has assigned and named his legions of demons also because he too understands the power of names.

Many of those in the ministry I've talked to have testified, during demon expulsion sessions, that evil spirits inside the possessed individuals would speak or screech out their names when commanded to by the name of Jesus (Phillipians 2:10). Names such as: Lust, Rebellion, Hate, Homosexuality are just some of the names of these demons (which identifies their assignment). I ,once, had a possessed and deranged ward on a psychiatric unit who kept laughing in a demonic creepy way while he was displaying bizarre behavior tell me in a deviant tone that his name was "malice" when I asked him in a commanding tone what his name was. Yet for that split second, he stopped laughing and became devilishly serious when he said the name. I knew by the Holy Spirit it wasn't him talking but a demon inside him identifying itself.

If Satan can name an individual what he wants, then he is likely to exercise his demonic prophetic forces over them, this goes in line with the spiritual laws. So when an individual accepts a name like Dirty D, Crazy, Lazy, Cocaine, Criminal, the power behind the name is often what they can become. Whether it was a name, which described a characteristic trait, or the trait of an older "O.G. Homey" (experienced and respected older gang member), the given name brought forth a prophetic manifestation. When an individual gives acceptance to a moniker or nickname which depicts a negative characteristic trait or is purposely named after an individual that embraced sin, this reinforces over and over, every time that name is said, the demonic power of the name over the individual's life.

Recently, I counseled a teenage boy in the community whose father was killed in a gang-related shooting when he was an infant. The father was a well known gang member. The son who I counseled had been given his father's gang name. Though he really never knew his father, he had developed an innate spiritual nature of his father's negative traits. People who called him by that name reinforced these diabolical traits over and over.

I advised him and his mother that the first step to deliverance was for him to disassociate himself from his nickname in order to be released from the evil, spiritual stronghold. Doing this would allow him to develop the identity that God had destined for him, which was already inside him. I explained to him that Satan had created an identity for him to accomplish his will. I then told him that it was Satan's will, to manipulate him into living a sinful lifestyle and then to kill him and take him to hell. I also let him know that God already had an awesome identity for him, and that God's identity would prosper him beyond his comprehension and that the only way he would find his true identity would be to develop a relationship with God by accepting Jesus as his Lord and Savior. Once he had done this, he should pray faithfully and develop the habit of reading the Holy Bible daily. During this process, God would reveal his identity to him through planting new desires (which are God's instructions) in his heart.

Names can be a blessing or a demonic stronghold. When you call an individual by a nickname associated with something negative, you indirectly curse them by reinforcing the stronghold.

Be careful with the words you say. The Bible instructs us that we will be held accountable on Judgment Day for every idle word we say. An idle word is a word said recklessly or out of carelessness. Remember, *"Life and death are in the power of the tongue"* (Proverbs 18:21).

Art of War or Art of Sin?

The two most requested books by the thug and gang population in our correctional facility are *The Art of War* by ancient warrior Sun Tzu and *48 Laws of Power* by Robert Greene and Joost Elffers. Some gang members have told me that these books are mandatory reading for members in their gang. They believe the strategies given to them in the book give them an edge over their enemy. Many have boastfully shared with me how they have deployed these tactics on others during their incarceration and how they live by them religiously for their day-to-day survival. I asked a small group of wards this week, "Do a lot of your peers read it (Referring to 48 Laws of Power)?" "Yeah, everybody reads it", another said," You have to read it three times to understand it." Another ward says, "It tells you how to manipulate and get over. You can use it anywhere."

"It's Been Proven by Myself"

Why I choose to live by these laws, is because these powerful and wise sayings have a lot of truth in them. It's been proven by myself and many others like me. Another fact is they will get you ahead in an environment like this. What I mean by ahead, is on top of this game. For example, Get others to do your dirty work but always take credit. To me this means to get others to do things for you, so you will never get your own self caught because your hands are clean. This type of thinking or belief brings a lot of manipulation and fear to others who are not aware of these laws, to the point that we feel they work. It gives a lot of power in a sense.

This is one of the laws I like because it keeps people confused and lost.

Keep others suspended in terror! Cultivate a cloud of unpredictability, make others guess what your next move is, keeping them wondering.

Gangsta icons such as Jay Z, Kanye West, 50 Cent and the late Tupac Shakur have all been believers of these texts and have used them to build their "gangsta" empires. These two books are essentially one in the same. The principles in these books both derive from the ancient eastern religion of Taoism. Let me give you some back ground on these two books starting with the Art of War.

During the third to fourth century, China was broken up into numerous states that were feuding against each other for various reasons. Sun Tzu was a freelance military leader who would sell his military strategies to various armies. His tactics proved very effective, thus making him a widely celebrated military hero. From this book of his military strategies came many other books which not only catered to armies, but business, sports and personal development. Many live by these principles religiously and swear by their effectiveness.

Here are some quotes made by those in the music industry whom are students of the doctrine:

"The only book I ever read I could have wrote: '48 Laws of Power,' " Kanye West

"In 'The 48 Laws of Power,' it says the worst thing you can do is build a fortress around yourself," Jay Z (Interview in Playboy)

"The book is like a martial arts manual for the business," said Quincy "QD3" Jones III

Law 28: Enter action with boldness.
The lesson: "If you're low, choose a big target and attack them as boldly as possible," he continued. "You have nothing to lose."

50 Cent has built his career from this law by verbally abusing a wide roster of hip hop stars, which includes Ja Rule, the Game, Jay Z and Lil' Kim, in his songs. He has even verbally attacked Oprah Winfrey, in an interview with the Associated Press he expressed his anger that she rarely has rappers on her program. How does he feel about this tension? "I'm actually better off having friction with her."

Let us take a close look at the core values of Taoism on which Sun Tzu based his war strategy on. In war, I understand there are skillful sometimes-deceptive tactics that must be utilized. We can see examples of this used by Israel in the Old Testament. Yet when a deceptive military mind-set is utilized in personal and business relationships for selfish gain and power to manipulate, it is called witchcraft, let me explain. Witchcraft is about attempting to control ones soul (mind, emotions, will). When you add the Tao spiritual component, it becomes witchcraft, because the methods and tactics being used are from a spirit other than God. There are all types of methods how witchcraft is applied such as: drugs, music, hypnosis, chants, tattoos and written doctrine, all which can open up and allow access to one's soul.

In order to understand Taoism, one must first understand Tao. Tao is believed to be a power or energy by which all things were created and work together. In essence, Taoism followers believe Tao is a god of creation. Ancient Chinese philosophers would say that Tao was the Alpha (beginning). Tao then divided into two spiritual principles: Yin and Yang. Yin represents negative energy and Yang positive energy. Yin and Yang then created the five elements, which are wood, fire, water, metal and earth.

The Yin-Yang symbol represents the on-going conflict of these two spiritual forces in every action. The religion believes Yin and Yang and the five elements are in control of our solar system. They believe each element is under the guidance of a planet, along with the moon and sun known as the seven rulers:

Earth-Saturn
Water-Mercury
Metal-Venus
Wood-Jupiter
Fire-Mars

All these planets can either be Yin or Yang producing an innumerable amount of astrological possibilities which many occult practices attempt to interpret.

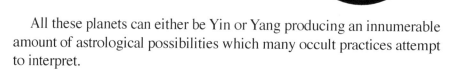

ShuShu is an ancient Chinese art of cultic ritual that practices divination, magic, dream interpretation, and fortune telling among others. The governing spirit they believe that brings a balance to the Yang and Yin is call Chi. Balance in Taoism is the key principal in creating holistic harmony in life.

Ancient methods such as acupuncture, acupressure, martial arts, yoga, tai chi, holistic massages, crystals, and other similar eastern art forms were created to conjure up the governing force of chi (also called energy) to bring balance to the Yin-Yang, in order for harmony to manifest.

In some belief systems, the Yin-Yang symbol represents a bisexual nature. The theory goes since there is some yin (female) in the yang (male), which is represented by the little dot, and some yang in the yin, it is interrupted as bisexuality.

One of the most disturbing principles of Taoism is its odd belief of good and evil. Taoism teaches that in order for harmony to exist a negative (yin) must balance out a positive (yang) and vice versa. In other words, the universe has to be balanced for all components within to be healthy. The belief is that good and evil compliment each other. Therefore, the only wrong is having a imbalance of right and wrong.

So in essence, what is this saying? It says good can be good and good can be evil and evil can be good and evil can be evil. So wrong is right and right is right as long as it's the same amount. These are the core values of books like _The Art of War_ and _The 48 Laws of Power._

Isaiah 5:20-21

20 Woe to those who call evil good and good evil, who put darkness for light and light for darkness, who put bitter for sweet and sweet for bitter.

21 Woe to those who are wise in their own eyes and clever in their own sight.

From gang members to mafia bosses to athletes, politicians and business professionals embrace these teachings like a cult doctrine. Below are some of the key principles from these two books.

Art of War

- "All warfare is based on deception."
- "When he is united, divide him"
- "If the enemy general is obstinate and prone to anger, insult and enrage him, so that he will be irritated and confused and without a plan will recklessly advance against him."
- " Offer the enemy a bait to lure him then disorder and strike him"

48 Laws of Power

- Law 3-Conceal your intentions
- Law 7-Get others to work for you, but always take the credit.
- Law 11-Learn to keep people dependent on you.
- Law 12-Use selective honesty and generosity to disarm your victim.
- Law 14-Pose as a friend, work as a spy.
- Law 15-Crush your enemy totally.
- Law 27-Play on peoples need to believe to create a cult like following.
- Law 37-Create compelling spectacles
- Law 42-Strike the shepherd and the sheep will scatter.

What type of impact has this philosophy had on our culture as a whole? Well, besides the standard of traditional morals, it has created a dog eat dog mentality. Self-empowerment is held in higher regard than self-integrity. It's been made acceptable to violate ones conscience and self-respect all in the name of greed, pride and power. However, we have seen a violent backlash in the principles of these two books. There is a critical law, which has been foolishly ignored. Written by the one true God, written in the one true book the Holy Bible, which states, "You will reap what you sow." This means individuals who practice these laws might obtain short-term gain but for breaking God's spiritual laws they will also obtain long-term pain.

Satan is always attempting to duplicate and corrupt what God has created. Taoism, with its governing spirit Chi (Ephesians 2:2) was conjured up by Satan to be a substitute for God's Holy Spirit. That's why God tells us to test the spirits (1 John 4:1). The spirit of Taoism was designed by Satan for mankind to give up their dependence on God to serve Tao, a false god, whose consequence is the eternal lake of fire.

Below is God's Answer to the principles of Taoism:

Galatians 1:9

9 As we have already said, so now I say again: If anybody is preaching to you a gospel other than what you accepted, let him be eternally condemned!

Proverbs 6:16-19

16 There are six things the LORD hates, seven that are detestable to him:

17 haughty eyes, a lying tongue, hands that shed innocent blood,

18 a heart that devises wicked schemes, feet that are quick to rush into evil,

19 a false witness who pours out lies and a man who stirs up dissension among brothers

Romans 6:23

23 For the wages of sin is death, but the gift of God is eternal life in Christ Jesus our Lord.

Ephesians 5:11

11 Have nothing to do with the fruitless deeds of darkness, but rather expose them

"Gangsta" Video Games: A Thug's Virtual Reality Training Camp

A few months ago, I was leaving a Starbucks in a Sacramento inner-city neighborhood known for its high crime rate, when I noticed numerous identical large artistic posters in a series of rows, advertising "Coming Soon, Grand Theft Auto, San Andreas." A new edition of one of the #1 selling popular video game series"Grand Theft Auto."

Of course, the title of the game and where it was strategically being marketed caught my attention. I couldn't wait to get back to work, to question the wards on whether they had played the game, and if so what was their take on it. To no surprise, most had played the previous "Grand Theft" auto game and loved it. They talked with enthusiasm and passion as they explained the game to me, as if describing their first love.

Other games they mentioned were "Real Crimes", in which the player can partake in numerous violent crimes in the community for points. Another was "Tony Hawk" where the player is a skater that goes around the city reaping havoc and vandalizing property.

Last week, while I was supervising an outdoor recreation program on a lock-up unit, I was intrigued at the dialogue about video games I heard going back and forth between the wards that were programming in cages. "Have you ever played G.T.A. (Grand Theft Auto) dude? Yeah I played it at my old lady's house," a White Power gang member yells out to a Fresno Bulldog gang member, in an enthusiastic manner as he animates how the video game character he was controlling "jacked" an innocent licensed driver for their car. The Bulldog yells back with mirrored enthusiasm, "You can have shoot outs with cops." Another ward from the cage across shouts, "You can kill cops." The wards then begin to smile and shake their head in agreement towards each other after reminiscing together about the violent acts that they committed playing within the video game world. They then, one by one, start rambling off a list of other violent and hostile video games on the market. A ward yells out with a passionate voice, "I want to see blood. I can't play a game without blood!"

At this time, I can't take any more; I have to ask them a question. "Why do you like these video games?" I ask in a subtle and sincere tone. The ward with the "mark of the beast (666)" and a barcode tattoo looks at me calmly and replies with sincerity and says, "You want a game that's going to show you how reality is, that's not going to hide it." Right after his reply, a ward yells out, "You play that "Sniper" game", as he chuckles he says, "I use to snipe civilians and everything."

Today, a Bay Area and Blood gang member told me that violent video games are "Therapy", that they actually used these video games to displace their anger. "Johnson, I bet you, if you brought a game system in, there would be a lot of less fights. I wouldn't even come out for program," the Bay Area ward stated. "Me too" added the Blood gang member from Compton.

There are two games which just hit the market that are selling out by record numbers, "Ryde or Die 187" (gang-related story line), and a game in which it's theme is based on gangsta rapper's 50 Cent biography called "Bullet Proof", in which the story line is for the rapper and G-Unit (his crew of gangsta rappers) to get revenge on the rival drug lords who shot him 9 times (which really happened in his life). The players' adrenaline playing this game gets to be pumped up by the gangsta artist's sound track playing   in the background of the game.

Unlike a music video where you are a spectator, in a video game, you become a participant. I remember hearing a Christian talk show host put it this way, " You see a book tells us something, a movie shows us something, music lets us listen to something, but video games allows an individual to actually do something." Role-playing is the most powerful method to condition and prepare some one to do something. Think about beginning pilots who first learn how to fly in flight simulators and policeman and the military utilizing virtual reality computer technology to set up real life scenarios, some of the new video games have become training simulators for future potential criminals and killers.

" I loved the game because I would love to do work for the mafia"

I had this one game called "Driver" and it was cool because this dude would ride around town doing business with the Italian mafia and they would send him on missions to kill certain enemies they wanted dead to rob and steal money from rich guys to wreck and crash into other enemy vehicles and to pick up women they called show girls that worked for the mafia. I loved the game because I would love to do work for the mafia for the amount of money they were putting out for this "driver" dude. He was making $50,000 a mission and in 4 missions that's $200,000 so in 10 missions you are making a cool amount of money so that's why that video game has me deeply entrenched.

"Grand Theft Auto, Vice City", this game also has a lot to do with mafia because this Italian guy himself is running around a city killing people for money, he has to eat, sell dope, do missions or hits for an extraordinary deal of a lot of money. It has entrenched me because I will do the same to sell dope, kill for money at the same time, do business with a mafia that is mandatory going to pay me some damn good money to make these hits I would put my life on the line for $50,000 a hit and the hits are not complicated you could do them if you put yo mind to it and you won't falter if you do it the way it is suppose to be done. 2nd have your mind set on accomplishing it not being shaky having low self esteem being paranoid and different feeling that you have when you know

you are doing things your not suppose to be doing. This is why
some negative video games pump me up and have me some what
deeply entrenched.

History of the Thug

Ask the average youth who they think were the original thugs?
You're likely to hear thug icons such as Al Capone and John Gotti, the
younger generation might say the late Easy E or Ice T. Ask them what
the meaning of the word thug is. You're likely to get a variety of answers,
such as a "down pimp", "baller" or "gangster". The dictionary's definition
of thug (Encarta Dictionary) is: *somebody, especially a criminal, who is
brutal and violent.*

Many might be surprised to know that the word "thug" did not
originate from the Italian neighborhoods of New York, nor South-Central
Los Angeles. The meaning of the word is about 700 years old and comes
thousands of miles away on the other side of the planet, from the city of
Bombay, India. There was a peculiar group of Hindus who worshiped
the goddess Kali, the dark consort of Shiva who is said to feed on the
blood of mortals and to haunt the burning-grounds where Hindus are
cremated. Kali's hideous image can be seen in temples throughout India
and now around the world. Typically, she was represented as a black
woman (one of her epithets, Kali Ma, means "black mother"), numerous
arms, and garlanded with human skulls and a long red tongue protruding
from a screaming mouth. Human sacrifices were once carried out in
temples paying homage to Kali. Worshipers called on her through
incantations. Kali worshipers from the 13th century practiced ritual
murder and the robbing of native travelers throughout the countryside.
These worshipers were from a tribe called Thuggee. Approximately
30,000 to 40,000 travelers a year, would mysteriously disappear, falling
victim of the Thuggee tribe, who estimated number was about 5,000.
These murderers came to be known as Thugs, which came from the Hindi
verb thaglana which means "to deceive," and reflected the mysterious
ability of Thugs to befriend their intended victims. The Thuggee
tribe was primarily a group of Hindus and Muslims that transcended
religion. It revolved around the fanatical worship of the goddess Kali.

After the thug gangs would murder the travelers, they would rob the bodies of their possessions and place them in graves, which often had been dug in advance. Every Thug expedition was planned in careful consultation with omens and signs. The secret society of the thugs lasted approximately 600 years in India. It was later almost dismantled by the British Government led by William H. Sleeman, who was a Magistrate in India. However sadly, the Thug's legacy, spirit and mentality continues to gain popularity and momentum in our nation and now throughout the world. One of the main catalysts of this movement has been the Hip Hop and Rock music industry. Russell Simmons who practices Yoga and Hinduism rituals, known as one of the godfathers of Hip Hop has a Kali statue in his house, which he meditates to daily, according to G. Craige Lewis of Ex Ministries (*The Truth Behind Hip Hop 3-video*). Is it not strange that many "gangsta" artists now refer to California as "Kali"; rapper Celly Cel has a song entitled, "Killa Kali." There is now a group that is called Thug Lordz that also has a song called "Killa Kali", which features gangsta rapper Spice 1. Marijuana use is on the rise among the thug scene. In some cultures marijuana is nicknamed "Kali." This is due to the fact that marijuana was and still is used as a part of the spiritual worship to the goddess Kali.

History of the Thug gods

The Holy Bible has the historical roots on this thug issue. We can go back as far as the first civilization in Mesopotamia, when Abraham was called by God to be separate from the idol gods, which were being worshiped in the land. Then we can move through the time when mankind continued to turn from God and followed the many false gods of Babylon.

All of these religions repeated the same sin Adam and Eve committed, which was to seek knowledge of the mysteries that God had not allowed them to know in the Garden of Eden. Satan is more than willing to reveal mysteries; however for the price of one's soul. Whatever path of knowledge Satan leads a person, it is always designed to lead the individual to self-destruction. We can find how the worship and religions of the many false gods of Babylon moved through out the world in Genesis 11: 1-9.

The Tower of Babel

1 Now the whole world had one language and a common speech. 2 As men moved eastward, they found a plain in Shinar and settled there.

3 They said to each other, "Come, let's make bricks and bake them thoroughly." They used brick instead of stone, and tar for mortar. 4 Then they said, "Come, let us build ourselves a city, with a tower that reaches to the heavens, so that we may make a name for ourselves and not be scattered over the face of the whole earth."

5 But the LORD came down to see the city and the tower that the men were building. 6 The LORD said, "If as one people speaking the same language they have begun to do this, then nothing they plan to do will be impossible for them. 7 Come, let us go down and confuse their language so they will not understand each other."

8 So the LORD scattered them from there over all the earth, and they stopped building the city. 9 That is why it was called Babel—because there the LORD confused the language of the whole world. From there the LORD scattered them over the face of the whole earth.

As stated in verse 9, as they settled throughout the world, they took these religious practices with them. They created temples for these false gods. Through out the centuries, each culture has modified their religion to their desired specifications; however, the seeds of all these false religions through out the world stem from the beliefs in the ancient city of Babylon.

The following is a brief history of Cabalism, which will explain how many witchcraft cults around the world derived from this ancient dark art.

When the Nation of Israel (Jewish people), began to worship the cosmic gods of nature, God punished them by sending them into captivity to Babylon. Some Jewish priests studied the ancient Babylonian mysteries (Witchcraft). The Cabalist's basic doctrine is to study what God has not revealed to them. Scientifically, this is called Metaphysics. Cabala is a Hebrew word, which comes from the verb kabel, which means to "receive."

This doctrine falls right in with the view of a satanist I talked to on our unit the other day. He stated that his denomination of satanism believes that they should pay homage to Satan because he led man to divine knowledge and mysteries by leading them against God to taste from the Tree of Knowledge. This is the whole premise of Cabalism, to seek the fruits of the forbidden Tree of Knowledge. This is basically seeking mysteries that God did not want us to know for good reason.

Thugs and the Stars

Astrology, the reading of the Horoscope was created from the Cabala religion. Let me first start by giving you a little background on this topic. Cabalists claim that the 10 Sefiroth (the ten characteristics of God, which make up God) is the Tree of Life from which the Universe came into existence, and that man can unite himself with, or become a god 'by rising through the spheres,' spiritually climbing the ladder of the Sefiroth to reach God. In magic, the sorcerer must experience and master all 10 Sefiroth in order to achieve supreme perfection and power, for the Tree of the Sefiroth is believed to be a cosmic diagram, the basic pattern which shows how the Universe is arranged and how its phenomena are connected. They believe man is a miniature model of the Universe (microcosm) and of God, and that man is able to spiritually expand himself to become God.

This is a blasphemous doctrine according to God's Word. This is the same sin that was committed in the Garden of Eden; *"Ye shall be as gods,"* (referring to eating of the Tree of Knowledge) (Genesis 3:5.). Those who practiced the Cabala teachings or Babylonian mysticism were known for centuries as the Illuminati. The Illuminati believed in and taught a doctrine of illumination or inner light (Illuminism). The teaching of the Cabala branched out to other occult beliefs such as Gnosticism (which the Da Vinci Code is based on) to the Knight Templers, which branched out to form the Free Masons, which went on to lay the foundation for America's government. The Gnostics were a cult during the Roman era, which practiced goddess worship, sexual rituals and parts of the New Testament. They rejected the Old Testament God, and paid homage to the serpent (devil) in the Garden of Eden, because they believed the male God, was withholding the divine knowledge from the female gods.

The Illuminati taught living a life of purity and service would open their so-called inner senses so that they would obtain spiritual insight or Clairvoyance, known as the Third Eye. They desired to become prophets and be able to converse with spirits (which were demons) and with dead saints.

Listen to these Hip Hop artists who embrace these teachings:

"Grand Puba says that he greets "brothers" with the Islamic greeting As Salamu 'alai kum." Grand Puba says that blacks are Asiatics, that he "loves Allah's mathematics," and black men have been taught to speak in ciphers. He uses his "third eye" to release the "black man" from mental chains, so that the "black man" will no longer be a slave."

RZA says that it is "time for the Wu revolution" and that "god is here to take over this sh@%." He says that on his side are Killah Priest, Sunz of Man, Killarmy, and Gravediggaz. ("Intro" from disc two.) They say that Allah is "heard and seen everywhere." They say that "innocent black immigrants [are] locked in housing tenements," and that the "85 Percent tenants depend on welfare." Stapleton federal housing project is "a concentration camp." RZA's "third eye" sees the following conspiracies: "babies have microchips inserted into their earlobes; blood is being contaminated; and the FDA is testing poison on the prison population (http://home.att.net/~phosphor/grammys/method/wu-tang.html).

Within these mysteries of the Cabala, there comes the 12 cosmic Zodiac signs in which we get astrology from. The twelve segments of our solar system they refer to as constellations, together called "the Zodiac." which forms a circle around Earth. As Earth revolves around the Sun, a different part of the sky becomes visible, and each month a different one of these 12 constellations can be seen above the horizon. The word Zodiac means "circle of figures" or "circle of life."

The ancient Greeks established the foundation for modern astrology. They associated mythical figures from the Greek Partheon(temples) to the stars and gave physical and emotional attributes to the planets of the Zodiac.

Millions of individuals from the time of the Greeks till today rely on their daily horoscope in order to make decisions throughout their day-to-day life. They depend on the mystical cosmic gods for guidance which are the false gods of Babylon. For one to say that "I'm a Gemini" or "I'm a Cancer", is basically making a confession that they're one with that false god and it's characteristics. It's the same as a follower of Jesus Christ stating, "I'm a Christian."

Thug Mentality Respects Evil

The thug culture embraces evil because evil is intimidating. The thug believes the more evil or intimidating their environment appears, the more they feel empowered and validated as a thug. That's why you have many gangsta artists displaying proudly the trashy, graffiti and crime ridden parts of their community, bypassing the positive and highlighting the negative. Why? Because, they believe individuals will associate them with their living environment, thus seeing them as intimidating.

Don't get me wrong, there is nothing wrong with being in or from the so called ghetto or hood, but it is wrong when someone boasts about the sinful elements and suppresses the righteous acts being done in the community.

I asked a ward the other day who I saw "pimp walking" throughout the dayroom reciting gangsta rap lyrics (paraphrasing), "Why are you promoting the very spirit, which is against you and your family?" The very evil spirit causing your family illness, that has them in bondage to drug addiction, manipulating their minds into criminal behavior which has resulted in long periods of incarceration, why are you promoting your enemy? I want to make them think about what they're doing, not just feel what they're doing. Listening to music is what gratifies their emotions. That's why they are so quick to defend their favorite music artists, even though they know the lyrics are sinful. They are deceived, just like a drug addict, in that they crave a substance that is destroying them, from the inside out. They take in the music to fill the emptiness of their soul, by tantalizing their emotions; however, they soon come to the realization that it's never enough.

God is the only one that can fill that void. There is always a price when the devil offers something gratifying. The price are curses- being left empty and with physical and spiritual death (hell).

Ephesians 5:6

6 Let no one deceive you with empty words, for because of such things God's wrath comes on those who are disobedient.

Pit Bulls

Many of the wards I talk to, speak with great pride about their pit bulls. Not how loyal and loving they are, but how vicious and full of malice they became after a brutal regiment of training for dog fighting. Pit bulls are often displayed on the front of rap and rock albums and in the music videos. Many of those young and old who embrace the thug culture are out strolling down the street, riding in their car and at the neighborhood park profiling with pride their pits as status symbols of their "thug machismo." This trend became more prevalent when gangsta rapper DMX featured the ferocious K-9's center stage in his music videos, growling and lunging aggressively from their chains as if to be blood thirsty for another kill.

Pit bull fights are common in the thug culture. Many wards have told me how they feed their pits from birth gunpowder and raw red meat, sometimes mixing street drugs in their food, along with beating them mercilessly all for the sake of creating a mean, insane killing machine. A gang member from the projects told me how dispensable these dogs can be in his hood. When a dog loses a pit fight, thugs toss the pit to their death from the roof of the housing projects where the fighting arena was. Others have told me, they have gotten so mad for losing their money; they just pulled out their gun and shot their pet. The thug culture promotes and teaches this pimp mentality. When you have gotten all the use out of something whether it's a woman, dog or an associate, they can become dispensable.

Thug Fatherhood

I can remember confronting two-gang members on the lock-up unit who were bragging about their gang's past evil deeds. They both stated that their goal was to go to the "pen." I knew both of them were fathers, so I asked them, why they chose to abandon their fatherhood responsibilities of raising and supporting their own children. They replied in order to help their gang to fight and riot for their so-called respect within the correctional institution. The thug culture has brainwashed so many gang members to neglect their aging parents, grandparents, younger sisters and brothers who need their love, guidance, protection and support. They are brainwashed by choosing to support these able-bodied men in their gangs rather than being with their families.

These young men had sent little to no money home for their children, because they were always in trouble within the institution. Therefore, they could never qualify for the prison jobs. Neglecting their responsibilities by supporting themselves and not their children, they had the belief that they should be respected as men, merely for being in a gang, having scary tattoos, muscles, an obscene mouth, and a violent criminal history. This is what the thug mentality's belief of what a man is. When I confronted and engaged these two in some dialogue about my observation, they became angry that I brought this to their attention. They began to curse and threaten me. They repeatedly stated that they were "warriors", referring to the fights and riots they had been in while incarcerated. They began to make crude jokes about me. I would then steer them back to our conversation, in which they realized they had no logical answer. Therefore, they went back to illogical antics. One told me, "fu%# my kids," then stated he would get out and kill the mother of his kids. The other replied, "I'll help you kill her, because I get out before you." Knowing I'm a Christian, they began to curse God, saying all types of sacrilegious comments, in an effort to disrespect me. Then one conveyed how he hated Christians, and stated that he wanted to stab his grandmother when he is released, because she is a Christian. The other ward laughed hysterically.

Though I realize where I work, I am often still amazed at some of the evilness that is displayed. By the way, these threats were reported to local authorities. We often hope that these statements are just talk; however, sadly, there have been many released from our institution who have gone on and committed the most heinous crimes imaginable.

How does an individual who has been given a conscience from God allow their heart to become so cold hearted and evil? I knew both of these wards fairly well, and at times have had pretty good rapport with them. I had counseled them on numerous occasions, and I was always amazed how both of these wards after acknowledging and seeing the impact of their crimes, could callously still look me in the eyes like they didn't care a bit about their victims or their victims' families. Nor did they show any real remorse or empathy in the pain they had caused their own family.

For the heart to become so cold hearted and evil, there is a process involved. To curse, abuse, steal and kill goes against the nature of our God given conscience. Drugs, alcohol and music are some of the major ingredients, which prep and condition the heart for evil. I will address this in detail later on.

The Mind Control of Music

The following will give you an idea how powerful the influence of music is over the mind. Roy H.Williams, Ph.D author of the book, _Thought Particles_, has a company which conducts seminars to businesses on how to create successful advertisements, which influences the subconscious part of the brain to draw people to their product or service.

Williams presents the brain in two parts: the left-brain as the skeptic which is our conscious state, the part of the brain that comprehends the words you are reading right now. Our right side, which is our subconscious, records everything we hear and see, even if we are unaware 24 hours a day.

He talks about the powerful effects of music. He states that music has the power to bypass the left hemisphere of the brain, which is our skeptic and go directly into the right hemisphere of the brain, which in turn takes the message and uploads it back to the left hemisphere which influences our beliefs and behaviors, often times, unknowingly. For example, a person says they listen to a "gangsta rap" song just for the beat, though they believe they are blocking the message consciously with their left brain, their right brain is recording everything, even any backward masked message. Our right side is so intelligent that it will take the message and transfer it back to our left-brain even without us knowing it, which will then influence our beliefs, emotions and behavior. Advertisers and the psychology industry have been utilizing music for years by discretely hiding latent messages within the music, in order to direct their message into peoples' subconscious without them realizing it. For example: Grocery stores have placed messages in music, to direct shoppers to specific items, in which they were trying to increase their sales. I heard about a store that placed latent messages about a produce item they were trying to increase sales on. The message they placed in the music was, "Strawberries are delicious, go purchase the strawberries" into the store's soft music. Soon after, the sales of strawberries soared out the roof.

Still think music isn't influential in our society?

"Holiday Blues "

Holidays suck, sh*% always seem to slow down, no ones really smiling around any more, the fights break out more, the loneliness makes you easy to aggravate. For real the days seem slower and the night too black, all you think about is the streets, don't matter if you got a place to go or not, you think back to when you once was a person not an animal. You remember the happiness, the smiles your family the closeness of it all the sh*% is crazy, I've seen fools try to cut on themselves for a little attention on these days, but it's pointless, no one cares here everyone is a bit%# that works, because they wanna be home with there family they remind you you're a burden to them as well as those you hurt on the streets. And when you lie in your cell you sit there with the atmosphere around you is so depressing, everyone is quite lost in their own world stuck on there own memories of there past. Holidays suck in jail, food sucks visits make it a little better, but we're always on lock down for the rioting amongst each other it don't stop, the fake war keeps on going on, the fighting never stops, the hate only grows, never does it stop or slow down. People think about their children, that's what I think about. I've been in jail 5 years I'm yet to see my child's

Christmas or birthday he spends his day with a man I don't know with his mother, all I see is my child. I'm used to being away from my mother and siblings.

I can handle it now I'm used to these Holidays, ain't sh%# no more, they have no meaning for me, just another day on my calendar. Another day away from my child, it's just more depressing, and the blues are in the air, ain't nothing you can do but mark the day off your calendar.

"Why I got Tattoo'z"

Tattoos are a form of art work. Most people (regular) get tattoos to symbolize a lost one, close friends, or just to have a nice piece of art work done on you that you like.

On the other hand people such as myself (gang members) get tattoos because a lot of the times they take pride in where there from, so they get there hood or gang affiliation symbol on the them. I got my gang related tattoos because I want it to be known that I'm a "Bulldog", without me having to communicate with people.

Another reason why I got tattoos is because it makes me look more of a gangster. People get tattoos on there body to symbolize history of their gang or something someone has done in the past. Another reason why I got tattoos is because I've been locked up for a long time.

The main reason why I got tattoos and why most gangsters get tattoos are to symbolize a specific gang or click your in, and I out of all people got nothing but gang related tattoos because I want people to know I'm a "Fresno Bulldog" and F*%# the rest.

Most of the people who get a gang related tattoo don't plan on getting them taken off because they where put there for a reason, and that reason from their point of view might still be unknown.

"It was like no one cared about females."

65

I saw all the dope dealers hustlers and pimps, they had it all: from money and fame to power and women. I wanted to be like that. I picked up on what they did and tried to put it to use in my life. So I started hurting people and doing what I had to do to make sure I had what I wanted. That's why I joined -- MOB. I mean, look at what it stands for; [th]Street, Money Over B#%@#'s. That's the kind of mentality that got me locked up. Not caring for anyone. Other than taking what I wanted, I tried to look out for my family. Those were the only people I cared for other than the people in my gang. Music was another thing that played a role in my thug mentality. Since I can remember I grew up listening to rap and a rapper calling females hoes and tricks – it was like no one cared about females – you hear them glorifying selling drugs or killing someone. Those are the two major things that come to mind when asked what played a role in my thug mentality.

"Wit-out money, you're a nobody"
(Ward said he didn't care about life after his brother was murdered.)

My life revolves around thugz, drugz and money. Being a thug isn't for everybody: you can't just wake up and say, 'oh I'm gonna start being a thug' and just start thuggin it out. Ta be a thug you gotta be born wit that mentality, it has to run through your veinz and mix wit you blood, because if you really think about it we really put our life on da line day in and day out wit out any fearz of dying and that is where drugz come into da picture. Drugz relax yo mind as well as yo soul and it keeps you motivated for what ever is on yo mind. Money bringz power, wit out money you're a nobody and wit out power your not important.
(A friend of this individual, also a ward, said this writer was murdered in 2005 in a drug deal gone bad.)

"No smiles, only mean mugs"

I'm a 24 year old male from Southern California. I been crippin since I was 13. I can tell you how music influences me, even till this day. I personally can not listen to no "gangsta rap". Specially hard core gangsta rap, like C Bo, Brotha Lynch, eastsidaz etc. and not have my mind be triggered by negative thoughts.

It's like 2 Pac said, "they planted seeds and they hatch sparking a flame inside my brain like a match such a dirty game." And that's how negative music is. See when I listen to C Bo or Brotha Lynch or da Eastsidaz for one, it's made for the negative street life, so anybody else listening to it is kind've infatuated by the gangsta life. I'll be the first to tell you that real gangsta music is not to be enjoyed by just listening to it. No, you live it, that's when it's enjoyed. See I couldn't see no other way of listening to C Bo, Brotha Lynch or Da East Sidaz, but 'grimmey". In the streets, my whole mood will go to darkness. No smiles, only mean mugs. And let someone look funny, we on they beanies (or on them) Because there already stating in the music, that there ain't no f---ing with our crew. Glorifying the macho image. So like Pac(Tu Pac) said it gets planted and it hatches, such a dirty game. Just think about it like this: you listen to love songs and you think about what? Your woman, sex, love. Now if you listen to hard core rap, then what are you gonna think about? It's just common sense.

"17 years old arrested for 1st Degree Murder. By the Lord's mercy, 4 months later I was sentenced to four years in CYA on a charge of Manslaughter..."

"I kiss my momma goodbye, and wipe the tears from her lonely eyes, said I'll return but I gotta fight the gist to rise, don't shed a tear cause mamma I ain't happy here, there be trials, no more smiles, for a couple years" (Song: I Ain't Mad At Cha: Tupac)

I've had plenty of time to analyze and evaluate my past. I was brought up in a home better than most. Financially we was more than straight and moms was able to be home to raise us boys. Seems pleasant enough yet I'm locked up for taking a life. Someone's son, someone's brother or friend, and possibly someone's father. I was exposed to a lot of negativity and noticed things that at a young age felt that was the way of life. My pops was the male role model for everybody in our family and in our neighborhood. Handsome, clean cut, confident and respected! He taught me things about respecting my elders, standing up for myself and taking pride in my appearance. But integrity, morals and dignity were absent. My pops was a dope

67

dealer and a womanizer. But he was my hero! Nice guy but don't take no sh*t. I quickly followed suit and shortly made a name for myself. By this time moms and pops separated and it was all struggle, I felt like a burden and hit the streets and became a juvenile delinquent. I stayed in trouble, which only added to my mom's stress.

"Jail"

Jail is a place where people go when they did something bad, jail is not cool at all, you have all kind of people in jail. You have gay people, you have people that's trying to go home, you got people that trying to fit in, you got people that just want to ride it out, and talking about they don't care, but down inside they really do, jail is where you have people that look forward to you doing stuff that you really don't want to do. I f you don't do it then they want to call you a punk or a case. I'm just trying to let you know a little how jail is run, so you could make up your mind and see that you don't want to live your life like this. I could tell you because I did hard times in jail. I know how it is to be taken away from your love ones, I will never tell you young kids out there anything wrong, based on I don't want you kids to live your life the way I did. I got into gangs because it looked fun to me and I saw a lot of nice things. But down inside I want to change my life, but my homies might try to kill me for that. They'll say I'm a "sale out". I have kids that I love dearly, that's why I want out. See where the gangs got me? And jail doing hard times, not knowing if I'm going to live or die.

<u>Notes</u>

Music and Satanism

I remember when I thought devil worship music was only associated to heavy metal bands, like ACDC, Ozzy Osborne and K.I.S.S. We used to call those who listened to this type of music "stoners", because of the ones we knew were always getting "stoned" from smoking marijuana and other drugs. My friends and I would sometimes talk about how insane they were, to listen to music that paid homage to the devil. "That's crazy", I used to say. Things have changed; it's not just the "stoner" or heavy metal groups any more who pays homage and gives worship to Satan. There are now many rap and R&B groups out there doing the same. For instance, there is a rap group rapidly moving up the charts at this time, which calls themselves "3 Six Mafia" (representing the mark of the beast 666 foretold in the Holy Bible).

Jay Z is featured on 2004's "The Grey Album," the underground album contains a secret message. Encoded in a backward or masked message, he says "666, murder, murder Jesus." These are the type of satanic messages that are coming into many souls unknowing to them, which is corrupting souls and producing behaviors of destruction and self-destruction. I was thinking the other day, how strange it is, that you use to have to prove you didn't have a criminal record to get a job, in the thug entertainment industry, you now almost have to prove you have one to get a record deal. Recently, I saw a title story on a well-known Hip Hop magazine, which stated on the front, "DJ Quick justifies his Thug". In other words, in order to be respected and have credibility in the thug industry, you have to prove to everyone that you're an immoral criminal.

Here are some disturbing quotes from band members in the entertainment industry:

*www.illuminati-news.com/art-and-mc/satanic-quotes.htm
*www.av1611.org/crock/dctalk1.htm
*www.jesus-is-savior.com/Evils%20in%20America/Rock-n-Roll/satanic_quotes.htm
(Jay Z/"The Grey Album" data from "Truth About Hip Hop II" video/Ex Ministries) 71

In 1966, John Lennon stated that Christianity would pass away and that the Beatles would become more popular than Christ. He referred to Christ as a character he named "Jesus L. Pifco, a garlic eating, stinking, little yellow greasy fascist bastard Catholic Spaniard" (John Lennon, A Spaniard in the Works, New York, Simon & Schuster, 1965 p. 14). John Lennon was murdered in 1980.

David Bowie, one of the biggest rock stars in 1976, declared "Rock has always been devil's music."

In a early interview with Rolling Stones magazine with David Crosby, from the group "Crosby Stills and Nash," Crosby said the following, "I figured the only thing to do was to swipe their kids... By saying that, I'm not talking about kidnapping. I'm just talking about changing their value system, which removes them from their parents' world very effectively" (Rolling Stone, vol. 1 p. 410).

In the journal "Jesserson Starship," Paul Kanter confesses: "Our music is intended to broaden the generation gap, to alienate children from their parents ." (In Tinglehoff Documentation of Expose, p. 4).

Mick Jagger of the Rolling Stones has remarked, "There is no such thing as a secure, family oriented rock and roll song" (same journal p. 5).

Jon of Bon Jovi observed, "I wanted to rebel against anything and everything, and it happened that I was able to do it by playing rock and roll in a band" (Metal Edge, Aug. 1987, p. 12).

John Cougar reveals, "I swear or cuss because I know that it's not socially acceptable. I hate things that are 'this is the way you are supposed to behave.' That is why I hate schools, governments, and churches" (In Tinglehoff Documentation of Expose, p. 6).

Nikki Sixx of Motley Crue comments: "We never set out to be anybody's role model. But since we have become that, we are trying to give our fans something to believe in. On the second album, we told them to "Shout at the Devil." A lot of people... think that song is about Satan. That's not true. It's about standing up to authority, whether it is your parents, your teacher or your boss. That is pretty good advice, I think. But I'm sure that any parent who hears it is going to think it is treason" (Rock Beat, 1989 p. 41).

From The Doors' Jim Morrison's mocking, screaming hatred of Christian prayer ("Petition the Lord with Prayer") to Skid Row's "Quicksand Jesus" ("Are we saved by the words of bastard saints?") to the more explicit blasphemies, rock culture has often identified its aversion to Christian faith. Ozzy Osbourne acknowledges "I'm not a born again Christian but a born again Hitler (Cream Metal, March 1986 p. 12).

"The Oath" by the band King Diamond: "I deny Jesus Christ, the deceiver, and I adjure the Christian faith, holding in contempt all of its works." "Possessed" by the band Venom: "I am possessed by all that is evil. The death of your God I demand. I ... sit at Lord Satan's right hand," and "I drink the vomit of the priest, make love to the dying whore, Satan is my master incarnate, hail, praise to my unholy host."

Billy Idol attempts "to show what a human rip off religion is." Leon Russell thinks that "organized Christianity has done more harm than any other single force I can think of in the world" and suggests that the religion of rock and roll replace it.

In an interview in Spin, Sinead O'Connor emphasized, "It's a huge abuse to teach children that God is not within themselves. That God is pollution. That God is bigger than them. That God is outside them. That is a lie. That's what causes the emptiness of children" (Spin, Nov 1991, p. 51).

In "Hymn 43" the band Jethro Tull conveyed this message, "We are our own saviors, and if Jesus saves, then He better save Himself" (Cream Metal, Mar. 1986, p. 12).

This genre of "inspired music" is now found in local record stores. Some "New Age" music is spiritistically inspired for specific occult goals. The "composers" of the New Age music claim it can foster meditation, help develop psychic power, alter consciousness, induce "astral" travel, and transform personality. Other contemporary rock musicians parallel these ideas.

John Lennon said: "It's like being possessed: like a psychic or a medium...." Of the Beatles, Yoko Ono has said, "They were like mediums. They weren't conscious of all they were saying, but it was coming through them..."
Marc Storace, a vocalist with the heavy metal band Krokus, told Circus magazine: "You can't describe it except to say it's like a mysterious energy that comes from the metaphysical plane and into my body. It's almost like being a medium..."

"Little Richard":I was directed and commanded by another power The power of darkness ... that a lot of people don't believe exists. The power of the devil. Satan."

Jim Morrison (of The Doors) called the spirits that at times possessed him "the Lords," and wrote a book of poetry about them.

Folk rock artist Joni Mitchell's creativity came from her spirit guide 'Aft." So dependent was she upon 'Aft" that nothing could detain her when he "called."

Superstar Jimi Hendrix, called "rock's greatest guitarist" ... "believed he was possessed by some spirit," according to Alan Douglas. Hendrix's former girlfriend, Fayne Pridgon, has said: "He used to always talk about some devil or something was in him, you know, and he didn't have any control over it, he didn't know what made him act the way he acted and what made him say the things he said, and songs ... just came out of him." (Dave Hunt, America: The Sorcerers New Apprentice, Eugene, OR: Harvest House, 1988, pp. 239 40).

Ozzy Osbourne noted, "I never seem to know exactly what I'm gonna do next. I just like to do what the spirits make me do. That way, I always have someone or something to blame" (Faces, Nov. 1983 p. 24). Osbourne, a former lead singer of "Black Sabbath" triumphantly summoned satan at one of his concerts in Canada. "Sometimes I feel like a medium for some outside force... " (Tinglehoff, Documentation of Expose, p. 21). Black Sabbath has also made altar calls to Lucifer at some of their concerts. In "Master of Reality" they sing that he is "lord of this world" and "your confessor now."

According to a Rolling Stone interview, Peter Criss, the first and most famous drummer of the rock band KISS stated, "I believe in the devil as much as God. You can use either one to get things done" (Rolling Stone, Jan 12, 1978).

Another guitarist when asked "From where do you draw the strength for such delivery?" He said,"Most probably from below, up there there is no Rock and Roll." Members of the group Iron Maiden openly admit that they are dabbling in the occult, including witchcraft (Cream, Sept. 1982).

One Iron Maiden concert in Portland, Oregon, opened with the words "Welcome to Satan's sanctuary."

Glenn Tipton of the group Judas Priest confessed that when he goes on stage, he goes crazy: "It's like someone else takes over my body" (Hit Parade, Fall 1984).

In describing what a Van Halen concert is like, David Lee Roth commented, "I'm gonna abandon my spirit to them [emotions], which is actually what I attempt to do. You work yourself up into that state and you fall in supplication of the demon gods" (Rock, April 1984).

Guitarist Mick Mars of Motley Crue described his band as "demonic, that's what we are" (Heavy Metal Times, May 1983). Nikki Sixx referring to their "Shout at the Devil" stage show commented, "We have skulls, pentagrams, and all kinds of satanic symbols on stage .... I've always flirted with the devil" (Circus, Jan. 31, 1984).

Stevie Nicks of Fleetwood Mac has several times dedicated their concerts to the witches of the world. An album of the rock group Venom entitled, "Welcome to Hell" contains the following words on the back cover: "We are possessed by all that is evil The death of your God we demand: we spit at the virgin you worship, and sit at the Lord Satan's left hand."

The "Rune" album of Led Zeppelin displays on the cover the famous black occultist Aleister Crowley. Led Zeppelin's Jimmy Page, a self confessed Satanist, bought Crowley's old mansion. John Bonham, a drummer for the band, died in the house in 1980; Robert Plant allegedly split the group up after his death and blamed Page's obsession with the occult for his death.

David Bowie in Rolling Stone magazine (Feb. 12, 1976), stated: "Rock has always been THE DEVIL'S MUSIC . . . I believe rock and roll is dangerous . . . I feel we're only heralding SOMETHING EVEN DARKER THAN OURSELVES" (Rolling Stone, Feb. 12, 1976).

In the song "The Conjuring" by Megadeth, the REAL mission of rock is clearly heard:

"I AM THE DEVIL'S ADVOCATE A SALESMAN, if you will . . .
Come join me in my INFERNAL DEPTHS . . .
I've got your soul!" At the end of the song • they chant "OBEY"!

Rocker Frank Zappa (who discovered the awful truth December 4, 1993 the second he died) proudly boasted: "I'm the devil's advocate. We have our own worshippers who are called 'groupies.' Girls will give their bodies to musicians as you would give a sacrifice to a god" (Peters Brothers, What About Christian Rock, p. 17).

* The super group, Metallica, in the song "Jump In the Fire", commands young people to jump into hell:

"Follow me now my child . . .
DO JUST AS I SAY . . .
Jump by your will or be taken by force I'll get you either way . . .
So reach down grab my hand walk with me through the land
COME HOME WHERE YOU BELONG
So come on JUMP IN THE FIRE."

In the cover song, "The Prince", Metallica openly sing:

"Angel from below . . .
I WISH TO SELL MY SOUL . . .
DEVIL TAKE MY SOUL
with diamonds you repay I don't care for heaven
so don't you look for me to cry
AND I WILL BURN IN HELL from the day I die."

* Rock star, Marilyn Manson, proudly boasts:
"Hopefully, I'll be remembered as the person who brought an end to Christianity" (Spin, August 1996, p. 34).

Manson, an ordained "reverend" in the Church of Satan, mutilates himself on stage (1 Kings 18:28), rips up the Holy Bible, and spews "blasphemies" against the Lord Jesus Christ. Manson's T Shirts declare,

"KILL YOUR PARENTS" & "I -- SATAN".

Manson claims his album Antichrist Superstar came via "supernatural inspiration":

"I heard this album as finished, I heard it in dreams . . . It was like the revelations of John the Baptist or something" (huH, Oct. 1996, p. 34).

Manson's "hope" for Antichrist Superstar,: "I think every time people listen to this new album maybe God will be destroyed in their heads. . ." (huH, Oct. 1996, p. 37).

Manson's "blasphemy" is not just an act. He goes on to let the public know his agenda:

"I don't know if anyone has really understood what we're trying to do. This isn't just about shock value . . . that's just there to lure the people in. Once we've got them we can give them our message" (Hit Parader, Oct. 1996, p. 28).

Manson admits his childhood longing for Satan:
"My mom used to tell me when I was a kid, If you curse at nighttime, the devil's going to come to you when you 're sleeping. I used to get excited because I really wanted it

to happen . . . I wanted it. I wanted it more than anything . . ."(Rolling Stone, January 23, 1997 p.52).

* Twisted Sister sings, "Burn in Hell":
"Welcome to the abandoned land
COME ON IN CHILD, TAKE MY HAND
Here there's no work or play Only one bill to pay
There's just five words to say As you go down, down, down
YOU'RE GONNA BURN IN HELL!"

Bon Jovi sings in "Homebound Train":
"When I was just a boy
THE DEVIL TOOK MY HAND
Took me from my home
He made me a man . . .
I'm going DOWN, DOWN, DOWN, DOWN, DOWN
On the homebound train."

In Smash Hits magazine, Bon Jovi says: " . . . I'd kill my mother for rock and roll. I WOULD SELL MY SOUL."

* One of the most popular groups in rock history is Slayer. Slayer sing of themselves, as:
"Warriors from the gates of hell . . .
In lord Satan we trust."

Slayer's albums sell in the millions! And song after song IS PRAISE TO SATAN! Their song "Hell Awaits" says:
"Jesus knows your soul cannot be saved
CRUCIFY THE SO CALLED LORD
He soon shall fall to me
Your souls are damned
Your God has fell to slave for me eternally Hell awaits."

The beginning of their song "Hell Awaits" contains an obvious backwards message. When played forward, nothing but garbled noise is heard, but when played backwards you hear the real message "JOIN US, JOIN US, JOIN US" over and over!

* The group Acheron, has an album titled, "The Rites of the Black Mass". On the album Peter Gilmore, of the Church of Satan, actually reads the rites of a Black Mass, as the group Acheron, in hellish growls, sings such lyrics as:

"Glory to thee almighty Satan . . .
We praise thee, we bless thee,
WE ADORE THEE . . .
THOU ART LORD, THOU ALONE, OH MIGHTY SATAN."

* The group Manowar, sings in "The Bridge of Death":

"Dark Lord, I summon thee
Demanding the sacred right to burn in hell . . .
Take My lustful soul Drink my blood as I drink yours . . .
LUCIFER IS KING PRAISE SATAN!"

* The group Morbid Angel, sings in "Vengeance in Mine":

"Mote it be Satan's sword I have become . . .
I burn with hate
TO RID THE WORLD OF THE NAZARENE!"

And to commit the ultimate blasphemy they sing in the song "Blasphemy":

"Chant the blasphemy Mockery of the Messiah
WE CURSE THE HOLY GHOST . . .
Blaspheme the Ghost
BLASPHEMY OF THE HOLY GHOST."

Trey Azagthoh of Morbid Angel claims to be a REAL vampire, and while playing onstage • he actually bites himself and then drinks his own blood!

Back in 70's one of the top songs was "Hotel California" by the Eagles. The song refers to the Church of Satan, which is located in a converted HOTEL on CALIFORNIA street! On the inside of the album cover, looking down on the festivities, is Anton LaVey, the founder of the Church of Satan and author of

79

the Satanic Bible! People say, the Eagles aren't serious, they're just selling records. That's what you think! The Eagles manager, Larry Salter, conceded in the Waco Tribune Herald, (Feb. 28, 1982) that the Eagles have attended and were involved in the Church of Satan! One of their songs is entitled "Have A Good Day in Hell."

* The group Kiss leaped on stage as rock'n roll demons puking blood, breathing fire and screaming • "God of rock'n roll, we'll steal your virgin soul." In their song "God of Thunder", they command young people to kneel before Satan:

"I'm lord of the wasteland, a modern day man of steel
I gather darkness to please me and I COMMAND YOU TO KNEEL.
Before, The God of thunder, the god of rock'n roll
I'LL STEAL YOUR VIRGIN SOUL!"

One of the most popular groups in rock is AC DC. In the song, "Hells Bells", they sing:
"I got my bell
I'm gonna take you to hell
I'm gonna get ya SATAN GET YA"

Their song "Highway to Hell" they sing:

"Ain't nothing I would rather do
GOIN' DOWN, PARTY TIME
My friends are gonna be there too . . .
Hey Satan, paid my dues . . .
I'm on the way to the promised land
I'm on the HIGHWAY TO HELL."

* The group Suicidal Tendencies, whose songs glorify suicide and have been linked to teen suicides, reveal a frightening truth in the song "Possessed":

"I'M A PRISONER OF A DEMON . . .
It stays with me wherever I go
I can't break away from its hold
This must be my punishment FOR SELLING MY SOUL!"

During a 1993 Oprah Winfrey interview, Michael Jackson, talked about why he makes sexual gestures in his performances: "It happens subliminally. IT'S THE MUSIC THAT COMPELS ME TO DO IT. You don't think about it, it just happens. I'M SLAVE TO THE RHYTHM" (The Evening Star, Feb. 11, 1993, p. A10).

* Pink Floyd sings, in the song "Sheep",
"The Lord is my shepherd, I shall not want . . .
With bright knives he RELEASETH MY SOUL
He maketh me to hang on hooks in high places . . .
For lo, he hath great power and GREAT HUNGER."

* The song "Sympathy for the Devil" by the Rolling Stones, is the official anthem for the Church of Satan. In it, Lucifer speaks in the first person and asks sympathy for all who meet him. Lead singer, Mick Jagger claims that Anton LaVey, the founder of the Church of Satan and author of the Satanic Bible, help inspire their music! Their album titled, "Their Satanic Majesties Request", leaves no doubt to their allegiance!

* The group Venom reveal the real reason for their music, as they sing:

"We're not here to entertain you . . .
I PREACH THE WAYS OF SATAN
Answer to his calls!"

In their song "Possessed", they sing:

"I am possessed by all that is evil
The death of your God, I demand . . .
AND SIT AT LORD SATAN'S LEFT HAND!"

* At the 1992 MTV Awards, the group Red Hot Chili Peppers, upon receiving their award and giving thanks, said:
"First Of all we want to thank Satan . . ."

Origin of Rock Music

Rock music derived from the 1950's era of "Rock and Roll." Alan Freed a Cleveland DJ and promoter coined the name "Rock and Roll."

Freed, concert producer, was attempting to cross over what they called rhythm and blues into the white community. He thought renaming the music would be the answer. The word "rock" was slang in the black community for "sex". Freed would call the music he was packaging "Rock and Roll," and it stuck. The definition of this word basically depicts "wild sex." It's not a coincidence that sex and drugs has become the main focal point of this industry. Freed ended up being charged with various crimes of corruption in the music industry. He ended up dying penniless on January 20, 1965 at the young age of 43. He was inducted into the Rock and Roll Hall of Fame in 1986.

Satanist Mentality Exposed

Knowing how evil the devil is, why would anyone buy music, paying tribute to God's arch enemy? Why are so many choosing to become blatant followers of Satan and his doctrine? I asked this question to two wards a couple of weeks ago on a lock-up unit. Both stated that they have chosen to worship Satan, because they could do what they felt like doing and get rewarded for it. They both conveyed that they loved sinning, and the idea of getting rewarded for having fun appealed to them. Listen to what they had to say:

"I met a lot of homies of mine who worshiped satan"

When I was growing up, I was being preached the Catholic faith. During this time I was about 7 or 8 and I was living in a good part of my town, I would attend Catholic services, go the Catholic school. I did believe in Jesus Christ, but then again I do still. I just don't believe everything that is said about him so I'm against him. When I turned 10 or 11 we moved to the bad part of my town, and during this time both of my older brothers had just got out of prison two months apart from each other. Now there was my two older brothers that gangbanged and plus we live in the hood now. So I started kicking it with them and their homies so when they got locked up I felt I had do what they did. So I started getting locked up a lot and I attend church services, but it didn't mean nothing to me anymore I felt if Jesus loved me, why would he keep me locked up. After a couple of juvenile hall programs and two boot camp programs, they finally sent me to CYA. I met a lot of homies of mine who worshiped satan so I started liking everything they did. You don't have to be good your whole life just to get what Jesus wants and that for people to go to heaven. I rather get out party everyday, sell drugs and do what I want to and enjoy my life instead of following the 10 Commandments. So I got more into worshiping satan and started tattooing my whole Body with gang related stuff all over my head, face, arms, and body and I got the "Mark of the Beast" tattooed on me "666" on my head. So now when I get out I'm going to become gothic and worship satan in every way I can. I can tell that that's were I belong and where I want to go. I like to self mutilate my body with tattoos. I got all the tattoos on my face, neck and head to represent were I'm from and what I am. It don't bother me if people won't give me a job, I don't care if I go to prison for the rest of my life. I will still continue to do what I do.

"The Dark Angel"

At this point and time I see my self as a gift to the world, I've been asked to see the good and bad the positive and negative, but don't know the reason why. After I had a vision of my best homie dying and three weeks later he died the way I told him. I saw him dying on the phone, I recognized it was real life, I was being told to look at. This was fun for me, because I knew when somebody was dead in my life that I loved, before it even happened or something bad was going to happen to them. That stopped me from worrying about what was going on, on the street.

Sometime in my visions I could see parts of hell and I could see, feel, hear and smell everything in my vision. That part opened up my eyes to acknowledge this sh*% is for real. And I had to pick a side to go to war with, so I picked the devil and told myself to go to war with God. Now I look at myself as one of the devil's dark angels, his kid as I call it now. I love everything that is evil and nothing that is good.

People might say I pick the losing side for a spirit war, but I know something they don't know. If you're not on God's side or the devil's side whose side do you think your on? And where do you think your going after you die? Just put it like this,

If you did not give your soul to God, then you sold your soul to the devil and I will see you in hell when the end of days comes trust me on that one. Those who follow the devil should not burn for him, but with him and all his dark angels, but the spirit war is not going to be over, just the fight. The war is yet to come after and it will be the devil's angel vs. God's angel and my lord vs. your Lord.

Sometimes I ask people do they think that a person can make them completely, religiously transformed? They tell me, "no!" But what they don't know when you do bad things and you think you got away with it, and you keep doing them because they make you feel good, your religion is now becoming the devil's and your soul is the devil's soul and until you get God back in your life, you belong to the devil and all his dark angels and let me tell you like this, hell ain't no walk in the park if thats what you think.

Innately, humans have a natural fear for evil; that's how God programmed us. The satanist I've interviewed believe that if they can make friends with the father of evil (Satan), they can live with out fear, and at the same time be rewarded for indulging in their sinful desires. However there is one big problem with this concept, by trusting Satan, they are trusting not only in the "father of sin", but also the father of lies," which is Satan himself.

John 8:44

44 You belong to your father, the devil, and you want to carry out your father's desire. He was a murderer from the beginning, not holding to the truth, for there is no truth in him. When he lies, he speaks his native language, for he is a liar and the father of lies.

I remember saying to two confessed satanists, "you know the Holy Bible refers to Satan as the "father of lies." They both agreed with me with no rebuttal. They had both told me that as a satanist, they believed that Satan would reward them for their sins, with great riches and power, once they die and go to hell. I then asked, "How are you willing to trust your soul to an individual whose nature is deceitful and known as the 'father of lies?' How can you believe, that all of a sudden, Satan will have integrity to honor his promise to you, once you go to hell? Wouldn't that be a bit naïve of you, to believe that?" Two blank looks appeared on these wards faces; some doubt appeared to be getting planted about their master.

Most satanists fail to understand, that Satan really hates them, and is willing to deceitfully bargain with them while their on earth, in order for him to get another trophy which is their soul. Why does Satan hate and attack the human? Because humans are made in God's image, which is the image of his judge, and Satan knows that God love us, because he sent his only Son Jesus to die in our place, for all of our sins (John 3:16). Satan knows it hurts God deeply when God loses a precious soul to hell. The satanist is a human made in God's image, who has been deceived by Satan to believe that Satan and his demons will win the war against God. All satanists have to do is what feels good to their body and keep sinning.

Satan's strategy is to mobilize humans as tanks in his war, by giving them evil desires which are really demonic instructions, which gives pleasure to their emotions and body, in order to get their will to line up with his will. He sometimes will empower them through witchcraft, and earthly blessings to do supernatural things, such as putting curses on people, levitation and astral travel (the soul comes out the body to travel). This is why movies like Harry Potter and shows like Raven on the Disney Channel are so popular. It makes witchcraft appear cool and exciting. Satan will use any type of bidding technique to get a soul to work faithfully and efficiently for him in this spiritual war, with promises of more blessings in the afterlife.

What better satisfaction could Satan get, then to have God's creation, a soul, work for him against God. At the end, Satan gets to kill them by torturing their soul in hell which grieves God. Satan relishes having their souls get the same consequence as him and his demons, which is to be thrown into the eternal lake of fire on Judgment Day (Revelation 20). Satan already knows he is fighting a losing battle, however his goal out of hate, is to take as many souls as he can with him. So why would he spare the souls of a satanist?

Satanism is not just practiced by those who proclaim they are satanists. Satanism is a way of life which is in opposition to God's commandments. With that said, there is a whole wave of Satanism being taught through our airwaves everyday. Whether Heavy Metal, Rap, R&B, New Age, Pop, Blues or Country and the list goes on, Satan is constantly looking for any platform to spread his message. The sad part is, that many don't even know that they're listening to satanic doctrine on a daily basis through their own musical selections, whatever styles it may be. I talk to individuals all the time who wonder why they continue to struggle and be overcome by sins such as lust and a host of other ones, and remain unaware or in denial that it is the musical message they are allowing within their soul which has corrupted their mind and driven their emotions and will (actions) against God's will in their lives.

The Ancient Roots of Hip Hop

"Hip Hop isn't just music, it is also a spiritual movement of the blacks! You can't just call Hip Hop a trend!" Lauryn Hill

Afrika Bambaataa is the founder of Hip Hop and The Universal Zulu Nation. "Zulu" means "heaven". Hip Hop is one of the strong catalysts for thug mentality, and it has cultivated a culture which encompasses not just music, but clothes, religion and philosophy. Before I start on the surface level of Hip Hop, let me take you to its root, back to Africa. Back to the Zulu Kingdom, founded in 1709 by Zulu KaNtombhela, but most known for the leadership of the great warrior Shaka Zulu. Shaka was known for his bravery and strategic battle plans. The Zulus paid homage to numerous gods. Their religious culture was heavily influenced by the Greek and the Chinese. Zulu culture was full of superstitions and sorcery. Zulus shared the belief with the Chinese and the Greeks that ancestral spirits take physical form in the shape of non-venomous snakes. The Chinese and Greeks believed they descended from Kekrops and Fuxi, who were half-man, half-snake. They venerated (paid tribute to) their ancestors and sacrifice animals to pay homage to their spirits. Zulus would perform a war dance called the Pyrrhic dance, a dance created by the Greeks. According to the theology of the dance; the goddess Athena invented the Pyrrhic dance to celebrate the victory of the gods over the giants who represented the dark and evil forces of nature. The Pyrrhic dance was a war dance for celebrating victories. Shaka never married and was against marriage and having children for him self. He had a harem of 1,200 women. When by mistake a harem girl would give birth to a son, shaka would kill the baby, because he believed the proverb, "A bull has perfect place until the young bulls-his progeny-begin to dispute his supremacy."

Shaka was callous and brutal in his ruling tactics. He massacred thousands who did not appear to him to show sufficient grief when his mother died. Once suspecting infidelity, he made a clean sweep of the whole harem. His tactic was often for the concubines to be rushed away, their necks broken by a sudden sideways jerk in transit and their bodies beaten with knobberries.

Today, the Zulu Nation pays great homage to Shaka Zulu so much that they formed a religion in honor of his tribe.

Is Hip Hop a Religion?

The Zulu Nation is the creator of "Hip Hop" which clearly has its roots in the pagan worship of false deities, which God forbids (Deuteronomy 5:7-9).

For more in-depth information on the roots of Hip Hop go to: Exministries.com, A ministry of Elder G. Craige Lewis. This ministries's web site and *The Truth behind Hip Hop*-video series was very helpful in the research of this book.

Lewis asserts in his video series, that the Zulu Nation channeled a spirit or deity called *"Hip Hop"* and that *"Hip Hop"* is actually a registered religion. The spirit of Hip Hop, has unknowingly introduced many into false god worship, along with the worship unto themselves.

From my own research, I have discovered there is now a church called *The Temple of Hip Hop* which has gone world-wide. These are the requirements for membership according to their website (www. templeofhiphop.org):

You simply must be; 12 years of age or older, registered with the Temple of Hiphop, own at least one copy of the Gospel of Hiphop (a study manual that accompanies the 'Hiphop' lifestyle) and you must love Hip Hop to call yourself an official "Temple Member". Apprenticeships, teaching positions, live concert and lecture touring apprenticeships are also available.

A recent slogan I have seen on T-shirts to promote the Hip Hop agenda and religion states, "I am Hip Hop." So if Hip Hop was a spirit channeled through an incantation, then the wearer of this shirt is proclaiming that they are one with this spirit or rather possessed with it.

The Zulu Nation's website states (www.zulunation.com/beliefs.html):

THE BELIEFS OF THE UNIVERSAL ZULU NATION

WE BELIEVE IN THE ONE GOD,WHO IS CALLED BY MANY NAMES ALLAH, JEHOVAH, YAHWEH, ELOAHIM, JAH, GOD, THE MOST HIGH, THE CREATOR, THE SUPREME ONE. WE BELIEVE,AS AMAZULU,WE WIL NOT FIGHT OR KILL OTHER HUMAN BEINGS OVER WHICH PROPER NAME TO CALL GOD.WE BELIEVE GOD WILL COME TO BE SEEN BY THE HUMAN EYE AND WILL STRAIGHTEN OUT THE PROBLEMS THAT HUMAN BEINGS BROUGHT UPON THIS PLANET SO CALLED EARTH.
WE BELIEVE IN THE HOLY BIBLE AND THE GLORIOUS QUR'AN AND IN THE SCRIPTURES OF ALL THE PROPHETS OF THE LORD.
WE BELIEVE THAT THE BIBLE HAS BEEN TAMPERED WITH AND MUST BE REINTERPRETED,SO THAT HUMANKIND WILL NOT BE SNARED BY THE FALSEHOODS THAT HAVE BEEN ADDED TO IT.

This theological statement contradicts itself; let me explain:

They attempt to make us believe that the names: Allah, Jehovah, Yahweh, Eloahim, Jah, God, The Most High, The Creator and the Supreme One, represent the same God. Jehovah, Yahweh, Eloahim, The Most High, The Creator and the Supreme One, describes the God of the Holy Bible. The names Allah and Jah clearly do not. This is why:

Allah: Muslims call their god Allah. Muslims often claim that their god is the same God referred to in the Holy Bible. Nowhere in the Bible will you find Allah. Because of Islam's dominance Allah became the common name of God across some cultures. Most Muslims I talk to don't know that Allah is one of the Babylonian god's of Baal, according to the Encyclopedia of Religion. In the Holy Bible, Israel was punished by God on numerous occasions for worshiping the many gods of Baal. The Arabs first knew Allah as the Moon God. They believed Allah had 3 daughters who were viewed as intercessors for the people into Allah (Remember the God of the Holy Bible had the son Jesus Christ, Allah had no sons). The names of his daughters were Al-uzza, Al-Lat and Al-Manat. The symbol of the Moon God Allah was the crescent moon. This symbol is an ancient pagan fertility symbol that is worshiped throughout the Middle East. The Arabs worshiped Allah long before Mohammed did, who is the founder of the Islamic faith who lead his people away from polytheism (worship of multiple gods). Before they chose Allah as their only true god, they had worshiped 360 gods. Allah was the god of the Qurish tribe, which was Mohammed's tribe.

The difference between Allah and the God of the Bible is that the God of the Bible is a loving and personal God, who sent his only son Jesus to die for the sins of the world so that the world could be saved from hell and the lake of fire, and inherit eternal life in heaven by accepting Jesus as Lord and Savior. Allah has never revealed himself to man, he relates to man only through his law and will. Jesus has called us to be his friend. (James 2:23)

Another issue with the Zulu Nation's doctrine is that there is no cohesiveness among these beliefs. For example, read what the Koran states about Christians and Jews who don't believe in Allah:

"Fight and slay the pagans [Christians] wherever ye find them and seize them, confine them, and lie in wait for them in every place of ambush" (Surah 9:5).
* "Fight those who believe not in Allah nor the last day, nor hold that forbidden which hath been forbidden by Allah and his apostle nor acknowledge the religion of truth of the people of the Book (the Jews and the Christians) until they pay the Jizya [tax on non Muslims] with willing submission and feel themselves subdued" (Surah 9:29).
* "Those who follow Muhammad are merciless for the unbelievers but kind to each othe" (Qur'an 48:29).
* "Enmity and hatred will reign between us until ye believe in Allah alon" (Qur'an 60:4).

* "Say to the Unbelievers, if (now) they desist (from Unbelief), their past would be forgiven them; but if they persist, the punishment of those before them is already (a matter of warning for them). And fight them on until there is no more tumult or oppression, and there prevail justice and faith in God altogether and everywhere; but if they cease, verily God doth see all that they do" (Qur'an 8:37 39).

* "And fight them on until there is no more Tumult or oppression, and there prevail justice and faith in God; but if they cease, Let there be no hostility except to those who practice oppression" (Qur'an 2:193).

* "Fight the unbelievers in your surroundings, and let them find harshness in you" (Qur'an 9:123).

* "For he who believes in the Trinity, "the Fire will be his abode a grievous penalty will befall the blasphemer" (Qur'an 5:72 73).

Notice the teaching from the Hadith (research):

* "You (the Jews) should know that the earth belongs to Allah and His Apostle and I wish to expel you from this land (Arabia)" (Hadith, 4363).

* "I will expel the Jews and Christians from the Arabian Peninsula and will not leave any but Muslims" (Hadith Sahih 4366).

Jah: This name for god refers to the Rastafarian's god, which is not the God of the Holy Bible. The Rasafarian's god is Haile Selassie. The Rastafarians believe that Selassie, the former Emperor of Ethiopia is the Black Messiah who appeared in the flesh for the redemption of all Blacks exiled in the world of white oppressors. Selassie claimed to be a direct descendant of King David, the 225th ruler in an unbroken line of Ethiopian Kings from the time of Solomon and Sheba (Queen of Ethiopia). King David came from the bloodline of the Tribe of Judah whose symbol is the lion. This is why some Rastafarians wear their hair in dreadlocks, to look like a lion. Another trait that is contributed to the Rastafarian's image is their use of "ganja" (marijuana). In their rituals they use marijuana as a sacrament and aid to meditation, Ganja is used in that they believe smoking it brings them closer to their god. Using marijuana to alter the state of the mind is called witchcraft. Rastafarians utilize various drugs for spiritual rituals also. Reggae Singer, Bob Marley, a disciple of Rastafarian, publicly made known his illicit drug use through interviews and his music.

In a recent interview, Afrika Bambaataa conveyed in an article *"The True   Meaning of Hip-Hop Culture" by Afrika Bambaataa*, and attempted to distant himself from the negative gangster rappers. He states :

The media does play a big role in destroying the hip hop culture movement, but many of you in the hip hop community are the biggest enemies of hip hop and you will be the ones who will help the enemies of hip hop to destroy it, or to bring it back underground, because of your ignorance of knowledge of hip hop
(www.globaldarkness.com articles true meaning of hip hop bambaata.htm).

Yet, some of the disciples of the "Zulu Nation" which he proudly presents on his website are gangster rappers themselves. The Zulu Nation states on their website:

Who is a Member of the Zulu Nation?

Diamond D, Ice T, Kool DJ Red Alert, Nikki D, A Tribe Called Quest, Brand Nubian, Leaders of the New School, Positive K, Yo Yo, Fat Joe, Jungle Brothers, DJ Kool, Funkmaster Flex, Q Bert, BIO, BRIM, King Sun, Rock Steady Crew, Roc Raider
As we are dedicated to improving and uplifting ourselves and our communities, all Zulu Nation members should be involved in some activity that is positive and gives back to the community. Hip Hop music is our vehicle of expression. We can learn to write, produce, market, promote, publish, perform and televise our own music, for our own people. There are too many divisions between males and females (www.zulunation.com).

However, listen to what their members have to say and the projects they are involved in, see how many contradictions you can find which conflict with their founder's mission statement:

Ice T:
Advertisement from Ice T's latest project: "The O.G. is back with his latest project: The Pimp Penal Code. Sit back and get ready to learn how to play the game from some of the world's top shelf players. The game is to be sold, not told. School is in session."

Ice-T's Pimpin' 101 is a x-rated documentary on the science of pimping. Ice-T illustrates the five different areas of the pimp game
http://www.icet.com/bio.html.

The Zulu Nation has expanded into another denomination on the West Coast, started by Ice-T. Ice-T explains the beliefs of "The Syndicate" during an interview:

Interviewer: "Okay, what's The Syndicate?"
Ice T: "It's the L.A. version of Zulu Nation."
Interviewer: "Great. What's Zulu Nation?"
Ice T: "Zulu Nation was the first organization of rappers who got together to agree to work together instead of against one another."

Drive In Movie Critic of Grapevine, Texas
1991 Joe Bob Briggs All Rights Reserve

artist: Ice T lyrics
title: Ice M.F. T
album: Home Invasion
Nigga step to me
But grab ya hoes quick
Cause the Syndicate's (West Coast name for Zulu Nation)
 throwin that crazy di#@
Punk motherf %#rs run up
You'll get done up
We'll have your as# gunned up
Before sun up
So what's the color I'm raggin?
Been a millionare for years
Still saggin

artist: Ice T lyrics
title: The Iceberg(Iceberg Slim is famous pimp, in which Ice
T derived his name)
album: The Iceberg Freedom of Speech
[Verse 1]

Before my posse makes a move on your mom's crib
Think we got knives and guns? We got bombs, kid
Blow up your whole block, ya hear the gunshots
Throw you in the Syndicate cellar and let your body rot
Cos I'm the coldest motherf%#r that you ever heard
Call me The Ice...or just The Iceberg

Positive K Lyrics

Carhoppers Lyrics

Uhh.. hey!
Carhoppers, car car hoppers
Carhoppers, car car hoppers
Speak on it now
Carhoppers, car car hoppers

Uhh, uhh! I call girls carhoppers
Cause I make em hit notes like they was singin at the operas
May I say, on anyday, yeah they with it
me

Artist: Fat Joe Lyrics
Song: Gangsta Lyrics

I went from grams into O's, pounds to bricks
On the strip pimpin hoes on some goldie s t
I'ma gangsta by destiny, OG's selected me
I earned my spot, my whole team elected me

[Chorus: children singing]
Gangsta, gangsta

I wanna be a gangsta
My daddy was a gangsta
Gangsta, gangsta
I wanna be a gangsta
My daddy was a gangsta

Yo Yo Lyrics
The Bonnie and Clyde Theme Lyrics

Ice Cube

[Ice Cube]
It's a man's world, but check the girl
With the Mac 11, 187
Hit the switch, front, back, side to side
Corner to corner, punk you a goner

[Yo Yo]
I'm the type of girl that's down for my nigga
I'll lie for my nigga, peel a cap for my nigga
See he don't mind me flirting, wearing tight skirts and
Cause when it's all over it's curtains

Industry Supporters of Hip Hop Doctrine:

LL Cool J

LL Cool J is an "old school" Hip Hop artist who has promoted the Hip Hop doctirine and publicly endorses and promotes artists from the 5 percent nation.

On the artist's 1993 Album, entitled 14 Shots to the Dome, he promotes Hip Hop artists such as Public Emenmy, NWA (niggaz with attitudes), Naughty by Nature, Ice Cube, A Tribe Called Quest and Ice T. In one for the tracks he dedicates it to all of the "Underage brothers with the rebel mentality". He also states,that women love bad boys and the "feds" can't stop him. He dedicates track 10 to "gangstas".

Jay Z
Album: "The Blueprint"

Song: Takeover

The takeover, the break's over nigga
god mc, me, jay hova
hey lil' soldier you ain't ready for war
r.o.c. too strong for y'all
it's like bringin a knife to a gunfight, pen to a test
your chest in the line of fire witcha thin a#s vest
you bringin them Boyz II men, how them boys gon' win?
this is grown man b.i, get you rolled into triage
beatch   your reach ain't long enough, dunny
your peeps ain't strong enough, f*#*a
roc a fella is the army, better yet the navy
niggaz'll kidnap your babies, spit at your lady
we bring   knife to fistfight, kill your drama
uh, we kill you motherf%#n ants with a sledgehammer
don't let me do it to you dunny cause I overdo it
so you won't confuse it with just rap music

Ja Rule
Album: "Venni Vetti Vecci"

Song:Only begotten Son

he who believeth in ja shall not be condemned. but he that
believeth not is condemned already. only because he has not
believed in the man and the only begotten son my Lord.
for he so feared the word, he left his only begotten son to
shed his blood, show that pain is love, but I won't cry. cause I
live to die, wit my mind on my money and my guns in the sky!
one of us; from the album "rule 3:36"
Lord, when I die pacify, crucify me
I rock a devil cross, one's for the soul one's for the body
if i'm built then god dies, I wanna see god cry
real tears from a burned out life in ten years
I sware I got the devil in me, with no fear
if I hear I can't see, if I see I can't hear

Ice Cube Go To Church Lyrics
(feat. Lil Jon, Snoop Dogg)

This song now has radio play

[Snoop Dogg]
Nigga you need to stop snitchin!
All that yip yappin and jaw jackin
Nigga if you scared, go to church
You knew the job was dangerous when you took it

[Ice Cube   (Lil Jon)]
I'm down with Lil Jon ain't got to pretend (YEAH!)
"Crunk Juice" nigga run the club that you in (HEY!)
You scary motherfu%#ers don't wanna bring the ruckus (NAH!)
You just spend all your time in the club tryin to duck us

[Chorus 2X: Ice Cube   (Lil Jon)]
If you a scared motherfu%#er go to church (GO TO CHURCH)
If you a gutter motherfu%#er do your dirt (A DO YOUR DIRT)
If you a down motherfu%#er put in work (A PUT IN WORK)
IF you a crazy motherfu%#er go berzerk (A GO BERZERK!)

Missy Elliott
from the album "So Addictive"

X Tacy
read between the lines,ecstacy, a place of fullfillment and
fantasies
were your dreams become reality's, mhm, ecstacy
it enhances your most inner desire, to become more free with
your guts and feelings
e e e ecstacy
boy let me free your mind, let's hook up tonight, take you on
a flight, high, high
make you warm inside, I won't waste you're time, my love is so
divine, it feels like i'm on..
ecstaacyy, i'm willing, to do the things I said I wouldn't do
on ecstaacyy, the feeling makes me feel like i'm in love with
you
dog in heat; from the album "so addictive"
uhh uhh.. cause this love right here is on fire (fire)

slide, wanna take a ride
i'm movin on; from the album "so addictive"
see, I had to make a record that gives thanks to my Lord and savior Jesus Christ. alot of people criticize me for the kind of music I sing, but see, they don't change my belief that I have in god, ya know what i'm sayin?

The Zulu Nation's Attack on God's Word the Holy Bible:

"We believe that The Bible has been tampered with and that White people, in preaching and teaching White Supremacy, took the Scriptures of the Prophets of God and rearranged them to push for White Supremacy, for example: 1) the painting of Jesus Christ White, 2) all of the Angels White, 3) in fact, even all the Prophets as White" (www.zulunation.com/beliefs.html).

They make a strong argument, however the only thing wrong with this argument is that you can't find any of these points in the Holy Bible. There is no painting of a white Jesus or angels in the Bible, nor does the Bible make written reference of Jesus' or any angel's ethnicity. Nor does the Bible promote that one race is better than another race. If the Bible had been tampered with, the tamperers would have definitely changed the story (Numbers 12:1) about Miriam, Moses' sister, who ridiculed Moses for marrying a Cushite woman (Ethiopian woman) and when God observed this, he cursed Miriam with leprosy. Hip Hop understands the power of music as stated on their website. They embrace many religions. Many other religious groups have now got on the bandwagon, such as the 5 Percenters and the Nation of Islam, both who preach cultic doctrine.

Bambaataa, a former New York City gang member from the streets of the South Bronx, who ran in his youth with the notorious Black Spades, states his spiritual views of music in an article on the Universal Zulu Nation Website:

"The body is a temple, and it's the feeling that you get from the music that makes you come alive. When the beats hit your body, it takes over. You lose control, you just have to do whatever you have to do" (www.zulunation.com).

Recently, I read about the country of Sri Lanka, an island lying off the southern eastern tip of the Indian Subcontinent. Some of the villages have practiced summoning demons through music since the first millennium B.C. The setting of the rituals takes on the form of a circular arena where dancers perform around a decorative altar of young coconut leaves with offerings. Masks are worn by those involved in the ritual as they dance and play instruments to conjure up spirits (demons) for guidance and their necessities.

A witness describes the ritual:

"The rhythm of the fast drumbeat, of the demon drum of "yak bera" vibrates through the air, building up suspense. An exorcism ceremony begins with an invitation to the demons to appear. The performers chant in time to the rhythm of the drumbeats. The sorcerer implores and finally threateningly asks the demon to stop harassing the afflicted subject and leave, in the name of lord Buddha, and King Vesmuni."

"Five Percenters"

Another religion that has married itself to Hip Hop is the "Five Percent Nation or The Nation of God's and Earths." This movement does not like to be called a religion but a "culture" and a "way of life." Clarence X founded the movement in Harlem. Clarence joined the Nation of Islam (NOI)Temple No. 7 in Harlem, New York back in the early 1950's.

They refer to their teaching as "Supreme Mathematics." Clarence started to question the doctrine of the Nation of Islam(NOI) in the early 1960's, when it claimed that God had appeared in Detroit in 1930 in the person of Master Farad Muhammad. Farad is the one who passed his teachings to his messenger, Elijah Muhammad. According the NOI doctrine, Farad the black man was the original man, and to Clarence, Farad looked white. Clarence X which later began to call himself Clarence 13X, began to teach that the black man was god. In 1963, he was reprimanded by the NOI, along with a few followers. They began to call him "Father Allah," after he had changed his name to Allah. They taught that only 5% know their divinity and use the knowledge to release the hidden resources of the black man. Once a man has tapped his hidden talents, he is a god. As a matter of fact, many in the movement prefer to be called gods rather than Five Percenters. The Movement believes that 85% are without knowledge. They refer to these individuals as mentally blind, deaf and dumb and headed towards self-destruction. Ten percent are referred to as the "white devil" or the "grafted" (they believe the white man was created by the evil scientist Yacub, approximately 6,000 years ago, according to Farad's teachings).

The Core beliefs of the 5 Percenters:

- Black men are gods; others who accept the knowledge of the Five Percent can become "civilized people."
- Education and family are of primary importance.
- Peace is central to teachings.
- The Five-Percents believe that as god themselves, the only one they must submit to is "self."
- That scientist created the white man from the black man, who in turn tricked the black man into slavery (Nation of Islam belief)
- Allah is the Supreme Being. Each man is god only of his own universe, his family and not of other people

*(http://en.wikipedia.org/wiki/The_Nation_of_Gods_and_Earths).

Below are excerpts of lyrics from songs of mainstream Hip Hop 5 Percent artists and supporters:

Group: Da Lynch Mob

Song: Buck Tha Devil

Buck the devil, buck the devil, buck the devil BOOM
Give the nigga, give the nigga, give the nigga ROOM
Must be a full moon, here comes a tune
Bullets fly by your head zoom zoom zoom
(A to the K to the 4 to the 7
Little devils don't go to heaven!

Last night I shot eleven at the record shop
Most of 'em dropped when my 9 went pop!)
Damn; see the f**kin cop with the flat top
standin over niggaz face down on the blacktop

<u>Nas</u>
Represent

Represent, represent!! [repeat 4X]

Yo, they call me Nas, I'm not your legal type of fella
Moet drinkin, marijuana smokin street dweller
who's always on the corner, rollin up blessed
When I dress, it's never nuttin less than Guess

Fugees
<u>The Beast</u>

[CHORUS:]
Warn the town the beast is loose,
Word 'em up y'all
C'mon

[LAURYN:]
Cool cliques throw bricks but seldom hit targets
Private DIC sell hits, like p*rno flicks do chicks.
The 666 cut W.I.C. like Newt Gingrich SUCKS D***

[CLEF:]
Let's get the confusion straight in ghetto Gotham
The man behind the mask you thought was Batman is Bill
Clinton.
Who soon retire, the roof is on fire
Connie Chung brung the bomb as it comes from Oklahoma
Things are getting serious, Kuumbaya,

On a mountain satan offered me, Manhattan help me Jah Jah

Wu Tang Clan
   Execute Them

[Raekwon]
It's real ("Execute Them"), diabolical
Logical, strange chokehold, kill is possible
Flip a wig blindfold, rewind the scroll
Clip full mo, flip on the glow, blow
[Masta Killa]
We roam, through the dark damp litter of the forest
Floor lies dough, wit a c note, throw em overboat
Slit his stomach so the body won't float

Five Percenters have been accused of cultivating racial hate within the prison system and the community. As you have read, some of the values and beliefs of these 5 Percenters are full of hate, violence, immorality and rebellion.

The Holy Bible states that *we will know them by their fruits* (Matthew 7:16). I can best sum this section up with this passage from 2 Timothy 3:1-5.

Godlessness in the Last Days

1 But mark this: There will be terrible times in the last days. 2People will be lovers of themselves, lovers of money, boastful, proud, abusive, disobedient to their parents, ungrateful, unholy, 3without love, unforgiving, slanderous, without self-control, brutal, not lovers of the good, 4treacherous, rash, conceited, lovers of pleasure rather than lovers of God— 5having a form of godliness but denying its power. Have nothing to do with them.

Music Questionnaire

Below are answers from a questionnaire I took, from the wards on the maximum lock-up unit in our facility of their favorite songs:

Entertainer:N A
Song: 3 Six Mafia
Message: Mak'en money staying on top living your life the way
you choose.

How does it make you feel when you listen to it and what does
it make you think about?: How they stay rappin about killin.
It make me think how they could kill someone when being
conscious about it and then it makes me feel attempting to live
life the safe way without being apart of the violence.

Do you feel the message is positive or negative?:Negative for
the fact killin people for money and petty moral values and
principle people die over.

Does the song promote or discuss any criminal behavior?: Yeah!
When teenager see this kind or behavior or hear it all they
observe is hella money. Casual cars and some fine females.
Then they make it their hobby or occupation to live life.

How do they rationalize or justify their criminal behavior?:
It's quick money they grew up in that lifestyle of they have
no choice to live life that way.

Are women respected in the song?: No they are not, because
every time they refer to a female their called bi*%es or sluts.

Does the song and video promote building a healthy loving
relationship with the opposite sex or does it encourage or
rationalize being unfaithful and sleeping around?: Encourages
being unfaithful. Women can never stay faithful all they want
is money and to have sex with ever man they see.

Are drugs or alcohol discussed in the song video?: Someone
either holding it or using it.

Do the entertainer's appear angry and intimidating?: Yes,
by talking about how they inflict severe damages upon
individuals. They also carry guns, knives which intimidate
people because they are scared to lose their life.

Would you feel comfortable listening to this song in front of your grandmother or an elder you respected? No! Because that's something they don't want to hear profanity, killing. There's no justification for this type of behavior to them.

If you were mentoring or counseling a youth would you recommend this song to them?: No! Because I don't want anything to influence them.

Would you or have you purchased the entertainer's music and why?: I have, to hear what they rap about.

Is this song or video appropriate for air play?:No! this selection would be appropriate for people who do it.

Entertainer: The Relatives
Song: The Life
Message: How they grew up in the hood and what the hood did for them.
How does it make you feel when you listen to it and what does it make you think about?: I feel that they being real because in my life I see bangin slangin lolo swangin and dirty big faces slugs and drug cases.
Do you feel the message is positive or negative?:.. If you a hood nigga and you understand it I say positive.

Does the song promote or discuss any criminal behavior?: Yeas lots of it but I'm from the hood so I can relate to it.
How do they rationalize or justify their criminal behavior?: Making dirty money either selling dope robbin or stealing or killing to get them dirty hundreds dollar bills.
Are women respected in the song?: No they have a song called being a hoe, all women are respected , but hoes and hoodrats expecially bit#%es are disrespected.

Does the song video promote building a healthy loving relationship with the opposite sex or does it encourage or rationalize being unfaithful and sleeping around?: Probaly all the above because they talk about having sex with a lot of different females.

Are drugs or alcohol discussed in the song video?: Yea, they talk about selling dope and drinking and smoking weed.

Do the entertainer's appear angry and intimidating?: Nope probably to people that's "unhood" but people that's "hood" no.

Would you feel comfortable listening to this song in front of your grandmother or an elder you respected?: I listene to the song in front of my mother so yes I feel comfortable.

If you were mentoring or counseling a youth would you recommend this song to them?: If they choose to listen to it which they might then they could. Wee all have choices in life so he she chooses to then so be it..

Would you or have you purchased the entertainer's music and why?: Yes. Because they are bloods and a lot of stuff I do they represent in the songs they have.

Is this song and video appropriate for air play?:Yes, any song is appropriate for airplay.

Entertainer:X Rated
Song: N A
Message: Gang Banging and survival.

How does it make you feel when you listen to it and what does it make you think about?: I like everything about I can relate to it. It makes me feel like I go to be on top and keep it real. I think about everything I do and done and allows me to see why I done it.

Do you feel the message is positive or negative?:Negative cuz all he says is negative and it gives us a negative message I also promotes negativity.

Does the song promote or discuss any criminal behavior?: It discusses a lot of criminal behavior and a lot of gang issues and promotes it.

How do they rationalize or justify their criminal behavior?: It minimizes it by making it look like you got a good reason for why you do it.

Are women respected in the song?: Not really talked about.

Does the song and video promote building a healthy loving relationship with the opposite sex or does it encourage or rationalize being unfaithful and sleeping around?: Not really talked about.

Are drugs or alcohol discussed in the song video?: It talks about using them but in a way that it's good and making it look cool or bad to do.

Do the entertainer's appear angry and intimidating?: X Rated intimidates people of opposite gang culture and give a attitude that says you can't fu%k with me.

Would you feel comfortable listening to this song in front of your grandmother or an elder you respected? No.

If you were mentoring or counseling a youth would you recommend this song to them?: No! It's not positive. I would try and help him out so he didn't go through with what I went through.

Would you or have you purchased the entertainer's music and why?: Yes, because that what I liked and did at the time of the purchase and cuz I related to what he did.

Is this song video appropriate for air play?:No, cuz it's promoting violence and gang behavior and it's just not right.

Entertainer: Rob Zombie
Song: Super Beast
Message: Bringing the dead back to life!

How does it make you feel when you listen to it and what does it make you think about?: What I lie is that it gives a message of death, a gift disguised as something prettier. It makes me feel that death is only the beginning. I think that life is a gift and should be given back to the maker!

Do you feel the message is positive or negative?:It positive if you believe in bringing the dead back to life.

Does the song promote or discuss any criminal behavior?: No.

Are women respected in the song?: It don't talk about women.

Does the song and video promote building a healthy loving relationship with the opposite sex or does it encourage or rationalize being unfaithful and sleeping around?: No, it don't talk about none of this.

Are drugs or alcohol discussed in the song video?: No drugs.

Do the entertainers appear angry and intimidating?: No.

Would you feel comfortable listening to this song in front of your grandmother or an elder you respected? Yeah, because nobody can tell you what you could listen to.

If you were mentoring or counseling a youth would you recommend this song to them?: Yes if they believe in the stuff that the song is presenting.

Would you or have you purchased the entertainer's music and why?: Yeah because it talks about stuff I believe in and yes I have purchased this.
Is this song video appropriate for air play?:Is appropriate because

Entertainer: Brotha Lynch Hung
Song: The Return of the Baby Killa
Message: It's about a person that has to do feed his kids some way, some how so he feed his kid's some way, some how so he feed his kids parts of human body's that he has killed.

How does it make you feel when you listen to it and what does it make you think about?: His whole CD are good it talk as about people killing. People he talks about, eating his victims a lot about cannibal sh*%. When I listen to it I get all pumped up and want to go put people on their back and eat some human parts just to see how it taste. I like to listen to it when I'm hella drugged out.

Do you feel the message is positive or negative?: It's negative it's all about killing people and eating human parts.
Does the song promote or discuss any criminal behavior?: It's all criminal, behavior any one that knows Brotha Lynch will say his sh%* is hella sick especially if him and X Rated make songs together.

How do they rationalize or justify their criminal behavior?: It all sounds good, but I don't think it's real, but a lot is. He's a gang banger from Sac. I mean I don't know what goes on up here.

Are women respected in the song?: No. In one of his songs it starts off with a Bit%# getting crazy and Brother Lynch loading a gun and blowing her brains out.

Does the song and video promote building a healthy loving relationship with the opposite sex or does it encourage or rationalize being unfaithful and sleeping around?: It don't really talk about a healthy relationship it's all bad, for women in these songs. It talk about the rapper putting a gun in the female pu%$y (vagina) and pulling the trigger.

Are drugs or alcohol discussed in the song video?: In this CD it really don't talk about alcohol it just talks about hard drugs such as KJ, heroin, acid shi% that will make you trip out when you listen to him.

Do the entertainers appear angry and intimidating?: Yes. Because all they talk about is killing Bi%$'s kids so that they could feed their kids.
Would you feel comfortable listening to this song in front of

your grandmother or an elder you respected? No. If I cared about someone I wouldn't want them to listen to it, it will have them thinking about doing some sick as% sh%#.

Would you or have you purchased the entertainer's music and why?: Yes, all his CD's are underground so you could only buy it in corner stores, you don't see them on t.v. and sh%#.

Do you agree with the over all message in the song?: Yes, you have to do what you got to do, to feed you kids when there crying, and want to eat.

Entertainer: Celly Cell
Song: It's going down
Message: It's about people getting ready to go for war at night time.

How does it make you feel when you listen to it and what does it make you think about?: I like this whole song. If your hearing at night time all drugged out with some homeboys it pumps you up to want to go hurt someone and just gets you ready for war it's a good song.

Do you feel the message is positive or negative?: Negative. It just pumps people up to want to go start sh%*.
Does the song promote or discuss any criminal behavior?: Yes, it talks about people getting ready to go pull a drive by or a robbery.

Are women respected in the song?: It just talk about after you do what you do just go to a party and get your fu*% on.

Does the song and video promote building a healthy loving relationship with the opposite sex or does it encourage or rationalize being unfaithful and sleeping around?: It talks about being unfaithful cause it says to go fu%# some hoes after your mission is done.

Are drugs or alcohol discussed in the song video?: Yes, marijuana and alchol. After you do what you did, go out get drugged out and drunk and celebrate your victory.

Do the entertainer's appear angry and intimidating?: Not really, they just sound cool just trying to pump you up.

Would you feel comfortable listening to this song in front of your grandmother or an elder you respected? No, I wouldn't want them to think it was right to get into hella fights or some other trouble, just because a song pumped them up.

Would you or have you purchased the entertainer's music and why?: Yes, I like more than half of his music , his sh*% is clean. I like getting pumped up when I'm drugged out.

Do you agree with the over all message in the song?: Yes, I like to listen to those kind of songs when I know me and my homeboys are getting ready to go do something.

The Feeding of the Culture

I was talking to a Christian friend at the gym this past year, and we engaged in a discussion about "gangster rap." "I just listen to it for the beat," he said. I asked him if he understood the financial cycle his money is contributing to in buying gangster rap. He responded with a surprised and confused look.

Many fail to realize that the dollars used to purchase these CD's are used to promote more of this doctrine, which leaks through our airwaves like a deadly gas, infecting minds, which contaminate society through installing destructive behaviors in a mass amount of souls. The deadly fact is that at the same time, it makes the entertainers, the catalyst for this thug doctrine, richer and more popular. It's giving tithes and offering to the devil's ministry in order for him to recruit more of his evangelists to propagate his doctrine around the world.

The Bible states that Satan is the prince of the air. It states: *"As for you, you were dead in your transgressions and sins, in which you used to live when you followed the ways of this world and of the <u>kingdom of the air</u>, the spirit who is now at work in those who are disobedient"* (Ephesians 2:1-2).

Ironically, Satan uses the high tech airwaves to spread his message through out the entire world. Again, the common justification for purchasing the music for those who claim to have moral values is, "I just like the beat." I like to ask these individuals, if Dr. Dre put a funky beat behind an Adolph Hitler speech and had rapper Eminem rap the lyrics of the speech, would you buy that single? When they say "no", I ask why not? I then clearly point out how the albums they are purchasing ("for the beat") boasts about killing, substance abuse, gang banging, murder and violence towards women? If they're just buying these for the beats, why not buy the Hitler single?

Some justify buying gangsta rap albums based on some of the generous donations and charity work some of these gangsta entertainers put on in the ghetto. Fans often assume it's done with pure intentions, and sometimes it is, but actions speak louder than words; not to mention the huge tax write-offs and the free advertising they get in the media.

I relate this to the analogy of having someone commit a major drive-by shooting in a community, then volunteer to assist the paramedics in the aftermath. These charitable contributions send a contradictory and confusing message to the youth. How can an artist present himself as a humanitarian against crime victims at a charity event when he is a gangster and thug on his album and videos?

"Marilyn Mason has been a true rock and roll renaissance man"

Rock music plays an important role in the minds of the young listeners today. It influences mostly white people in my point of vew. A lot of it is about what has happened in someone's life and it is locked deep down inside somebody's soul. It's mostly actual events that have happened to them or that are happening as we speak. There are many rock bands out there that support devil worshiping and in white supremacy. But also there is a few Christian bands also. For example a rock star and a legend. Marilyn Mason has been a true rock and roll renaissance man. He enjoys this role. He is an open white supremacist. Having concerts in Germany with wide screens in the back showing the rise of the Nazi's. Rock music expresses a lot of hatred towards ethnic groups that are not white, but most people just can't understand it or they support what certain rock bands are expressing in there music. Rock music has gone a long way from classic rock to now days heavy metal. Very few bands have switched and stayed on top but a long time legend and a very real band Metalica has made it through thick and thin and they still dominate the music world. Rock music to me is a real go getter. I've listened to it my whole life and I still can't get enough of it. It supports my very active role and still growing white supremacist beliefs. And it explains day to day life. It has a lot of different stuff to it too. A band called 'Disturbed' for example is into the Jewish beliefs and expresses it through his music to gather more believers. It's basically a war of who can rise to the top. But people will have their views and on looks about rock. But for me it helps me relate to tragic events that have happened in my life, or it is down right telling the white supremacist may through lyrics. But for one thing that has been proven time in and out rock music will never fall it will continue to dominate the rock world, from all ages and back grounds. Like my influence White Zombie that broke off and formed his own group call Rob Zombie. He is a heavy metalist, that has directed and written two successful films. In my opinion he has dominated both areas in song writing and in film making.

"I tried to walk in the shoes of Easy E"

The person rapper who I looked up to, who inspired me, was Easy E. The way he conducted himself was in my eyes seen as good. Because of rap, I felt it was right to refer to women as b*tches and hoes. That it was cool to push and slap them and dehumanize, and look at them as a nobody. Because of rap, I felt it was cool to rob and steal when you didn't have nothing. Because of rap I thought it was cool to assault and victimize people. Then I had converted to a gang. I tried to walk in the shoes of Easy E. I tried to be like him. Rap and the negative vibe was my way of getting the attention to be liked to be accepted to get the girls from around the way. And because of this so call thug mentality, look where it got me. Behind bars at a young age of 13, even then I came in here with that thug gangsta, mentality and lost 7 years of my life. It took this place and seven years being here to get me to open my eyes and see what I was doing wrong. That this thug mentality was keeping me longer away from my love ones.

Now, the key for me coming out of this mentality was my family. I noticed that I was causing them great pain. Let me just make it short, the key to coming out of this state of mind was self love, self respect ,respect for others the love of family and most of all the love of Jesus.

"You could feel the power of the dollar bill, while in their presence"

As me growing up, I was raised around a lot of negative things. Being born in the mid 80's it was the era of gangsta rap. As I got old enough to listen and understand what artists were saying and what message they were putting out, I immediately took a liking to it. My father was the provider, so whenever we went somewhere, Easy E, Ice T, Ice Cube or Too Short was blasting in the tape deck. That's when I really felt that these rappers had a talent, to put words together and have a rhythm with a beat. I feel that emotionally these men grew up in the cold streets of LA and put something together to get out of the dangerous lifestyle. Gangbanging, selling drugs, and making fast money was all that they knew and experienced, so that's what they wrote about. After some years past, I grew a very liking to Tupac. He has lyrics that are heart touching and you can feel every word that he's saying and it's true. He wrote about struggle and daily life situations. There is more to rap than just, smoking, killing, robbing and the other stuff that is glorified. People just look at the negative and attack without seeing the positive. There are a lot of artists out there that rhyme about the positive side of rap but it's hard (these days) because the youth don't want to hear it, so they're not noticed as much. But there is always a negative to the positive and vice versa.

I never really realized how much the rap culture influenced me until I sat here and took a self inventory of my life. Even in jail, I hear a song like "Wanksta." I ask around find out what it means, fake gangsta, then I add the word within my vocabulary as if it was "fly." I have done this exact cycle throughout my life so much it has become habitual, sometimes with me not even being aware. Almost like a subconscious thing. Knowing what I know I ask myself, what positive and negative things have I learned, from the music industry?

When it comes to positives, I confuse myself. Because, I consider myself a thug from the streets. Rappers are looked at as kings of their own dynasty. They have women, money, cars and jewels. What else does one need, respect? Money brings respect. So from a thugs perspective I can say boom, there's the positives. I learned money and respect. But in my heart I know the truths and how I'm blind to the truth. I can call a woman a "bi#*%", but I get mad if someone calls my mother a "Bi#*%". When I rap to myself this question always appear. The women I disrespect many not be mine but another's mother or grandmother. I need to start reminding myself of that, as well as rappers in the industry. I never did understand how negativity brings money and publicity. 50 cent, from the group G Unit, made 11 million dollars by disrespecting the entire Terror Squad, Fat Joe, Rimmy Ma, etc

I was raised around people who listen to rap and chose to become famous rappers. Shawn and Anthony know too many as C Bo and Brother Lynch are just a couple I know personally. Both are known as two of the notorious under ground rap artist, I loved as well as envied them. As a child, when they would come to the hood, they would have all the attention, almost as if they demanded it. You could feel the power of the dollar bill, while in their presence. It was so unreal. I wanted that respect, that glory to feel like a king. I know as well, I knew what I had to do, "ryde or die". In the process learning the negatives, learning the street life. Enabling me the ability to call a female a "bi#*%", in my rap or who I hate and who I almost killed. People don't want to admit it but most music is a bad influence on the children. From my rank in the hood I shouldn't say that, but to know that my admitting could eventually make one person life change positively is worth it. A girl once asked me" why do I listen to such music?" I said, because what I've been through, they don't mind putting on the radio for the world to hear. I t makes me feel better knowing I'm not alone. Even though they may put it with downing another with obscenities. How we can end this hate for one another within the rap culture? I will never know. People suffer from historical and cultural amnesia including myself.

"Just take it for what it is, entertainment"

To me I think that Rock and Heavy Metal are a way of life for people. They get drawn into the sound and messages of music.

Me personally, I don't really try to dissect songs or look for hidden meanings in lyrics, but do I believe that they are there?

I think that people get deep into the lifestyle and live it to the fullest. That with the combination of drugs and alcohol can influence people by the masses. Some people become die hard fans that will support and promote their favorite band and become emotionally and somewhat spiritually attached to the performers. An example is when performer and guitarist for the well know heavy metal band "Pantera", Daryl Abbot aka Dimebag Darryl was shot and killed on stage at a club where he and members of the new band he was in "Damage Plan" were having a show. The crazed fan was a dedicated and obvious till death fan of Pantera and blamed Dimebag for the band splitting up. He showed how upset he really was when he went on stage while the band was doing their set and shot and killed dimebag and two others before being laid to rest by a security guard with a shotgun.

That's just one example of the affect music has on people. Another is quoted by To Araya of "slayer" a known Heavy metal Band with Satanist views: "Our fans are the best, though I think a few of them take it a little too far, they'll see me walking down the street and they'll come running up with blood in their eyes shouting at the top of their lungs. It's great, but if your not used to it, you start to wonder what kind of power you have over these people. If we didn't have a real good understanding of ourselves and a healthy perspective on what we were doing, that kind of power could be real dangerous."

I think that goes with most performers. Most of them do it for stardom, money and the love of Rock & Roll lifestyle.

I think the music is what you make of it. If you get too absorbed in lyrics it kind of takes the fun out of it. Just take it for what it is, entertainment.

"I viewed women as Bit#es"

I grew up in the projects of West Oakland living with a single mother on welfare, a younger sister and brother, without enough income to support all of us. I didn't have a positive role model in the household to lead me in the right direction, so I looked toward the streets seeing the people from the hood with these nice cars and clothes. I wanted that for my family not to be struggling so I resorted to selling drugs even though I knew it was wrong I conned myself into believing it was okay. The rappers that influenced me were local Bay Area rappers like Seagram, R.B.L, Bad Influence, Click, E 40 etc. From the experiences I've had with women, I viewed them as Bit**es and hoes from the rappers I listened to and the way some women displayed themselves on the street, being easy and not having respect for themselves."

"They would give me a natural high"
(incarcerated for murder)

I was conditioned with the belief to be a thug was from the attention from all the peers that had respect. I was rejected as a child. So since I believed I needed the respect to survive in my neighborhood, I could kill two birds with one stone and get the attention and respect from acting like a thug. Being rowdy, boisterous, disrespectful and wild was passed on to me from peers. I had beliefs of if I don't beat him somebody else will, or this is free money so I'm going to get it. I t was important for me to be serious and get over on the system more I became deep in the mentality as a hustler.Too Short, E 40, and Lil Ric were a couple of main Bay Area rappers that I like because they talked about all types of killing, drug dealing and how they kicked it by drinking and smoking. They would give me a natural high and get me pumped with negative adrenaline.

"I'm not a role model"

I started listening to hardcore rap around the age of 6. Artists such as N.W.A., Too Short, 2 Live Crew, and Kool G. Rap, just to name a few, were the ones who had my head nodd'in. Since I was growing up around the type of stuff they talked about, I found it to be nothing less than real beauty. I could be listening to Will Smith on a day that I may be feel'in good and his music may keep me feelin good all day. But since that ain't my reality, I'd rather listen to those who I can relate to, and eventually try to emulate them and act out the things they talked about. They never put any ideas in my head, but at the same time, their music may have given me an extra boost of motivation to do the things that I had already chose to do at the early age of 6.

How do I feel about the image that I put out? Well, I don't want to see people getting victimized because my music (I rap) may have helped push someone to do something that I may have said I'd done just to make a rhyme, and then try to say I made them do it. Everyone makes their own choices in life, bad or good. Just this last comment to all parents of kids who listen to hardcore rap... "If your kid listens to my music for the beauty of the art of hip hop rap then let him give me my "props", but if you see your kid trying to live like me, talk to your child because there's something wrong going on in your home and your child's life, I'm not a role model.

"I saw rappers as role models"

Don't get me wrong I'm not blaming any of these rappers for what I did, I'm just saying their lyrics was a big contributing factor in my behavior. I saw these rappers as role models because growing up in an unfortunate situation and seeing people from my same situation end up having all sorts of money, women gold teeth, cars etc., was very enticing.

IV.

Thugs & Drugs
The Conscience Hardener

This week we had five new intakes on our unit. During the interview process, all five told me that they had done "E Pills." Two of them informed me that they believe the E Pills have caused them brain damage because they told me the drug has slowed down their thinking process. A former ward called my supervisor today saying, "They're going crazy in the Bay; you can get 2 'E Pills' for $10.00."

These types of drug habits are the root of much of the new mental illnesses in our society. These individuals told me how popular the "Hyphy Movement" was in their cities. This made me think about the inevitable health care crisis coming to our nation regarding the mental illness epidemic, which our nation is being propelled into at a rapid rate.

Marijuana, Meth, Sherm and E Pills are some of the main culprits of mental illness. With these drugs being in style now by the music industry, millions of naïve youth will fall victim to mental illness which will continue to escalate the crime rate and lead the health care system into a financial catastrophe.

Drug use opens the door to one's soul for demonic spirits to come into torment, influence and eventually take possession. No amount of medication or treatment sessions can undo all the damage from some of these drugs. It will take the savior Jesus Christ to fully deliver and transform these drug addicted individuals back to sobriety with a sound mind.

What's wrong with Marijuana?

"Marijuana relaxes me, it mellows me out"…"It's a natural herb"…"it should be legalized." These are the arguments from the pro-marijuana movement that I hear all the time at the correctional facility. Many have vowed to me and others that they will give up their gang banging, robbing, stealing, drug dealing and committing violent acts on others, and go to school and get a job, however very few are willing to honestly commit to leaving a drug such as marijuana. "I love it", I hear a lot. "There ain't nothing wrong with it." They tell me that they have used it for years and they aren't hurting anybody by doing it. They say they just want to be left alone after a hard day of work to kick back with a beer and "fire up" a joint.

To get a clear understanding and knowledge of any plant, you have to go to its root. In this case, I'm going to take you back to its historical and spiritual root.

Why is God against substance abuse other than the physical and brain damage it causes? Because, it's sorcery. That's right, it's witchcraft. I know that sounds extreme, but let me explain. The Greek word "*pharmakia*" is used five times in the New Testament. One time in Galatians (5:20) and four times in Revelations (Rev. 9:21, Rev.18:23, Rev.21:8, and Rev.22:15). According to W.E. Vine's expository dictionary of New Testament words, the word "pharmakia" refers to a sorcerer, one who uses drugs, potions, spells, and enchantments. The word "pharmacy" is derived from "pharmakia." This Greek word does not refer to all drug use, but rather drug use which is related to sorcery. Sorcery involves using drugs to open up oneself to the influence of evil spirits.

Revelation 9:21 states that after God poured out his wrath on rebellious humanity through plagues, people did not repent of their *"murders, sorcery, fornication or their thefts."*

Dating back to ancient times, the occult used mind-altering drugs as part of their rituals. Years ago, marijuana was practiced in Shamanistic rituals in India, China and Assyria. In an ancient Chinese writing, the Pen Tusuo Ching (100 AD) noted that, "If taken over a long term, it (marijuana) makes one communicate with spirits." A Taoist Priest wrote in the fifth century B.C. that marijuana was utilized by "necromancers (sorcerers)... to set forward time and reveal future events." Today, many groups such as the Rastafarians, the Tepecano

Indians of Mexico, and the Kasai Tribes of the Congo use marijuana as a sacrament in their religious functions. The Kasai considers Marijuana to be a god- "The Nector of Delight".

The Menninger Foundation did a study led by Dr. Charles Tart, published in *Nature*(a scientific journal), about the effects of marijuana. In a survey of frequent marijuana users, eighty percent said "I get somewhat paranoid about the people with me, I am suspicious about what they're doing." Twenty three percent said "I lose control of many actions and do antisocial things that harm other people." Twenty percent said, "I have lost control and been taken over by an outside force or will which is hostile or evil in intent for a while" (http://sosmin.com/TRACTS/marijuana.html).

Marijuana weakens the natural moral restraints people have against engaging in immoral activities; it corrupts one's conscience. Back in the 1960's as millions of people were introduced and started smoking marijuana, these people who once embraced the values of the Holy Bible were now embracing eastern religion, new age thinking and occultism.

They adopted a hedonism lifestyle which has the philosophy "if it feels good, do it." In ancient times, even today, a witch or shaman prepares these drugs. They are used to enter into the spiritual world by inducing a pleasurable altered state of consciousness that allows demons to take over the mind of the user. Today, many say they use drugs for so-called recreation; however, one can not negate its cultic ties. While marijuana impacts one's mind and soul by changing an individual's personality, beliefs and thinking process, it also damages the individual physically. Here are some of the detriments of marijuana reported by *Parents, the Anti-Drug Foundation:*

Effects of Marijuana on the Brain. (THC-Tetrahydrocannabinol)

"Researchers have found that THC changes the way in which sensory information gets into and is acted on by the hippocampus. This is a component of the brain's limbic system that is crucial for learning, memory, and the integration of sensory experiences with emotions and motivations. Investigations have shown that THC suppresses neurons in the information-processing system of the hippocampus. In addition,

119

researchers have discovered that learned behaviors, which depend on the hippocampus, also deteriorate."

Effects on the Lungs.

"Someone who smokes marijuana regularly may have many of the same respiratory problems that tobacco smokers have. These individuals may have daily cough and phlegm, symptoms of chronic bronchitis, and more frequent chest colds. Continuing to smoke marijuana can lead to abnormal functioning of lung tissue injured or destroyed by marijuana smoke. Regardless of the THC content, the amount of tar inhaled by marijuana smokers and the level of carbon monoxide absorbed are three to five times greater than among tobacco smokers. This may be due to marijuana users inhaling more deeply and holding the smoke in the lungs."

Effects of Heavy Marijuana Use on Learning and Social Behavior.

" A study of college students has shown that critical skills related to attention, memory, and learning are impaired among people who use marijuana heavily, even after discontinuing its use for at least 24 hours. Researchers compared 65 "heavy users," who had smoked marijuana a median of 29 of the past 30 days, and 64 "light users," who had smoked a median of 1 of the past 30 days. After a closely monitored 19- to 24-hour period of abstinence from marijuana and other illicit drugs and alcohol, the undergraduates were given several standard tests measuring aspects of attention, memory, and learning. Compared to the light users, heavy marijuana users made more errors and had more difficulty sustaining attention, shifting attention to meet the demands of changes in the environment, and in registering, processing, and using information. The findings suggest that the greater impairment among heavy users is likely due to an alteration of brain activity produced by marijuana." (http://www.theantidrug.com/drug_info/)

Marijuana is also known as the "gateway drug", in the "Dawn Report" led by Dr. Harold Voth, senior psychiatrist for the Menninger Foundation. He found that 90 percent of those using hard drugs such as heroin started with marijuana. A quick foot note, a predecessor to the gateway of Marijuana is cigarettes, which statistics have proven that the majority of individuals who start smoking tobacco products go on to try marijuana. Marijuana has been proven to open the gateway to drugs such as cocaine, heroin, ecstasy, LSD, methapehinimies, PCP, "sherm" and a host of others. All which are known by the medical community to be deadly and to cause a multitude of health problems, but also cause irreversible brain damage. Towards the end of this chapter you will read some bizarre testimonies from wards incarcerated who tell about their drug experiences.

A ward on my unit, who is a former crystal meth dealer revealed to me the secret ingredients in the deadly addictive drug. I couldn't hardly believe it at first, but another former meth dealer on the unit confirmed it. Take a look at what many individuals are willing to put in their body for a cheap high:

Some of the Deadly Ingredients of Crystal Meth
- Raid
- Red Sulfur (from matches)
- Ajax
- Bleach
- Sudafed

"My Insight on Various Drugs"

The effects of drugs that I've done and taken are many: good,bad,fun, scary. I've explored a lot of drugs in my short life of 20 years. From weed to heroin to acid to extacy.

Hallucinogenics are my favorite drugs, but being hard to get my drug of choice is crank/meth. I was once up on meth for 1 month and 3 days. That's burned into my memory because it was the last month and 3 days I spent on the streets before coming to YA. Marijuana was my first drug I started smoking it at the age of 11. My cousin gave me the joint to calm me down because I was hella mad. He didn't like me getting in trouble so weed was the only option to calming me down. Every smoke after that was to mellow me out. Running from my problems? Hell yeah! But so would you if you had so much anger wanting to be released in a way that would end up with me in here a lot sooner. So weed was just a mellow me out drug.

Cocaine (the powder) was a drug that I would use to help me drink my alcohol and to numb my spirits. If that sounds weird to you then I apologize for I know no other way to express it.

Meth was a way to stay up and not miss out on the opportunities of the coming days. The parties, sex, drinking, fighting and more meth. I done heroin one time as a type of experiment, I didn't like it.

Cocaine (rock form) I've also tried once and it was a high to good so I've never done it since. Acid (LSD) is a mind trip drug that I love. Though my first experience wasn't very nice I did it again.

It's a drug that alters your vision, "inhances" your hearing . My second trip was Coo. I would wave my hand in front of my face or anything for that matter and would see about ten more following the original object. "Trails" were fun when you did a pass a couple of times and try to find the real thing. I could hear colors changing and blending like clashing or crashing waves.

I once seen Mario and Luigi (from the Mario Brothers) fighting to see Mario the victor and then tearing off Luigi's head.

I like watching trees on a windy day and frying balls when it's raining. The rain seems to slow down and when it hits the ground it's really a beautiful sight. My worst experience was with liquid form acid. My thing was I thought I was surrounded by death. A rotten stench wading in blood. That was too much for me especially with O.J. which enhances the effect. The trick with acid is knowing before you take it is that everything that will happen will be controlled by you and your mind. For example if you think you're going to go and see rabbits, then rabbits are what you'll see. Peaceful minds have good trips while troubled worried minds have bad trips it's all in the head.

Mushrooms are weird too. They taste like crap when eaten alone, but when eaten with some food the shrooms have a little bit of flavor added to the bitterness mushrooms unlike LSD never gave me any bad trips. My cousin said it's because the shrooms are a gentle and friendly hallucinogenic.

I've had the same hallucination of Mario and Luigi fighting but with a slightly different ending the roles were reversed. Extacy or "X" is a drug that has you in that state therefore obtaining it's name properly. There are many different types of "E"; clovers, pyramids, daisies. There are so many I'm sure not even the biggest law enforcement agency with all it's evidence on drug busts would have even half! Each pill has different effects but similar sensations. I myself like to have a baby pacifier In my mouth with a lot of Gatorade because you can dehydrate quickly. The pacifier to keep from chewing my tongue off or trying to swallow it. If you were to start chewing your tongue you probably wouldn't stop because it wouldn't hurt. It would feel good.

Extacy helps you to gain energy and flow with the music. House music catches my attention on "E" and it's the most amazing sound and music that someone, anyone could have invented.

There are three forms of the pill: single double and triple stacked. This is the thickness of the pill. The thicker the stronger. I think this is what leads to the seizures that a first time user has. If they took a single stacked pill I don't think it's likely that they would O.D. as they would with a triple stacked one.

I've also taken a certain cold medication to get high. The pills? Triple C Coriceden cold and cough. The pills gave me the weirdest high I've gotten in my drug history. I was drunk, stoned, wired and strong as satan on steroids. I remember getting into a 1 man fight (me) with 6 guys and knocking four of them out at turns. I s@%t you not. The other 2 I beat up one at a time first then I ended my rage with my older sister by my side telling me to "be coo already" and handing me a beer, Bud Light. That's not my choice beer, tastes like crap. Budweiser then she got pushed and I went into a rage again and was hitting the poor guy so hard I broke or fractured his eye socket and busted his ear with a rip. They took me inside and I passed out. I woke

up in a cold as# shower was dried off by some hina I never met
(which is good for me because I ain't very well endowed) and was
put to bed with a "guard" and ordered to keep me in the room
if not in bed. I woke up and the next morning with my hands
swollen, the knuckle to my ring finger pushed back behind the
rest and the middle knuckle I would later come to find out was
shattered.

Drugs can be enjoyed but they're looked down upon by today's
world because of the financial aspect becoming greater than the
country's own. If drug were legalized there would be no killing,
now women having sex for drugs or guys taking advantage of the
addict in that way.

I've dealt drugs and have been offered sex with women and their
kids for a 20 sack which ain't very much at all. That's enough
for one hit of meth maybe 2 and 1 very small line of Crystal meth
which is more expensive. There would be less robberies for fixes
and less everything that a drug addict analysts connect or blame
on the actions of addict there's my view and my explanation or
insite on drugs I've experienced."

"I Started Doing Drugs to Stay on My Feet"

I had to maintain on the streets because I was wanted by a lot
of enemies, because I always robbed them and was taking dope
and money from them. Every time the dope dealer saw me they
would shoot at me or they go to my house looking for me. But
I was never at home, it was one time when these dope dealers
went in my house with guns and pointed it at some of my family
members looking for me. They told my people that, "If we don't
get your son we are going to kill you", but then I start doing
drugs to stay on my feet, because I never know when they going
to come to kill me. I always snort cocaine because it makes me
stay up. I never got to sleep because the people who I robbed
could come any time. Sometimes at night I would walk around
on crack because it makes me stay up and in the daytime I be on
the corner nodding my head.

My mom always told me to turn myself in to the police, she

always tell me she can't sleep at night because she is worried about me, she told me one of these days I am going to give her a nervous break down. I love my mom, but I never tried to put her in my mix. One day I got so tired of all this sh*% and the streets and I was stressed that my mom was depressed. People wanted to kill me, so I had to do something. I was walking down the street and the police rolled up. I was like, I'm glad this sh*% is over with, I told them to take me to jail, I was kinda happy in a way, because my mom did not have to worry about me, and I did not have to watch my back or duck from cars any more, but I have to still keep my head up, because it was a tough war. To this day, my mom and grandma still happy that I am in jail and I love them for it, because they know I'm safe.

"I wish to never use it again"

When I was 13 years old I used meth which wasn't a good experience and I wish to never use it again, but I remember we would use it so much we would be up for days and after a while of using it so much no matter what I would always feel paranoid and dirty. So one night around 2 or 3 in the morning, I was in my room with a friend who was also using it, we heard something out the window or at least we thought we did but anyway we began to think someone was out there watching us so we went to take a look and all we seen in a distance was shadows behind cars, bushes, houses and we thought we were being watched by cops and thought they were trying to bust us, so we went in the house and started flushing all our drugs down the toilet breaking all our pipes and getting rid of any evidence that coulda been found and after all that come to find out there was nothing even out there at all it was us just us tripping out off of the drugs which made us do that and I ain't gonna lie I really seen those shadows but that was a bad experience for me on drugs.

"Meth Trip"

When I was high on meth I didn't sleep for two and a half weeks. I was taking rests here and there, wake up, try to eat, like a candy bar or something. For those two weeks and a half I was hallucinating people and animals.

This hallucination of people scared me. People that I saw in my hallucinations are described as aliens. Aliens that I thought that were trying to take my friends to tell them or do some type of experiments. These people that I was hallucinating on, they looked as any normal people. 5 fingers on their hands, clothing, driving, the only different thing was their face. Big eyes, small mouth, it looked as if they were wearing masks.

On animals, they were normal, bears, deer's, quails, but didn't belong in the environment that they were in.

"Doing crime gave me that rush"

With women such as my mother, the things I did and the attitude I had stressed her out. We weren't close anymore and my life had to do a lot with the things my mother did and went through. Then my relationship with my grandmother got worse. I had no love for her anymore and it seemed the other way around also. I also started acting more disrespectful towards women in the way I treated them and talked to them.

I grew up in Hawaiian Gardens (South East, Los Angeles) during my younger years, where I started hanging around older gang members during elementary school. It felt good having big homies, but it was even better knowing that they were gang members. I felt the love and protection. As I grew up it got more serious. Just about all my friends were gang members, and that was who I rolled with. During those times I was neglected, hurt, and abandoned, and I thought that I could never do good and satisfy my family. I had nothing to go home to. After a while I felt there was no family. There was no Christmas, and we never did anything. Doing crime gave me that rush, the sense of power made me think that I could do something good and instead of being looked down for it, my friends did the same thing. Since I had no family at home I felt that love around the homies felt like family and felt like control, because of the love and all the things we did and went through. I kind of felt obligated and that was the only thing separating us, me not being in the gang.

"I careless about my mom and dad because my anger won't let me feel for no strangers."

Growing up as a Hispanic male in a family of 8: 4 males, 4 females, I was in between of all of this, my mom was a drug dealer when I was a baby, back in 80' she got busted for manufacturing crack cocaine in an Oakland residential area. She left my life for 3 years, I was put in a foster home. In the mean time out in Modesto, California my grandmother was staying out there at the time so I was able to stay with my grandmother after a year or so. I grew up with no father figure. During the time I was always at the foster home I experienced a lot of drama. The foster care lady would mistreat us and call us degrading names. She fed us powder milk, powder eggs and other food of that nature. I was relieved when I finally left the home.

Living with my grandmother now, I was eating right, and felt comfortable and safe with no worries. My grandma's house burnt down just a few months before my mother got released on parole from prison. During that time I was living with my great grandmother until housing authorities found a place for my grandmother to live.

When my mother was out of prison we returned to her. She was on parole and still selling drugs so she can provide for the family. She completed parole with a honorable discharge. 8 weeks after her completion of parole the Modesto Police Department raided our house on suspicion of drug deals, they found nothing. After that, my mom discontinued selling drugs, and started using them.

When this started, life started to get even more miserable. Things started to come up missing and slowly but surely we went from having stuff to having nothing. Mom use to do the drugs in front of my face, also she would make me go by the drugs for her. At that time I was 10 years of age when this started to occur. Shortly after this I began to runaway from home.

When I was on the run at 11 years old I experienced going to juvenile hall for 1st Degree Burglary, 3 days later I was released on probation back to the custody of my mom. Shortly after I was released I skipped probation school and court after I left home again. I was out committing more crimes for the greed of money and excitement of doing the crime. I started using drugs not only weed and liquor, but smoking crystal meth. It got bad, so I started using all my money to support my habit, so that meant more crimes. I got busted again for car theft. Released once again back to my mother. I was rebellious to probation so I did it moving again. Back on the run again I experienced the same lifestyle over again, but this time it got worser I started committing crimes with weapons. I needed the drugs so I could cover up the pain, when I was high off drugs I felt problem free and it felt good. Back in jail for another burglary, a car theft along with a firearm in my possession. So now I'm on my way to come to the Youth Authority with only 18 months and end up doing 7 years. I involved myself in fights, group disturbances, and in possession of drugs and prison made alcohol. I've been careless about life and don't give a fu** about what goes on because I only got one life to live so I'm a live to the limits. I careless about my mom and dad because my anger won't let me feel for no strangers. They say I'm wrong and I'm heartless, but all along I was looking for a father, he was gone.

"I use to love the name 'Hot Boy'"

The anger in my heart, hurts real bad every time I think about my childhood, sometimes I wish that I never was born in this life, because it hurts me every time I think about what I did to my family.

This is how my life started: I was born in Oakland, California with my mother and father, with my little brother and me. As I remember when I was two years old my father had rollin' stone jobs, and my mother had welfare and every time of the month for rent, she would pay rent and use drugs. She smoked "coke" and my father used heroin. They were drug addicts, we had food in our house enough to last us the next month. As I got to go to school, I use to act out, because I could not get much attention as when I was at home. When I got older I use to run away from home at age 8. I use to sleep outside in the "cuts", beneath the house. My mom used to look for me, but I never want to go home, because she always use to hit me with her fist and my dad use to tell her to stop. Then the next thing you know, my mom and dad started to fight, I used to hate to see my mother and father when they used drugs, they do it in my face, sometimes when I used to run away from home, I go to the store and steal food for myself, because I had to make it on my own. When I turned ten years old, I told my father on the phone that I am not coming home no more and said that I was going to call the police and say that I was a runaway, when I called home I could not take the pain anymore so I never came back until I went to jail, I went to jail because I was so angry that I beat somebody up real bad. Then people call the police on me, police took me to juvenile hall, I spent one month in there then they sent me back home. When I went home my parents beat me real bad.

After that, I start to run away again, because my mom and father start it again, now my brother use to always runaway too. Sometimes he use to get in trouble a lot, just like me, we always use to talk about the pain in our heart, but sometimes me and my bro use to go out and rob people, because we had to make it on our own.

My mom and father did not care about what we did because they always used drugs and got "high" and then it started to get worse, because I start to get guns and drugs when I was 13, that's when everything started to begin. Now it was time for me to get money fast, quick and smart. I started to sell drugs and make fast money, my brother used to rob people all the time, now we start to have lots of money, we always make victims and take they money and I never use to feel sorry for nobody because I use to have a lot in me that I never care about. My brother shot somebody, because he had lots of anger in him, he did not care and he got away with it, the person he shot did not die only he got shot in his leg.

Me, I was to go home and get beat up for no reason, because my mom and dad had a lot of anger they self, I will go back outside and rob more people and take things that do not belong to me. I always use to love to rob people because I get a lot of money doing that, people use to tell me that you a "hot boy" people looking for you "hot boy", I use to love the name "hot boy" because I was known for that name when people see me and they ask who I am to say "hot boy" and they belike all that's you always robbing people, you got heart, I respect you, that made me feel good, because people knew who I was, "hot boy", then I caught a dope case and I went to jail, then when I went to jail people used to know who I was, so I used to fight all the time in juvenile hall, because I had a lot of pain in me. I was sent back home from juvenile hall, I got out feeling good because people knew who I was, but I still had anger in me everyday, I did not care about nobody. I keep on catching case after case and the judge sent me to CYA, then I start to fight because people use to test me and now they still do and I want to fight everyday, because I want other people to feel my pain, because I always never feel sorry for nobody, now every time I wake up I feel angry because of my family's habit, and it still hurt from this day.

Since I was young I always had a lot of hate in me because , I always remember my past. I been hurt it's hard for me to stand up and be a man about it, because I can't take the pain away of what I been through. People always say leave the past behind me, but it's hard to let go, if you was in my shoes, what else would you do?

I always tell myself to let things go, but it's hard for me to let go, now sometimes I wish that I can change the way I think, but now I can't change, people always use to tell me to be more good than bad, but it seem that I do more bad, because that's what I am use to doing I always do more bad than good, my family always did drugs and got high, so I look after my dad a lot and I did drugs because my dad did it, and now drugs kinda messed my brain up and I can't think straight. I always try to let things go out of my way, but I seem to adjust to the bad things, it seems at night time when I go to sleep it haunts me in my sleep, if I think about my childhood, it's always give me flash backs and it hurts me real bad. If I try my best to be positive it seem like the devil always give a flash back when I was doing something bad and that hurts, after that I start doing bad because that flash back always try to haunt me and it does every night. So now I am just going to have to deal with it everyday , so I am still keeping my head up and try my best to be positive.

"The most scariest and darkest day in my life"

December 20,200# was the most scariest and darkest day in my life. It's hard to explain it to everybody, but I'm going to do my best. I was given some trees(weed), and not knowing what it was laced with I just accepted it from a person that I called my homie. So me and my other partner started smoking and off the first hit I was already high, but at the same time I was like, trees(weed) Don't suppose to hit you that fast. So I thought it was just some good as* trees(weed). So I kept on smoking and when I felt I was too high I put the rest of the tree(weed) out and then I started to feel like I wasn't off no trees. My movement was a hundred times slower than usual. I felt a little bit paranoid. Then my partner that smoked with me he was in the room next to me, he start to panic so I told my partner that smoked the weed with me to call staff I got up ran toward the door, and I started to bang on the door, and as I was baning on the door I said, a staff man! A staff man! (ward's name)! Up here tripping out all I could see was pitch white and every thing that moved froze. At that point and time the only thing I remember was a staff man! (ward's name)!up here tripping out and what I heard other people saying that sh#t replayed over and over and over, then I seen staff and I was telling him something but it seems like he didn't understand me or something like I was from a different planet or something so then I layed down on my bunk and just thought that this is the end of my life I'm dead now but I thought life was suppose to be the other way and which way was that, however everybody die in there own way. As I was laying there staff came to my door called my name like five or six times before I answered them and when I did I felt relieved because I was still alive. So they handcuffed me and took me to this classroom where they called the M.T.A.(medical technician). They started talking and I thought they was trying to kill me. Then that's when I seen that white light again and as I started to blink my heart started to blink at the same rate and as it was slowing down my heart started to slow down that's when I realize that I was running out of time and life so I fell to both of my knees and started to pray cause I knew I was dying my soul felt funny like it was waiting to jump out on to something I wasn't ready and then I blacked out and then I came back but scared as hell to move they took me to the hospital where they checked my blood pressure and they said my blood pressure was 240 that was passed a stroke and a heart attack rate. I kept on asking who was God and kept on saying I need God then I started to get weak and I started to lay down and I took the easy way out and my eyes rolled in the back of my head but for some reason they wouldn't close and the staff kicked the gate and told me to get up so I go up started to watch tv but didn't understand. Then they put me in a camera room and watched me from there.

I would like to thank my vent mate cause If it wasn't for him I'll be dead, I would like to thank the staff, M.T.A. , but the person I would like to thank the most is God. I understand that God is real now. He is not a joke . Take it from somebody that almost experienced death. I see life as a whole new meaning now. And the devil will try to get in any way he can everything might seem all fine and dandy, but he just waiting til the time is right. I'm straight now, I don't do drugs no more never did like drinking, I'm not selling no drugs when I go home.

If I would of died it would have been fxxx up because I only had 15 days until I go home. So that is my almost encounter with death, but God saved me from that and I appreciated my Lord.

"Vent mate's Story"

The other night I got some bad marijuana, but anyways what it had done to me it was a bad feeling, I almost died off of it. It really had me going crazy and my friend almost died himself when the nurse came to get him he was passed out. When they came and got me I found my friend was almost gone. They wanted to take my blood pressure so I wouldn't have a heart attack in my sleep. So when they did my blood pressure it was 231 over 130 so they take me to the hospital and they said I had to stay overnight until my blood pressure went down. When I got there my friend was praying to God and he was shaking and that had me really scared, I really didn't know what to do, but me and my friend got released from the hospital the next day. He is alright and I'm alright. We just happy we living.

But to tell the truth I really don't know if I'm going to stop smoking marijuana, I probably just won't smoke in jail and just do my time and go home. To experience death isn't cool at all, so for the young ones that's not smoking now, don't never start, cause it's not good for you, it will kill you.

might try to kill me for that. They'll say I'm a "sale out". I have kids that I love dearly, that's why I want out. See where the gangs got me? And jail doing hard times, not knowing if I'm going to live or die.

A gang member recently told me that he utilized drugs on the street to quiet his conscience of all the evil deeds he had done. He stated, "It keeps me on point (sharp)," when asked why he had to use them. He went on to say that without drugs he walks around paranoid. When he uses, he believes it calms him and gives him a boldness to continue his gang banging activities with little or no fear.

This is part of Satan's plan, to create a desire of evil and boldness in individuals so they can either do his sinful deeds or meet dangerous opportunities for them to be killed. Ancient worshipers of pagan gods did marijuana for the purpose of communicating with the spirits (demons). During the state of their "high", these demons gained access to their soul, in order to place new desires in them. The desires placed inside them were sinful. This is why there are so many youth living rebellious lives. So many individuals love the feeling of the "high" (which is a spiritual sensation, created by demons entering the soul), therefore an addict continues to crave a fill up which creates more sinful desires, because of the feel good sensation. You wonder how a gang member can kill someone by showing no remorse. The desire was cultivated in them through a process of drug use and music over an extended period of time. Moral desires are God's instructions for us, sinful desires are Satan's. In other words, drug use gives an individual, instructions from Satan.

"Cult Leader"

(This ward convinced six other wards on his unit to join him in a suicide pact.)

"I guess my words are so strong I can kill you."

Brain washing or as I call it mind fu*%#ing. What I do is make someone feel bad and tell them they're no good and pretty much keep it up for a long time some time's weeks months and then you become their friends and keep it up even when you become their friend. Because people are more willing to believe someone they trust and sometimes someone with a weak mind just wants someone to listen and that is when you tell them about death and how it could all stop the problems that the victim is going through.

And what I did on ------- is just this, they thought I was their friend and they were wrong because they were wrong, because they wanted to die and when they were hanging, I was asleep. I guess my words are so strong I can kill you.

One out of the five became my friend and I knew he was dying as I faked being asleep, so I kicked the door to stop his death and I did but he almost died from the bleeding, from cutting himself and the loss of blood. I guess I have a heart and it's for the best that I do because I saved all six of their lives. And why I wanted them to kill themselves? Because I wanted to see how far I could push a person until they break.

"For the Rush"

Occasionally when I confront an individual for breaking an institutional rule, I often hear, "It doesn't matter Johnson, I got 30 days to the house" or "go ahead write me up, I max out next week." Those that are "short timing it" (getting out of prison soon) are excited about their second chance to get out in society. When I ask many what there plan is, some will respond, "Get drunk, kick it with my girl, spend time with family and then hit the clubs with my homies." Many of these wards re-offend in less than a year, sometimes months or even days; some end up dead. Their state of mind is to live mindlessly day by day.

They crave immediate gratifications, and have failed to develop the skills of patience and self-discipline. They are blinded by the horrific consequences that are to come. There behavior makes them a magnate for law enforcement and rival enemies. What is sad is that many wards are being released from our correctional facility to "death row" and they don't even know it.

The Unhealthy Lifestyle of the Thug

Watching a "gangsta music video", you're almost always likely to see attractive and shapely women and muscular pumped up men with "ripped" abs. This is the appealing picture the entertainment industry paints of the "gangsta paradise." But this picture of health doesn't align with the lifestyle that they teach through their music?

You have mega Hip Hop performers like Jay Z, P-Diddy and Tyrese portraying a godfather or crime boss figure profiling with cigars in their videos. Hard liquor being consumed at party scenes, mixed in with high-speed street car racing and reckless sex escapades promotes the scenery of the thug. Reckless driving is being promoted at an all time high in the entertainment industry, such as in the "Hyphy" and "Crunk" movements, along with recent hit movies as the *Fast and the Furious* and *Waist Deep*. These movies are purposely being marketed to the youth and young adults. Many have tragically met their fate attempting to emulate the car stunts in movies such as these.

With obesity at an all time high, especially with American kids, you have many of these gangsta entertainers proudly parading their glutton and lazy lifestyles. They refer to their excessive overweight frames as a status symbol of wealth and prosperity. Therefore, you now have young obese kids who identify with there overweight idols taking on the same mind-set of them.

The medical profession and statistics relate the following consequences to the thug life style:

- High Blood Pressure
- Diabetes
- Rapid Body Aging
- Heart Disease
- Mental Illness

- Suicide
- Kidney and Liver Failure
- Cancer
- Emphysema
- Brain Damage
- Fatal Car Accidents
- Sexually Transmitted Diseases
- Paraplegic
- Prison
- A Violent Death of Self or a Family Member or Friend

The Adrenaline Rush, the "In-House Drug"

I remember engaging in a conversation with a small group of wards on a lock-up unit about their past drug use. We were discussing their hallucination trips and weekly and daily usage amounts, when one of the wards spoke out and said something very profound. He stated "You haven't talked about the most powerful drug", the ward said as his eyes lit up with excitement. "What is that?" I asked. He responded, "The adrenaline rush." He went on to tell me that the adrenaline rush is the most exciting drug of them all.

I've been familiar with the definition of the adrenaline rush, and know that the adrenaline rush is sometimes a good thing, which can boost our physical or mental ability to accomplish difficult tasks. However, I never looked at it as a drug. That night I went on the Internet to search some medical sites, and discovered that our adrenaline is a chemical which actually produces the drug dopamine within our body which gives an individual somewhat of a narcotic "high".

The article went on to explain how the "adrenaline rush" can become a serious and sometimes fatal addiction. The addiction guides many into substance abuse and other criminal activities. The "thrill", "adventure", "the rush" of living on the edge, is an exhilarating high that many can't get enough of. These are often the A.D.D (attention deficit disorder) individuals who find it difficult to sit still, or concentrate on a task, which extends longer than a few minutes.

Music is a great instigator of the Adrenaline Rush. Just look at "slam dancing" on the punk rock scene or the emotional hype stirred up by the entertainers at a rock or rap concert. They can emotionally stir the audience to get them tapping, rocking, bouncing and sometimes escalating into a frenzy: fighting and rioting. You just read about the "Hyphy Movement," must I say any more?

Those who self-mutilate, are exhibitionists, are sexually promiscuous and are gang members fall into this category of the Adrenaline Rush. It is the "in house" drug which can provide them a temporary coping intervention from a painful feeling.

What cultivates the Adrenaline Rush Disorder?

- <u>Victims of Abuse</u>- Those who are victims of past abuse, often crave the excitement of the adrenaline rush, because it provides a temporal fix to alleviate the pain of the memories and emotional hurt they suffer from. On a psychiatric unit that I worked on, many wards would cut themselves and bang their heads against hard objects; some would go to the extreme of spreading and eating their own feces. When I asked them why they did this, the majority would say to me that their bizarre behavior brought them temporary peace from the hurt that was going on in their lives. Abnormal behavior was an escape from their reality.
- <u>Guilty Conscience</u>- Those who feel great shame from their past deeds use the adrenaline rush to escape their reality. At the correctional facility, many say they can't stand it to be quiet, because that's when their conscience starts talking to them. They must engage in interaction with their peers or enemies to drown out the voice of their conscience. Verbal disrespect and physical threats are a "high" for them, because they know that it might lead them into something even more exciting, which will give them an even greater "high," such as a fight or riot. If it doesn't, just the mere fact of them believing that they have created some fear or agitation in someone, will give them that adrenaline rush. As they say, "misery loves company."
- <u>Boredom</u>- Those with no worthwhile goals or vision, who go through life aimlessly seeking a thrill to rid themselves of their

boring existence, often gravitate to the adrenaline rush.

- Insecurity- Those who feel a need for control or seek attention get a high when they feel in full control and obtain attention from others. Outbursts of anger, lying and "needy" codependency are methods some individuals use to control others.

One of the most dangerous and destructive methods in stimulating the "Adrenalin High" is anger.

Anger in itself is not a problem; it's how we manage it and the mind-set it derives from, which can become the problem. For example, Martin Luther King Jr. was angry over the injustice in America towards minorities, yet instead of acting out in hostility, he utilized his anger through non-violent peaceful demonstrations and in doing so, he accomplished more than any other civil rights activist in this nation's history. So we see that the emotion of anger can be a positive which can motivate us to take appropriate action against injustice or a negative circumstance.

Unfortunately, there is a significant portion of our society that equates out of control anger as power. The "Thug Mentality" culture is fueled by unhealthy anger which utilizes and transforms it into a weapon of intimidation. This weapon is used to intimidate others to supply their immediate gratification. It is also used as a stimulant or emotional narcotic, which works the individual up through a temper tantrum, until they're into a state of euphoria to where they feel invincible. In the Thug Culture, music is the method of choice to stimulate the dopamine high.

I have seen wards in this state in their rooms attempting to lift bolted down beds and desks, banging on metal doors with their heads and yelling out challenges to their enemies and sometimes correctional staff. They have worked themselves up to an illusion (through the dopamine high) of a super power state, such as how the "Incredible Hulk" would. They are high off the emotion just as one under the influence of PCP or meth. They deplete most of their logic believing they can lift bolted objects and bang their head and fists against metal doors with little or no injury. When they come down off their high, reality quickly reminds them that they have been fooled. I have observed wards displacing their verbal abuse and threats on innocent bystanders in an attempt to hook them into returning an insult or a threat back at them. The slightest reaction from someone would escalate their anger, simultaneously giving them a feeling of empowerment. On-going verbal combat keeps their fuel line in tact to maintain the high. This is the mind-set where bad decisions are made which can negatively impact a person and others for a life-time. The first principal I teach students in my anger management group is to stop, relax and think, it is vital to make this a habit.

Great coaches instruct their athletes to relax, because it is a proven fact when the muscles are relaxed we are quicker, stronger and better focused than when we are tense. In sports we often see players given fouls for mental mistakes made when they are angry after being frustrated by a past play or a foul that they feel was unjustified. Out of control anger causes us to become unfocused, which results in mental mistakes, which can have lifetime detrimental affects. The best thing we can do when we feel the emotion of anger is to relax, so we can plan a successful game plan.

7 Steps to Overcoming Hostile and Impulsive Emotions:

1. Practice viewing the positive and humorous side of every situation. Remember it is the challenges in life that build strong character, if we react with the proper response.
2. Associate with positive peers and get involved with positive activities and organizations.
3. Obtain counseling from a wise Christian counselor for any unresolved feelings from past abuse or unpleasant experiences or memories.
4. Read, listen and watch positive materials, eliminate the negative. Remember we must watch what we download into our mind, "junk in junk out."
5. Make a list of positive interventions and coping skills with a counselor or mentor and utilize them when your anger and negative impulses are triggered. Test them out; find out what works and what doesn't until you find your niche.
6. Visualize over and over a variety of scenarios where your anger is triggered and role-play in your mind giving the proper response. Visualize yourself being disrespected or tempted or in an undesirable situation. Then rehearse in your mind giving the appropriate response.
7. Recite positive self-talk; tell yourself, "I'm doing this because it's best for myself and my family." Remember the big picture.

"The game was to see who can pass out"

Well I was about 9 years old running around my neighborhood with friends looking for something to do we were just little bad kids, you can say we were little outlaws and disobedient with our parents. Well one day we were just chilling at a spot we usually hang out at it was a bunch of us and one of the cool kids brought to our attention a game and the game was to see who can pass out quicker. You breathe in and out 10 times and lean against a wall. Well your buddy is putting pressure on your neck and once you pass out they let you go and then catch you before you hit the ground. It's like a drug it makes you feel cool cause your dizzy and laughable, like you just want to laugh a lot and you just want to keep doing it over and over, it's fun because well there passing out they make funny looking face expressions, so it's fun to see that. We'll I'm 19 years old now it's not good to do that stuff because it kills brain cell. I know better now, but youngsters don't know they just want to get excited off of passing each other out, well that's it.

"I have met and cheated death twice"

My story begins with my first battle for life in August ＿th of the year 197# when I came into this world and soon after into my mother's arms. I am originally Mexican born, but was raised on the east side of Los Angeles. I came to the south side of California from what was once know as the beautiful city of Tenochtitlan (Mexico City) at the young age of two where I then became a street warrior. I had two elder brothers who were no more than strangers in my trials of a young life. However, I had a wonderful loving mother who worked too much and too hard to pay me the undivided attention she would've liked to. Not having much homely attention at home, I took to the streets where I learned every crooked trick in the book; as well as how to survive which I have done just fine so far, although I've had some reeeeal close encounters. I have met and cheated death twice.

You have to respect death in order to understand life. Death is part of living and will one day come knocking on our door, although it doesn't necessarily have to be bad. Everyone will one day take that walk with death, everyone! Though some with that ol' bag of bones sooner than later. In my instance death came at the age of twelve. Death came and left without my company on it's long journey to the land of the dead, which according to my Mexican indigenous culture is in the underworld known as Mictlan. I like to imagine death as an attractive, voluptuous spirit woman dressed in the dark clothes of mourning, picking me up at the age of twelve on a street corner headed to Mictlan. I on the other hand, construct a lie believable enough to keep that ancient woman waiting for me on that East L.A. corner while I flee to leave her standing for eternity, or until she finds another poor fool to take my place. However, it isn't as easy and it didn't happen like that. My encounter with death happened on a sunny day of October, 19 . Dressed in my full street warrior regalia I took to the street of East Los Angeles, after a strenuous day of school. I should've known something was amiss, now that I think of it. After all those undetected subconscious hints I got from homies, teachers, and girls around school. "Be careful", they told me "look what happened to Spooky" or "don't be out on the boulevard too much, it's hot right now, ese." One school counselor asked me, "What are you gonna do with your life Dam? Life's too short to keep doing what you do. Look at you you are a walking target with all those tattoos and gang attire. Do you want to end up dead? Or in a wheelchair? Oh, I know: how about doing life in the pen? That's what you really want, huh?" Boy, was I in for the ride of a lifetime! I found myself on Whittier Blvd. Being the hardest cholo I could be, throwing up gang signs and announcing to everybody in earshot my affiliation to the barrio --------gang. Like every superhero has his consort, I couldn't go without mine. After a while of no activity on Boulevard, I decided to call my "Baby" on a nearby payphone down by the corner on Whittier Blvd. After a short conversation of sweet nothings with my "Baby" a green 85'---(car) materialized full of havoc and chaos in the form of gang members – rival gang members. Hard, murderous looks were exchanged, as well as insults. Insults not an up and coming courageous cholo can ignore; insults that were blasphemous to the gang protocol; insults I would avenge no matter the consequences – words that almost cost me my life. As the brave, young street warrior I believed to be, I had to react as one. Having neither fire power nor a knife, much less a sling shot, I threw a 40oz beer bottle at my estranged enemy arrivals. My intentions were to provoke these guys enough to make them get off and fight me; or should I say jump me. I was outnumbered two to one, but that didn't bother me. As long as I'd prove my point and show these intruders they couldn't just come around my territory without any static, nor even a word said. To my surprise and relief they just kept going. I wasn't really up to the idea of being severely beat, but I couldn't lose face, which I didn't ..It wasn't too bad a day after all. Yeah, right! My girlfriend advised me to leave and call her from home; she was afraid they might come back. I gave her a macho reply of some sort in disagreement, but she won me over and I left. I didn't go far though. I guess they had just left to load up, because they came back with intentions to take me out the game for good. As I walked around the corner and up the street, I heard a car motor, I don't know exactly why, but I remember everything else in slow motion. I turned around and spotted the same car approaching, I noticed the car door was slightly ajar and the passenger sitting shotgun was concealing something from view which I knew to be most likely a gun. My first reaction was to run, however my conscience told me to stay put and ride it out' this is my neighborhood and I shouldn't run in my neighborhood. This is where I'm from and nobody's going to chase me off! Is all I could think about.

Homeboy in the car, for reasons I don't understand, asked me "where did you say you were from, ese?" After our previous encounter, I told him again I was from the Varrio ---------

Gang Anyway, to which he then leveled his gun and fired his first shot, the thunder sound echoed in my ears while I was shocked motionless to the point of not feeling the bullet strike me on the right side of my twelve year old belly. The second deadly slug missed me, but sure as hell snapped me out of my initial shock making me realize this ordeal was way too real to just stand there dumbfounded. I ran and ducked for cover behind a curve side car, but it wasn't enough because my rival had just got out his car to finish what he had started. We played a deadly game of "pickle" around the car for some very, very high stakes and I ended up losing. Six shots were fired and five of them were now part of me. After my assailant emptied out the gun's magazine, He fled the scene, leaving me for dead. I stood up and inspected the damage while walking to my homeboy's house, not noticing the overall destruction he had caused me. To my knowledge only my left arm was wounded and bleeding. As I took a few steps towards my homeboy's house my legs gave away and I collapsed to remain there immobile until help came. People seemed to materialize out of nothingness while I laid there in a battle between life and death, in a haze of confusion and disbelief. I had always heard of things like this happening everyday, but I never thought it would actually happen to me.

I was aware of the possibility of it happening to me, of one day being face to face with death. I just didn't realize how real it could be until I was laying there with death reaching a hand out to me, laying there a bleeding mess. My homeboy "--------" and my home girl "--------" made their way up to me with a gun in their grasp ready for war and to annihilate any intruding force. As they noticed who I was and what had happened they asked who they were and which way they had fled. I gave them all the information I could, and sent them on their way telling them to "get them fools for me, dawg! Hit'em hard, ese." My homie promised me they would, and told me not to worry, I'll be around to hear about it and will get my chance to go too. Under the circumstances it was hard to believe. I knew he was as scared as I, and was just boasting about a future that might never be. Before he left though, I stopped him to tell him to tell my mother "I loved her" and to take care of her. To which he angrily replied, "f@#% that s@#% ese! I'm not doing s@#% you're going to do that dawg, you're gonna take care of her and tell her whatever you want, fool!" Meaning I was going to be alright. He fled and left me to what I believed to my last thought, which were filled with my mother's hardship and anguish. All I could think about was her anger and hurt at the realization of her baby being fatally hurt. Boy, was she going to be upset! My present situation became distant during those pensive moments filled with thoughts of my precious mother. All I could think about was her and her pain, not mine, but her pain.

The paramedics and cops arrived at the scene moments later — right on time! Everything had begun to go dim, and sounds became distant, sort of like when you get up too quick and experience one of those quick dizzy spells. Although I didn't feel much pain, I knew I was in grave danger. My breathing became labored and my body grew tired. The cops and paramedics began to ask questions and began their death fighting techniques. It became a real battle between life and death, where only one would win. This is also where fantasy took place Fantasy? Yeah, lies began to form about the whole ordeal. Green cars became red, two armed gang rivals became one unidentified assailant,' 5 Buick turned into '9 Honda ----, eastbound became southbound, etc,.."Why?" you ask; well, simply because that's the way people in the barrios are raised, and because it is an important rule in the gang culture. Never snitch people off. Times might have changed since my incarceration, but I remember the old days when a Mexican mother would scold her young for "telling" on people and their doings. It was a tradition. Protocol. Not to mention the fact that vengeance is in order and one cannot bring vengeance while the perpetrator is behind bars. Cops will sometimes bring justice, but such act of disrespect can only be brought to justice in the proper form by the law of the streets. Police know this fact, but cannot do anything to stop it. The police at the scene asked their questions and proceeded with their wild goose chase, while I was lifted onto the ambulance. On my way to the hospital I experience an overwhelming fatigue which my whole being revolved around. All I wanted was to fall into a deep sleep, but the medic guy just wouldn't allow me to at least close my eyes. He badgered me with annoying questions that I am now grateful for. We reached the emergency room of the famous East Los Angeles "General Hospital" where USC medical staff prepared me for surgery "Go USC Trojans!" It was chaos in that ER people screaming, yelling, crying and most likely dying. I made it to the operating room where tubes and machines were everywhere. I was strapped on and ready for the ride. Some type of mask was placed over my nose and mouth and I was told to count to ten while some powerful over head light beamed down on me one two three..four five six sev eig   I   passed out and didn't wake up until the next day or so. What followed was two and a half months of blood tests, x rays and looonng lonely days of hospital life. My mother, my homeboys, and even some girls from around the neighborhood came by frequently, but my life had been touched by that ancient woman who was full of death and sorrow. You would've thought I'd change my ways, right? .naw, I was nearly killed a second time by bullets now lodged in my neck and back. One was directly headed either for my spine or throat, and the other one was bound to penetrate my right lung. What's funny is that you would've figured all the hardship would've slapped me in the face and woke me into realizing how precious life is. Instead, I am now deprived of my freedom, doing what somebody did to me.

V.

"Thugs and Women"

The other day I was talking on a cell door with a ward from Watts who wanted to show me photos of himself from the "Out's" (In free society). In one of the photos, he was dressed up in the latest style Hip hop clothes and the majority of his teeth were plated in gold. In another photo, he was holding a wad of money as if they were playing cards. We had been discussing his perspective of a relationship with the opposite sex. As we were conversing, he kept referring to women as "females." When I asked him why he kept referring to woman as "females" he conveyed to me that he believed he was being respectful, knowing the majority of his peers in conversations about the opposite sex, refer to women as "bi*%#'s" and "hoes."

This individual and I had been talking about his life for the past couple of months. He is a highly skilled artist, who is very bright, yet his downfall has been a strong taste for "fast money." In past talks, we had weighed out the pros and cons of the drug dealing and gang banging lifestyle, and he himself came to the conclusion that there were far more cons than pros, and that he knew he really needed to change his ways. Yet, the biggest roadblock he felt about changing his ways was that he believed women would have nothing to do with a hardworking student, working a part-time job, with a modest to low-income salary.

He, like many I talk to within the institution, believed that large amounts of cash, jewelry and fast cars are the only way to bait a beautiful woman to come their way. They read the latest music magazines and see the music videos of half-dressed, beautiful women, lusting and falling all over the entertainers with all the riches. They see the entertainer lying back like "King Cesear" having his selection of a modern day harem of women, who if summoned, will run to the rock or rap star, with complete submission. In many videos, it appears that the meaner or more disrespectful these entertainers are with the women, the more

147

the women are attracted and committed to them.

Two gang banging dope dealers from Compton shared with me that some of their "Big homies" who are the "king pin" dope dealers of their "hood" have bought mansions in places such as Las Vegas, where they employ women to be a part of their harem, and serve them drinks and perform other household duties while wearing bikinis. These wards truly believe this type of lifestyle is the meaning of the "good life." This is what keeps many of them so motivated to keep risking their lives in the crime, gang and "dope game." When talking about their "gangsta paradise" goals, women are mentioned in the same itemized object list as money, jewelry and cars.

However sadly, young girls and women are being groomed through music videos to believe that in order to get a man and the finer things in life they must dance and dress provocatively. To many of them, a tough thug who has a lot of riches equates to security. Unfortunately, security is what many young women are growing up without, due to the epidemic of broken homes and being victims of physical and sexual abuse. They believe a thug will scare off all predators and take care of them like a fairy tale, but sadly enough, it's the thug that they get who often becomes their worst nightmare.

At the time I am writing this, the #1 song and video in the nation is a song by gangsta rapper Ludacris, titled, " *Money maker.*"

Artist: Ludacris

Album: Release Therapy

Song: Money Maker

[Luda]

You know I got it

If you wanna come get it

Stand next to this money

Like - ey ey

[Verse 1]

Shake, shake, shake your money maker

Like you were shaking it for some paper

It took your momma 9 months to make ya

Might as well shake what your momma gave ya

This song blatantly portrays women as sexual objects and clearly sends a message to women that if you want money from a man, shaking your body or your "money maker" in a sexual way to please a man will earn them a high income. This song is cultivating a prostitute mentality in many young women.

Girls are being taught at a young age, that women are to be treated as objects of sexual pleasure. As stated earlier, the ward kept referring to women as "females" as if they were objects. I have heard some wards ridiculed by their peers for mentioning their faithfulness to their girlfriend or wife. To be faithful or monogamous to one woman in the "thug culture" is often considered being a "punk." However, the "pimp" is held up in honor. One pimp on my caseload put his philosophy or ideology this way, concerning the relationship between pimps and "whores":

<u>"The reason why whores need the pimp."</u>
<u>Notes from an incarcerated pimp</u>

"After all, whores are not born they are "turned out""

The career pimp lives by a rigid code of self discipline which projects an image of icy composure in the face of the constant stresses and threats of the turf. He keeps his cool despite the most voluptuous sexual temptation within his stable or in the streets he's a gut god who has put his emotions and sex drive into a kind of commercial cold storage.

He never gets sweeter than the amount of a particular whore's money. The codes, the rules the attitudes of pimping are passed along to new young pimps who if imaginative will discover something new and cunning to add to the pimp book.

The reason why whores need the pimp. The practical reasons are the whore needs the pimp to protect her, to advise her and keep her out of jail, for another, no less urgent reason, she needs the pimp to drive her to punish her, to make her suffer so that painful guilt for her "bi*%# dog" existence can be relieved.

After all, whores are not born they are "turned out", they are kick outs from broken homes, students, waitresses, entertainers, barflies, middle class kooks, and even daughters of preachers, but all have some conscience and know of society's contempt and loathing for the hooker.

Whore need and use the flashy from, notoriety and phony glamour of pimps to get a sense of personal importance and worth. I don't think I ever got a dime from a whore because of any sexual prowess I possessed.

A career pimp literally working every waking moment, sounding out potential whores for his stable everywhere he goes. A pimp's next whore could be the young girl working the elevator or desk at your hotel. Whores are like quicksilver and twice as hard to hold.

When a pimp meets a girl with a curvy body and a weak mind and she is not a whore he must turn her out. This can be difficult when a girl has strong moral inhibitions against selling her body. The "turnout" is an art within an art. However pimps have an exciting aura of wicked bravado and raw sexiness that would threaten even the mortality of a nun in long exposure. A girl with strong inhibitions but who has been weakened and stricken by the pimps poisonous personality will have her inhibitions brain washed away by the pimp.

The pimp in teaching the inhibited young girl to unlearn and will point out moral hypocrisy and greedy materialism rampant in the so called square world he will constantly portray socialites and actresses who marry older men as merely glorified prostitutes who have bartered their bodies for money. In cases where a girl's inhibitions stand firm to this approach and to his corrupting aura, the pimp will probably dump the package. But if she really has great commercial potential he will try to trick her into her first whore transaction through the use of a prearranged con skit or min psychodrama. The turn out hinges on one clear cut sexual act for pay that whether performed in awareness or in trickery forces a sharp emotional and moral transformation from square to whore. (Ward uses quotes from his pimp idol "Iceberg Slim")

The thug culture commonly views relationships with the opposite sex as "pit stops" of convenience, which they utilize to get their living and sexual needs met. To validate this point, I'll let some of the wards tell it to you in their own words:

"Females want to have fun just like us."

On this subject I feel that when we're young we should be able to have fun and what I mean by that is not being with one female because I believe that a relationship will not work with people my age we're still finding out new things and stuff like that, but I do believe in settling down when I get older. Females want to have fun just like us. I don't believe that a female's job is to do what ever I say I feel they can do what they want if they want to work they work and so on.

"I think of them as a lower level."

I view all the women about the same. Besides on the simple fact that when I was growing up all I seen was my older brother and all his friends with multiple girlfriends. I hardly seen any of my cousins, friends or uncles with just one girlfriend. So when I was growing up I started getting at girls and I always had more than one and I thought it was a good thing to do. When I was getting more into girls I was starting to get caught up with other girls and I never even cared about breaking someone's heart. Now that I'm older and in the system all I look for in a woman is support so I still write to more than one female. I try to get every girl to send me different things such as money, magazines and even 3 ways to call up homeboys on the phone. I don't view women as being equal to us men. I think of them as a lower level. All us men do all the hard work, while they stay home and kick it. So I ain't going for all that, they do all the work while I stay home and kick it with the homeboys.

I feel that while in lock up, they should be the ones working and sending me what ever I want. And I got a lot of tattoos so I'm still going to be the same when I get out, cause I can't get no job, so I need to be supported.

"I look at females like a piece of meat"

My perspective of females is down grading I know it's wrong, but yet I look at females like a piece of meat they should clean cook take care of the kids and do what I say. It's not right to have two or three females at one time, but again it's more of a challenge like a thrill trying not to get caught and when you do get caught you try to talk game to her and depending on what happens you brag to your "homies" saying females are way too easy to manipulate. Your "homies" are on the same pages as you. So all they think about is having sex, how many times and how many women. It's important for us to accept our women as a equal partner.

"Why I call women B's"

I'm writing this essay because the way I come at females tends to be a problem area for me. I figure this based on since I've been locked up I'm seem to always get in trouble when I talk to female staff. Most of the time I don't mean any harm, I just talk to ladies the way I was use to. I tend to call females bit%#*'s because in my neck of the woods the way I come at females is welcomed.

The females in my area I think find some type of sense of belonging or connectedness and to me I think they find some type of comfort, because when one of my "potnas" or somebody is messing with my girl I'll tell them to leave my bitc% alone and she seems to respect that. And I think I call females bit#%'s because they call themselves bit%#*'s. They tend to let it be known that they area bit%#*'s but good one's and they call each other bit%#*'s among themselves but in a friendly way so like I said I call females bit%#*'s because thats what I'm use to calling them and the ones in my area don't seem to mind.

A week later, the same ward that wrote the above statement, called me over to his cell and told me he wanted me to see something, he believed it would validate his above statement. He slid under his cell door a letter from one of his so-called girlfriends, and in bold writing on top of the page, this young lady wrote the statement, addressing the ward:

"I'm digin you, you my daddy, I'm yo Bit#%."

As sad as it sounds, the ward did make his point, in conveying that some women desire to be called such names. Sadly some have embraced the thug culture and have accepted the role given to them in the culture. Reflecting back, I would have to say for myself, I have also heard woman proudly refer to themselves as "bit%#." Many women have accepted this role as a "badge of honor" in the thug culture. In playing this role, some believe they gain power and respect in the eyes of others by being feared or envied by other women, through their relationship with their "gangsta" or "thug" boyfriend. There are many lady gangster rappers who refer to themselves in derogatory names, the following are a few examples:

Artist:Lil Kim
Song: Queen Bi#%h

I am a diamond cluster hustler
Queen bi#%, supreme bi#@h
Kill a nigga for my nigga by any means bi%#h
Murder scene bi#ch
Clean bi#%, disease free bi#ch

Da Brat

Song:Chi Town Lyrics
The pimps got the hoes pinned up on the wall
Just pass me the blunt and I puff it all
In the summer, winter, fall, or spring
I love it when my bit%#es and my ballers sing

Artist:Foxy Brown
Song:Broken Silence

now i'm the type of b tch that's one of a kind
y'all know, the kind of b tch that like to sip that fine
wine

Why are so many young men trying to be thugs? The entertainment industry has promoted the thug culture, which tells them that the prettiest women are attracted to thugs. Read the lyrics of the song below. The song entitled *"Soldier"* is performed by the #1 R&B group Destiny Child. Examine the message they are giving young male youth and how they present a new ungodly standard to young women of what they present a real man as:

Soldier lyrics
Artist: Destiny's Child
Album: Destiny Fulfilled

We like them boys that be in them 'lacs leanin' (leanin')
Open they mouth they grill gleamin' (gleamin')
Candy paint keep that whip clean and (clean and)
They always be talkin' that country slang we like
They keep that beat that be in the back beatin' (beatin')
Eyes be so low from the chiefin' (chiefin')
I love how he keep my body screamin' (screamin')
A rude boy thats good to me with street credibility
If yah status ain't hood
I ain't checkin' for them
Betta be street if he lookin' at me

```
I need a soldier
That ain't scared to stand up for me
Known to carry big things if yah know what I mean
```

I remember when this thug image really started to gain popularity. It was when the attractive pop singer Janet Jackson debuted the hit song and video *"Nasty"* from her 1986 Control album that went gold.

The female pop icon boldly proclaimed in the song "Nasty" that men with good moral values, in her eyes, were a "turn off", but that guys who lived an immoral lifestyle were of her liking. Here are the opening lyrics of the hit single:

```
Nasty Lyrics: 1986
Album: Control


Gimme a beat!
Sittin' in the movie show
Thinkin' nasty thoughts
Better be a gentleman
Or you'll turn me off
That's right, lemme tell it


Chorus:
Nasty, nasty boys, don't mean a thing
Oh you nasty boys
Nasty, nasty boys, don't ever change
Oh you nasty boys
```

The music video of this song, which is very sexual in nature, features street thugs who are projected as tough, "cool" and exciting. They dance along a sensual moving Janet as she randomly gazes at them with lustful and desireable eyes.

Jackson's star power through this song gave her influence to reinvent a new ideology of the boyfriend and girlfriend relationship to a younger generation. The traditional innocent and cute relationship was now seen as obsolete, leading to a new hip relationship which is now illicit, immoral and dangerously exciting.

Rapper Mc Lyte dramatically increased her star power when she jumped on this bandwagon with her hit song, "I Want a Roughneck." Her message came across even bolder than Janet's as the song earned her a Grammy nomination and also went gold.

Check out the song's lyrics:
Ruffneck Lyrics 1993

Artist: Mc Lyte
Album: Ain't No Other
  (chorus)(x3) Gotta what yo Gotta get a ruffneck (verse one) I need a ruffneck I need a dude with attitude Who only needs his fingers with his food Karl Kani saggin' timbos draggin' Frontin' in his ride with his home boys braggin' Lying 'bout the Lyte how he knocked boots last night But he's a ruffneck so that's alright Triple o baldie under the hood Makin' noise with the boys up to no good C low on the down low cops come around so ruffneck front like he gotta go Evil grin with a mouth full of gold

This promiscuous mind-set has caused an increase of sexual transmitted diseases that has infected and killed millions. Absentee fathers and mothers are on the rise. Thug mentality teaches that relationships are for the purpose to obtain bodily pleasure and for convenience. Many of these youth behind these prison walls were raised by grandparents, or other extended family members, often because the biological parents were too irresponsible, running the streets, neglecting them and going to prison. This resulted in the child being raised up in the system, because there aren't any family members competent to care for them. These children often go through life feeling unloved, emotionally hurt and feeling like a burden to others. These beliefs often ignite feelings of anger, hopelessness and low self-worth. I have talked to ward after ward, where this is the case in their own life (you have already read some of their stories). Thug Mentality provides an illusion of an opportunity of hope for these individuals, to gain a new identity and an exciting lifestyle. Unfortunately, the masses are running to it like hungry mice to a mousetrap. Many look to the gangsta entertainers as the father figures they never had. These entertainers are willing to give them advice and support through their lyrics on how to obtain the finer things in life. This is why you have so many youth conforming to their favorite gangsta artist, because typically a son wants to be like their father.

Stopping the Destructive Cycle

First, we can start by getting back to the basics, by treating others how we want to be treated. Next, we must destroy the myth that a decent guy can only get the woman of his dreams, only if he has rolls of cash, an expensive car, $200 shoes and a gold plated grill (cosmetic dental work). Girls and women must be educated that everything that looks good isn't good for them. Whatever happened to self-respect? If one's idea of a meaningful relationship is just to get sexual fulfillment, neighborhood status and material wealth, than these types of relationships might meet their needs temporarily, however the long-term affects can be deadly. Besides, if you are a guy and you are able to obtain what you think is the woman of your dreams by flaunting and giving them material wealth is a loose foundation. All it will take is for another to take your woman is for him to have more material wealth than you.

Here is a quote a music video model made during an interview of a popular Hip Hop magazine:

Interviewer: So you want a man who's both honest and thug?

Model: I love guys who are street. I won't even give soft guys a chance. Menace II Society is my sh@%! Caine was like my first crush. Actually, O Dog was my true dream guy. I was in love with him, from that opening scene where he pops the convenience store worker. He had me from that gunshot [laughs]. He was 'hood, and I loved that.

These days there are now a growing number of modern day gangsta love novels selling like "hot cakes." Youth are gobbling these books up by the masses for the entertainment of feeding their own personal fantasies of the thug love they see glamorously featured in the entertainment industry. This week I was in a popular bookstore chain, and they were featuring a new book entitled "Thugalicious." This word by the way has been added into the Urban Dictionary.

Urban Dictionary Definition:
thugalicious

a joke that actually means the opposite of thug usually said with sarcasm. a comical stab at words with suffixes like "licious" such as bootylicious which are generally just pretty stupid

She's a thugalicious as a tall white girl can be!

2.
thugalicious

A pimped out gangsta with lots of ice

Whoa look at that thugalicious pimp.

3.

```
thugalicious
```

A brutha with street style that isn't ghetto. Is smooth and has some class when he opens his mouth.

Dre is so thugalicious, I would love to get next to him.

```
4.
Thugalicious
```

A thug that's real fine

damn, that boy thugalicious

The Benefits of Sexual Purity

The thug culture promotes behaviors that desecrate sexual purity, as did pagan societies for thousands of years. Perverted sexual rituals to pagan gods were believed as a way to obtain life's necessities and special blessings.

Sex was a gift created by God as a love covenant between a husband and his wife. Did God prohibit sex out of marriage just to be controlling? No, he did it because he loved us and wanted to protect us. Protect us from what?

- Sexually Transmitted Diseases.
- Neglected and Abandoned Children (Many of the incarcerated youth at the facility where I work, express that their hatred and anger towards rival gang members and authority is really the hurt and pain from their childhood from being neglected or abandoned by a father or mother or both.
- Abortion The murder of millions of children every year and the emotional pain and guilt that lingers for a life-time.
- The Emotional/Physical Pain and scars from break ups, adultery and divorce (many murders are related to the results of these sins.).
- Molestation/Incest

- <u>The Consequence of Sin,</u> which is eternal damnation.

Never during any time in history has there been such an attack on the institution of marriage. Marriage represents the covenant between Jesus (the groom) and His church (the bride) (Revelation 19:5-9). This is what the coming of Christ or rapture is all about. It is about Christ coming for His bride the church before all hell breaks loose during the tribulation here on earth. Afterwards, Satan and his followers will be cast into the Lake of Fire (Revelation 21:8, Revelation 19:20). Satan hates Jesus and the church; therefore he is always attempting to make a mockery of the covenant between the two. Thug mentality, along with the same sex marriage agenda is on a destructive course in leading the way for Satan's plan to desecrate sexual purity. You see, sexual purity is God's will for all our lives, and His will is the most joyful, fulfilling and safest place to be in this universe. If it's your desire to marry, God has a wonderful person made just for you. This individual for you is in God's will. Therefore, to meet them, you must enter God's will. How do we enter God's will? By being obedient to God's Word the Holy Bible.

Ephesians 5:3

3But among you there must not be even a hint of sexual immorality, or of any kind of impurity, or of greed, because these are improper for God's holy people.

Does the Thug Culture Promote Homosexuality?

I have never observed in my lifetime where I seen more young men carry themselves in a feminine way then ever before. I remember going to school where I might be able to identify less than a handful of gay or overly feminine boys. Being gay or feminine was considered to be taboo and as we would say "nasty." These days many consider a male being feminine as "cute", "chic" or a metro-sexual. Nowadays, it appears there are almost as many male youth being feminine and homosexual, as there are trying to be thugs.

The entertainment industry for years has been slowly desensitizing the public to accept homosexuality. Recently on national television, during MTV's Music Video Awards, well-known pop star and cabbalist Madonna exchanged a prolonged, open-mouth kiss with a young Britney Spears as they performed a song together in front of millions of viewers:

When Spears was asked if she would "do it again," she squealed, "No, I would not do it," but then added, "Maybe with Madonna."

Listen to what Madonna said in a magazine article after the incident, regarding her explanation to her nine-year-old daughter:

Madonna says she had some explaining to do when her daughter, Lourdes, asked about that kiss with Britney Spears at the 2003 MTV Video Music Awards. "(Lourdes) is really obsessed with who is gay," says Madonna in an interview in Out magazine's April issue.

"And she even asked, 'Mum, you know they say that you are gay?' 'Oh, do they? Why?" And she says, "Because you kissed Britney Spears."

"And I said (Madonna talking), No, it just means I kissed Britney Spears. I am the mummy pop star and she is the baby pop star. And I am kissing her to pass my energy on to her'."

Even more recent, Lance Bass, band member of the popular N'Sync, came out to the let the world know he's gay and in a "very stable" relationship with a reality show star. Bass stated to CNN, "The thing is, I'm not ashamed that's the one thing I want to say," Bass added. "I don't think it's wrong, I'm not devastated going through this. I'm more liberated and happy than I've been my whole life. I'm just happy."

The gay cowboy movie "Brokeback Mountain" recently received the most Oscar nominations, which was eight. It also won best picture honors from the Golden Globes (drama).

The homosexual agenda has now found it's way into Hip Hop. Look at these lyrics from rap artist Nelly's #1 hit song *Country Grammar* (2000):

Now I'm knockin like Jehovah   let me in now, let me in now
Bill Gates, Donald Trump let me in now

Spin now, I got money to lend my friends now
We in now, candy Benz, Kenwood and 10"s now
I win now (Whoo!) <u>Fu#%'in lesbian twins now</u>
Seein now, through the pen I make my ends now

Check out this song from female rap artist Missy Elliott as she conveys her acceptance to the Bisexual lifestyle:

Artist: Missy Elliott Lyrics
Song: Pass That Dutch Lyrics

Pop that, pop that, make that money
Just keep it going, like the Energizer Bunny
Shake that, shake that, move it all around
Spank that, yank that, dutch back now
<u>Freak him, freak her, whatever ya choice</u>
<u>Didn't come to judge,</u> I came to get ya moist
Scream - (WHO DI WHOOOOOOO!) now my voice is lost
Can I get a ride on the white horse? [horse neighing]

There have now been a number of female rap artists which have come out the so called "closet" as bisexual. The entertainers in the pop and rock industry have come out years ago, many boastfully. Yet, this has been taboo in the Hip Hop industry until recent as you can see from Missy Elliot's lyrics, and now some of her colleagues have followed her lead, also coming out and preaching homosexual tolerance.

Homosexual Roots of Sagging

Another way the spirit of homosexuality is creeping its way into the thug culture, is through the stylish trend of "sagging", in which you have men and boys displaying their underwear to the public, by pulling their pants down to the middle or just below their buttocks. Something that would of appeared odd, even freakish in years past, is now the norm in mainstream society. I ask these individuals if they know where sagging comes from, some will guess right and say "prison." However when I ask why? Some say, "They didn't have belts, because they

didn't want the prisoners to commit suicide." This might have been the case at times, however the core origin of sagging begins through male prostitution. Male prostitutes were instructed by their jailhouse pimps to sag their pants down to their buttocks and walk up and down the tier for advertising. The purpose was to sexually arouse perverted inmates to proposition them for business. Why else would a man want to show his buttocks to the world?

However, the argument of the "sagger" is, "I don't sag for that reason." The fact remains that they have allowed a homosexual trend to influence their dress style. This is another example of how this ancient Babylonian homosexual spirit is now covertly impacting the youth culture of today. The entertainers who introduce these styles are like cult leaders because they know they can get their fans to do anything after hypnotizing them with their music.

Along with the sagging pants, we see males wearing the feminine color pink more than ever, feminine hairstyles, along with two earrings, which has been a practice by bisexual men for centuries, especially in Greece and Rome. This spirit of homosexuality is creating a tolerance for these feminine trends, by reintroducing them now as "hardcore". Now, there are some gangsta rappers that rap about raping other men in their songs. This is portrayed as masculine because some in the culture believe that raping another man is taking their "manhood." It is viewed by thugs as the most degrading method you can use against an enemy.

Though it has been public knowledge that homosexuality has always been part of a portion of the prison culture, in the masculine mainstream, homosexuality has been taboo (unacceptable) as far as I can remember, especially in the thug street culture. Now, this has become disputable. Let me explain:

A few months ago I had a flamboyant homosexual ward on my caseload. I addressed him one morning during an outside recreational program as "Mr." Immediately, a few of his peers became angry with me, stating I had disrespected "her", by calling him "Mr." The ward himself did not appear offended by my comment. We had talked previously about his sexuality, and he had conveyed to me that he knew within his conscience it was wrong and that he wanted to change. He had confided to me that he had been molested like so many of the other homosexuals I have had on my caseload throughout the years.

Back to those wards who came to his defense. They went on and on how I should respect him wanting to be a woman and should address "her' that way. What was odd to me was that some of these same wards who came to this ward's defense, adamantly denied they were homosexual or bisexual. Yet some would describe in very vulgar words and publicly, how they desired to have sex with other men during their incarceration. Some admitted that they already had homosexual encounters, however still would deny that they were homosexual. Kind of like someone admitting to getting drunk every night but saying they're not an alcoholic. They justified their homosexual acts by saying they "punked" their victim or their victim was the "fag" not them (because they were the aggressor) and during the act they were thinking of a woman. During incarceration, some thugs (not all) look at taking someone's manhood (raping another inmate) as a way to build up their thug status. A while back I talked to a respected gang leader on our unit, who often boasted openly about having multiple homosexual encounters with other wards since his incarceration. Some whom he stated he raped, and bragged about it to his peers. During our conversation he discussed his first encounter of being seduced by a homosexual which he says led him into a homosexual addiction. He volunteered to write me an essay about his mentality which he entitled "The Mind of a Booty Bandit." He writes after describing that first homosexual encounter:

When I came out the bathroom I felt a way I never felt before. I almost seemed like I was a new person. When they let us back to our units I looked in the mirror and hated myself for what just happened all of a sudden I felt dirty, filthy less than a man almost to the point of suicide but not quite that felling lasted for almost 3 days until I finally went to school and attacked him and when my peers asked why I did that I said 'I don't know I just did.' Then my peers said it's okay it was your first time your getting use to it. Don't worry let it go you'll forget about what gender your screwing by the third or fourth one. And that's what happened I forgot.

He explains after raping one of his roommates: He was crying and didn't know what to do so I threatened him if he tries anything or tell the staff everybody's going to know and he had a reputation he didn't want to be destroyed so he stayed silent and let me penetrate him and gave me oral copulation when I wanted it and the time was right if I wanted to bring somebody emotional destruction I would make sure every time that person used the bathroom and brushed his teeth he would think about me.

He concludes with: I am not gay and don't consider what I tell you because it's a way of life inside the vicinity of the bob wire fences even though I learned to sexually manipulate people and use everyway possible to destroy a normal mans way of thinking, I still look at females as I would on the streets.

History of the Homosexual

Homosexual is synonymous with "gay." Many believe the word gay comes from the dictionary definition of "full of light-heartedness and merriment and having or showing a carefree spirit." You might be surprised to know that this word does not come from that meaning at all; it comes from the name of Gaia a Babylonian goddess.   Listen to what self-proclaimed "warrior dyke" feminist Judy Grahn says: "Gay comes from the grand old earth goddess Gaia, who reigned long before the patriarchal invasion overthrew and replaced her. Western homosexual people truly deserve to consider them selves the children of Gaia, [after] having kept her name alive for thirty or forty centuries after her fall from grace."

Most would be surprised to know that homosexuality is rooted in the cultic worship of the goddess Semiramis that originated in ancient Babylon, which grew throughout the world. Ritual worship to Semiramis included: sacrifice of children, orgies, in which every conceivable form of sexual perversion was practiced: Homosexuality, Lesbianism, incest, sodomy with both male and female prostitutes and transvestites. These acts were a vital part of the worship of the various pagan gods and goddesses.

What was the motivation behind the homosexual worship of these gods and goddesses? It was for the purpose to invoke or appease the gods and goddesses (most were both male and female) in order to gain fertility for one's self, clan or the tribe. Appeasing the gods always meant that a ritual had to consist of actions that were an abomination to the one true God.

A common form of worship, which spread through out the world from Babylon, was to erect a phallic pole on a hill. A phallic pole symbolized the male's sexual organ. Cult members would erect these poles to give honor and praise to the male gods. After a pole was erected, the cult members would perform perverted sexual rituals under it which were often homosexual in nature. There would often be male prostitutes nearby the poles, shrines or temples, in order for members to participate in these abominable rituals. The cult members believed that when they performed these acts, it would please the male gods, and in return the male gods would fertilize "Mother Earth," which was the goddess Gaia. They would receive blessings from the goddess such as a plentiful crop harvest, increase in livestock and fertility for an abundance of children.

Cultures around the world have varied in their worship and rituals to their gods; however the concept has remained the same: to defy God's commandments and divine order.

"I'm a Gang member and I like the Laws"

First off, I would like to start off by saying laws are needed in America, but not all of them. I think laws should be strict based on without them America would be a disaster. People would do what they want, when they want and so much stuff would happen. Like the laws against gangs and drugs, when a person in a gang gets locked up for a possession of a fire arm, if he's documented as a gang member he she will receive a certain amount of time that, goes the same with drugs. I'm a gang member and I like that law, I say if a gang member displays his herself in such a manner, they should receive the consequences. There's a lot of laws I disagree with and agree with like legalizing mari-juana, what for? If that happened they are going to wish they never did that because the people smoking it are going to take it all out of proportion. Smoking in theaters, little kids going to elementary intoxicated off marijuana. Everybody except the one who voted against it would be smoking it any and every where. What I think should be done about all this law stuff, there should be people who don't do it and people who do it, that would hopefully straighten things out with laws. If not then America has a big problem, people will continue to break the laws. I'll be honest I break, I get the consequences that's how I learn from my mistakes and just move on, because I'm not going to break the law my whole life.

"Kicking it"

I got attracted to the thrill of "kicking it" with the older homeboys. My mother and grandmother started noticing that I would always want to be with my uncles and knew that they had no control over me whatsoever. If they tried to stop me, I would rebel and do what I wanted to do. They knew that they had lost me the way they lost my uncles to the gang lifestyle. They would come home drunk or high and I would come in right behind them. I know it hurts my family to watch the men in their family get caught up in the web of death and incarceration.

"I always had that sense of obligation to rebel"

Why I have such a lack of respect toward those who hold any type of authority? Is mainly the simple thought that those individuals who are marked by official positions or stand over me have the ability and power to tell me what to do. I have always been the type of individual that wants to do what I want when I want and where I want. And that's when the authority figures step in the picture (police, probation officers, parole officers, your authority staff etc..) attempt to stop my negative actions by laying down and enforcing the law.

But just because they stepped into the picture does not mean that I will stop doing whatever I was doing. I'm bound to resist and inclined any type of authority and rebel against their set guidelines one way or another. Whether I try to be sly and do it on the unders and try not to get caught, or do it in the opens where the eye can see. I would still do it regardless of the circumstances and what the repercussions maybe. I always had that sense of obligation to rebel.

When I was younger I would always do what I was not supposed to do to get that little rush of excitement because I know I am not suppose to do it and there is a good possibility that I could get caught. This went from small things when I was young such as my mom telling me not to eat the cookies, but as I got older it gradually changed to bigger things such as stealing from the store, using drugs, skipping school and stealing cars breaking into house and so on. But as the acts of rebellion (crimes) grew bigger so did the punishments. First it started out with me getting verbal warnings, to getting grounded or restricted from things I liked to do. Then I started getting arrested and the more times I got incarcerated the longer my stays were. After a while the courts felt that my mom had no power over me and didn't have the ability to control my actions so they declared me a ward of the court and started sending me to placements. This didn't stop the way I acted or help me gain more respect for authority figures. I still did what I wanted and a majority of the time I would be out and about having fun but I always found some reason to bring attention to myself and end up where I started, back in juvenile hall. I would keep repeating these actions over and over and then the court system felt like they had no control over me and they exhausted their resources and decided that the Youth Authority would be better suited for my needs.

Since I have been in the youth authority, it has not really been able to change me, I've changed myself. During my current stay I've had the time to mature both mentality and physically. I've changed my old ways "A lot" I'm sure I still rebel against the authority in change but not like I use to. I've forced myself to adjust to a lot of the petty rules and regulation that are established for all wards that reside within these walls of confinement and I show the stall the respect I think they deserve on an individual basis. I know I'll always have some type of hate towards authority figures, it's not going to change. I'll just learn how to better control it.

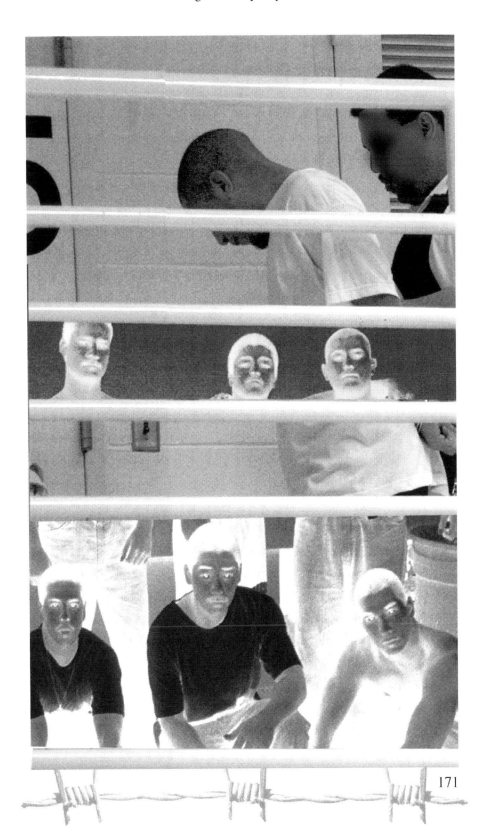

VI.

<u>Gang Banging</u>

I was always taught that a real man lives by his values and convictions, which are regulated by his God given conscience. This means that he won't join or be persuaded to do anything that he believes deep within isn't right, no matter what the consequences. This was called self-respect and having integrity.

There was a time when integrity (doing the right thing, even when no one was looking) was valued. I was raised to believe that if you did or joined something that violated your conscience, you were violating your self-respect. I was also taught that a real man sought after his God given talents and purpose with diligence and a strong work ethic. He would not let anyone or anything stop him from obtaining it.

Today, I see and talk to youth; many of them gang members who want to demand immediate respect from others. If they don't get the respect they feel entitled to, they often unleash verbal epithets or even escalate to physical violence. Many have been given street names by their gang such as, "Do Dirty", "Puppet" and "Creeper", which is usually associated with their reputation. They have allowed their street names to replace their birth names which has given them a new identity.

As a correctional counselor, when I ask, "Why are you in a gang, and what are the beliefs behind the mission of your gang?" Often, I get a puzzled and defensive look, followed by a run off of shallow and illogical answers such as:

- "That's just who I am."
- "I'm not allowed to say."
- "Because I'm a gangsta."
- "I grew up in this."

- "I'm protecting my hood."
- "That's my family."

When a gang member is faced with the above question, they often come to realize it is a question that they cannot logically answer in good conscience. It's a question all of them try to avoid, because within the truth, there is no logical answer that will sit right with their conscience. Meaning, there is no honorable purpose in their violent, reckless and immoral pursuits. That's a hard fact to absorb and live with. This is where drugs, alcohol and reckless behavior come into the picture. These destructive methods can soothe their conscience temporarily by giving them a false sense of peace. However, when they come back, their conscience is still there waiting and pleading for them to change their ways in order to have some inner peace. This is a soul battle that every thug goes through, and one, which many run away from.

Our conscience is what leads and guides us into our true Godly purpose. It is what motivates us to strive for our fullest potential. When we get off course in what our conscience is telling us, we will never have true peace.

When I talk to gang members, I frequently ask, "Are there things that you do as a gang member which goes against your conscience?" I would say 99% answer "yes." Ninety-nine percent violate their own self-respect, and are so adamant about demanding respect unto themselves from others. This is insecurity. They want something from someone else that they can't give to themselves.

Knowing the history about various gangs, I show the gang member how their gang was started by one individual's vision. An individual who obviously had a lot of charisma, an individual who created an organization that persuaded a multitude of others to give up their own God given purpose and identity to follow him. To say with simplicity: gang members (or those in the thug culture) are individuals who have basically given up their own identity to become an identity or dream someone else has created for them.

Conversing with a gang member recently, I confronted him on the issue of violating his self-respect as a gang member, which he adamantly denied. His rebuttal was, "I'm Catholic." I then asked him if he had asked for forgiveness for the sins he committed as a gang member? He paused for a while, and just smirked as he reluctantly confessed. I went on to inquire: why would he be involved in a gang or organization, which activities violated his Catholic beliefs? I find many gang members wearing crosses and rosaries and other religious symbols on the outside; however what's inside them, represented by their actions symbolizes just the opposite. How can someone willfully live by two sets of values which contradict each other, wouldn't that be living a hypocritical lie? How do you respect yourself and have peace knowing that?

In summary, a gang manipulates individuals to lose their God given identity, conditions them to violate their self-respect, and then heads them down a road of temporary gratifications towards self-destruction.

<u>"The way I had to live my life in Compton"</u>
(Referring to family, being rivals of own family)

I been living in Compton all my life and I didn't really like it that much, because I couldn't walk out of my house with out getting shot at. One day I was walking out of my grandmother's house with my uncle when one of my other love one came up with a gun and began to shoot at us. I didn't get hit, but my uncle and his lil girl got shot in the head. They die right there in front of my grandmother's house. I really didn't know what to do because I was mad. My uncle and his lil girl die for no reason. My uncle was not in no gangs at all. He had a job and was taking care of his family. So when all that went down, two weeks later he tried to kill me, but one of my homeboy push me out the way. At that time the gun went off all ready, and hit my homie in the head. I turned around because I didn't know what was going on by that time the car was getting on. So I turned to my homeboy and seen him with blood all over his face. So I pick him up and tried to talk to him, he tried to say something but I couldn't make it out. Then he died in my arms. He laid out there for nine hours before they took him away. Then we put him away, may he rest in peace.

What About Your Convictions?

The excuse is often everybody does it, or I have seen Christians do it too. What is it about individuals that use the norms of society and its cultures as a barometer to gage their own morality? What is it about an individual that they'll bypass their conscience, their own inner convictions of self respect, to meet the moral standards of others? This displays a lack of integrity by the individual believing that the respect of others is more valuable than their self-respect. This only shows how insecure an individual is.

I hear gang members talking about "I'm down for the cause." When they let me challenge them on the purpose of their cause, it has been my experience that they all will reluctantly admit it goes against their conscience. I reiterate to them, over and over, that a true man only takes up a cause that is in alignment with their true inner convictions. Violating that inner conviction would be to violate their self-respect. Where is the honor in that?

Jesus the Real Man

The thug mentality attempts to define what a true man is. This culture portrays males with characteristics of: violent behavior, selfish motives and reckless behavior. This is only an imposter of the one true role model of man, Jesus Christ. Jesus, the author of man, demonstrated that a true man is loving, brave and unselfish. He displayed this by humbling himself in taking on the most excruciating, emotional and physical pain beyond human comprehension. He knew what his task was ahead of time, but still bravely, heroically and lovingly walked the course to the most horrific death in history to save man. Jesus is the only one who qualifies to define and set the standard of what a true man is.

Self Worth

On a daily basis, I talk to individuals who have gone through the most horrific childhoods imaginable. Full of abuse, neglect and tragedies, many I talk to feel that they are unwanted or a product of an accidental pregnancy. They believe that they are unloved and of little or no value, and live their life according to this belief.

Many gang members have told me that the reason they act so crazy and "hard", is because they don't care about living: putting their life in danger is no big deal to them. Some say they prefer to be killed than commit suicide. The majority convey to me that they feel suicide is a cowardly act to get out the "game" (life).

On the lock-up unit where I currently work, the classic cliché is "I don't care," or "I don't give a f%#@!" The majority of the wards I work with have been abused as children. Many have expressed low self-worth they developed after the victimization.

Basic psychology tells us that individuals strive to obtain a purpose in life, to love and to be loved. In a small group a couple of weeks ago. I made a statement in front of six gang members on a lock-up unit, who were seated in individual cages. I said that there would be a lot more suicides if it weren't for gangs (said not in a way to condone gangs). They looked inquisitively at me when I said that. It got quiet, but as I scanned each individual, I began to see nods and heard verbal confirmations of the statement I had just made. During our discussion, it was conveyed by all of them that their gang was their substitute family, from which they obtained support, praise, encouragement, love and purpose. They believed that almost everything they needed in life was encompassed within their gang. Many of the wards at the correctional facility have taken bullets and done time for members in their gang. There is often a sacrificial, sincere love and camaraderie among gang members. That is why so many of them tell me it's hard to get out, even when they know it's sending them down a road of self destruction.

Telling them to quit their gang is like telling them to abandon their family and give up their purpose for living. In their eyes, it is asking them to give up not only their family and purpose, but their friends, excitement, money, parties, respect and most importantly identity. They spent years earning their respect, building a name for themselves, and developing relationships that exemplify that of a close-knit, loving family. Many of their "O.G. homies" stepped in as their father figures when their own fathers stepped out.

Many of these wards have admirable qualities. Their manifested qualities utilized in their gang culture are: commitment, creativity, bravery, unselfishness, confidence and teamwork, to name a few. Not condoning the gang culture, I don't believe that you necessarily have to totally tear someone all the way down to the ground in order to build them back up.

We must learn to build up others, and see all individuals as God sees them: as gifted, unique and valuable. I look for these hidden qualities, even in their negative lifestyle. I make it a practice to find the good qualities in these individuals and to consistently compliment them, no matter how they continue to act in other areas.

Whether it's a good sense of humor, the gift of gab, a disciplined work-out routine, good reading habits, or a clean and organized room, I let them know that I notice it by complimenting them. I then explain to them how that characteristic can be an asset to them in the future.

In my years of working with incarcerated youth, I have seen some amazing artistic talent. I have seen a ward make spectacular, detailed sculptures from state soap. Another ward has made realistic colored roses from toilet paper and Kool-Aid. Also others have made paper frames, plant holders, baby shoes and a variety of animals, all out of potato chip bags. I have known wards who have figured out how to make grilled cheese sandwiches on their metal desk seat, and how to use their toilet to boil noodles. I was talking to my co-worker the other day about this topic, and he told me he knew a ward who made a satellite dish out of a toilet paper roll, tinfoil, and some copper wires. He was able to get ESPN.

Many of these individuals have never or rarely received any sincere praise or compliments outside of their gang; however, within their gang, they receive an abundance of unconditional love, attention and praise from their peers.

Some of the most spectacular buildings in our cities were buildings that were once condemned. All it took was a contractor who looked past the damage to see the value in a building's design, brickwork and frame, and renovated it into something spectacular and valuable. God looks at us in the same way; he finds the good qualities in everyone, whether on the surface or deep within the destructive facade. His desire is to go in and help us renovate and refurbish the splendor that is within. The way he looks at us is the way he wants us to view others, so make it a habit to search for value in everyone.

"The Soap Artist"

I acquired a skill that I now use to keep my mind mentally strong for anything. I refuse to lose the battle of "self gratification". Things, which please me being an individual who is incarcerated is that my talents are placed at a certain limit. That of which I daily try to break in any way possible, where there's a will there's a way whether it's using ink as dye or colored powder kool aid as a coloring. How I acquired my skill is by being in the worst position I've ever been in while being incarcerated.

It started about 2 and a half years ago what I thought was going to be a simple five on one premeditated attack turned into a four on two incident which soon led me to the holding cell where I ended up on "Chilly Willy" (A time out which you are striped of your bedding, clothes and all personal items. Due to the fact that I instigated the incident I was placed in this position where all I had to my name was a bar of soap and toothpaste. Mentally I was close to the point of a break down, but I'm stronger than that and I refused to go out like that to any individual somewhere deep down in the resources of my mind I began to create chess pieces with the soap using the broken toothpaste lid as a tool. I succeeded in winning the battle of self gratification mentally. I told myself if I can get through this then there is no limit to what I can do. I was actually enjoying the position I was in as awkward as that may sound.

Almost two days later I received my personals and bedding, I hadn't slept for a few days so I fell into a deep sleep when I awoke I saw what I had made two ponds and a castle. It actually impressed me. Homies started making orders of things they would like letters of their varrios, roses, hinas (women), "smile now, cry later", the Raiders shield, ash trays with a weed leaf in the center. Tinker Bell, Winnie the Pooh, Snoopy, full scale Martain Luther King speech and much more. I began this particular endeavor to teach myself a lesson that of which I learned a lot more, it's hard to tell how far my creativity will take me in life, I don't do it for other people I do it because I enjoy testing my limits and seeing the reactions of people who so wrongly judge inmates who are incarcerated. I take joy in this and many other arts and crafts so hopefully I continue when I'm out which most likely I will.

The Rich Suburban Thug

The other day, on a lock-up unit, I was talking to a ward who was locked up for stealing a computer. This ward came from an extremely wealthy family: His father owns a very successful business worth in the very high millions, lives in a multi-million dollar mansion which includes an 11-car garage, has maids and a full-time chef. When I asked about his parents, he told me that his parents were church-going individuals and well respected in their community. He hadn't experienced any abuse or neglect, he believed both of his parents loved him very much and still remained faithfully in contact with him during his incarceration. So what happened? I asked him directly. He told me that his parents had set extremely high goals for him, which stressed him out. They wanted him to be a lawyer or doctor. They and their church-going friends disapproved of his peer group, which he says made him cling to his friends even more. He felt that, though they loved him, they didn't care what his aspirations and goals were. They had his life plans set in stone, and attempted to keep him focused on the course that would make them proud of him. When I asked what he wanted to do with his life, he said he wanted to do something adventurous, but wasn't sure exactly what. He told me of his adventures of running away from home and jumping on a train and letting the train take him where ever. Money didn't matter to him; he said he had no desire to be rich. He just wanted to be free to live out his life in his own uniqueness. At an early age, when the pressure from his parents got too much for him, he rebelled by going 180 degrees from whatever they told him. He thought by doing this, they would give up hope and leave him alone (paraphrasing), "it didn't work," he told me. He lifts up his right shirt sleeve and shows me a demonic looking tattoo of a dragon on his bicep. "I thought this would piss my parents off, that's why I got this." "I'm in here for something my friend did, but I didn't want to see him get locked up again, so I said the computer was mine. My dad tried to get a lawyer for me, but I told him I didn't want one. I didn't think they would send me to Y.A. for stealing a computer, that's why I admitted to it. My parents were really mad at me." He said he didn't gang-bang, because he didn't want anyone telling him what to do. When he arrived in Y.A., many of the white supremacist gangs approached him to join them. "I'm on site (a target by gangs) by almost everyone." "Why?" I asked. "Because I flipped their dead sh#t (term used by gangs to ultimately disrespect someone, by referring in a disrespect manner to their dead loved ones). Again, I asked him why? "I don't know," he replied. "Don't you know that your making it dangerous for yourself in here?," I asked. "Yeah, I guess," he said. Below is more of this ward's story, told in his own words.

"The Rich Ward"

I'm inmate 8#### doing a 2 year sentence for receiving a stolen laptop computer. In reality I had nothing to do with the computer, I just didn't want a homeboy to get violated and go back to prison for eight years. If you believe me or not that's totally up to you. What you should know is, "If I really wanted a laptop computer, I could go and buy a hundred million of them and still have money left over to buy about ten houses the size of the white house, a couple of Jags, BMW's, Porsches and a Rolex watch. Then still have money in my pocket. I was born to a mother that is a doctor, and a father who owns an -------- company making around 130 million a year. My dad dies, leaving a nice chunk of change for the family. Well, my mother remarries to a man who owns his own stock broking company, making around 45 million a year. So what I'm trying to say is I've always been around lots and lots of money.

I'm not writing this to brag, I'm writing this to tell people that being born to a rich family is not what it seems, that you just have an easy life with no strings attached, well think again! Growing up, I always went to private schools, I was taught that being rich makes you better than everyone else. There a lot of expectations you have - or more like you parents have for you. My parents wanted me to have straight A's, to speak 4 or 5 different languages besides English, they wanted me to be the most popular kid, they wanted me to go to Princeton, Harvard, Stanford or West Point University. They set the goals for me, I didn't get to choose, it's what they wanted, not what I wanted.

So at 16, I rebelled. I started hanging around middle class people, even people from the ghetto. I felt they were more down to earth. I started smoking weed and drinking once in a while. I got so sick of being around rich little snobs and even more sick of being someone I'm not. So I dropped out of school, sports, out of church and completely changed my life.

My parents tried to bring me back. They put me in drug rehab, got me counselors, shrinks, but I didn't want anything from them. I kept telling my parents, "You can't help a person that doesn't want help!" but they didn't get it! Even to this day they tell me that I'll grow out this phase. For some people it's a phase, for me it's a journey I wanna take, and it only just begun.

My dream is to become a S.W.A.T. member, sky diving instructor, a preschool teacher, or just a drifter going from there to here to there.

"Girl Gang Banger"

I always looked at girls to be a lady, so I never went out my way to call them out of there name until one day I was in my hood and this girl came by, she was looking very good. Me and some of my other homies was talking about who was going to go over there and get at her. So when we was doing that one of my lil homies, who was a new nigga on the block went over to get at her. So one of my other homies saw that he was going to get at her so he went behind him. They were over there talking to the girl, then out of nowhere she came out with a gun and shot my lil homie right in the head. It happened too fast for me to react, so one of my other homies came out with his gun and started to shoot at her, when he was doing that a car came from down the road and my other homie began to shoot at the car, in the mean time, ol' girl was shooting at my homies. She then jumped into the car. So they took off going back to their hood. One of my homies was who was in his car took off behind them, but the bad part about it was that I was on the hood of his car when they start to shoot at him. I didn't get hit or anything, but I was in the middle of a shoot out. So we didn't get them, they got away. So we turned the car around and went back to the hood. When returning back to the hood the homie who got shot in the head was dead. So what I'm saying , girl gangbangers will set you up too, so be on the look out, cause they will turn you on with sexy looks and let you get your n**, then have some niggas come and wet you up. I wouldn't wish this on no man, because I feel every man was put here to do good work, no matter if he like it or not. The only reason the girl shot my lil homie was to get her name for her hood. She killed him right in front of his mama and his little sister. They were coming down the road from the store, his mama use to be on his head for being out there with the homies. So when he use to see his mama coming he use to run and hide, because he knew that she was going to be on him for being out there with us. She told him one day on the block, that if he stay out on the block with the homies that he was going to end up in jail or that he was going to get killed. Sorry to say it, but she was right, may my lil homie rest in peace now, he is in a better place now, I hope that he is doing the plan that God got going for him. I'm sorry that you had to die young homie, you knew what they say, the good die young, but it shouldn't be that way.

"Recruiters"

I've been a member of the ------ -------- Pirus since April 19--. I use to hang out with friends that were gang members. My mother, brothers, uncles, father and cousins were part of my gang and other gangs, so when my friends finally asked me if I wanted to become a member it was easy for me to agree due to the fact I already accepted the lifestyle being in the surroundings I was in. My friends took me to some older homeboys and told them I wanted to be a Piru and one ask me "lil man you sure you want to be down wit the Pirus", I said yeah I want in. "At that point I became nervous because I already knew how the initiation goes, but I told myself my brother made it so I will to. The older homeboy called seven young Pirus over and told them they gone put me on. So some of them started taking off their shirts putting their guns on the grass and tying there shoes tight. The only thing the older homeboy said when it was time was "He got family from the hood so don't stomp him", and the punches started. All I could really do was close my eyes and swing. The beat down lasted for about a hundred and # seconds because all the initiations in my gang are for a hundred and --- or a hundred and ---- seconds because those are two major streets in my hood. Afterwards my eye began to swell shut immediately my nose was busted, my lip was split and I had numerous knots all over my head. I was congratulated and told this is a job, the hood is more important than god, school, and everything else. The older homeboys started saying what we gone call you? and I said I don't know. The older homeboy that was doing most of the talking said, " I like you blood you gone be my little homie and be a c-@# killer just like me." His name was Big -------- and so I went on to become Little ------. I was told everything I need to know, meted with everybody I needed to meet and started officially gangbangin as a new recruit on the rise to become a gang recruiter.

The Facts:

A gang recruiter is someone who gets you the proper resources and certification you need to be a gang member. There's two types of gang recruiters in every gang: 1. A part time gang recruiter and 2. A full time gang recruiter.

A part time gang recruiter could be anybody that is officially from a gang, which was what my friends that recruited me were. What a part time gang recruiter would do is take the person who wants to become a member and go and meet with the members that have authority to make the decision to accept or reject that persons proposition of wanting to join. For example: If you meet somebody that never been to church and have become interested in becoming a Christian after a talk about god and doesn't know how to pray, you can teach them how to pray and how to seek Christ, but you can not get them into heaven, so basically a part time gang recruiter shows you who to go to and get initiated but cannot do it by there self due to the fact the mass majority of part time gang recruiters are members with little or no respect, beginners in the gang, don't care about finding recruiters part time of fulltime, or focus there time mostly on shooting enemies, selling drugs, robbing people and patrolling the neighborhood. Every part time gang recruiter will eventually run into someone that's cool and wants to join there gang or someone who's been rejecting gang banging and is now ready to accept life as a terrorist and so it would be handled accordingly by the part time gang recruiting standards.

A Full time gang recruiter can only be people with high levels of respect, knows the history of the gang, and is not a freshman (A freshman is considered 5 yrs. Experience and under.) This is needed because being able to initiate name and eliminate members if need be is considered power in the gang community, also being able to say something without nobody objecting is considered major respect. Ninety eight percent of all fulltime gang recruiters have done time, murdered people, is known practically by everybody in the gang. Is feared and usually are the one that take the new recruiter on there first shootings and test the recruits mentally and physically for combat. Every fulltime gang recruiter has something in common regardless if it's crip, blood, piru. They are chamillions they change their character to fit your persona. For example: if you were a youth that goes to church it is common for a fulltime gang recruiter looking for new recruits to tell you, " I go to church too, if we go on Sunday it's okay for us to gangbang Monday through Saturday and I know it happens like that because I've recruited gang members right out of church before. I remember another incident when I found a potential member at the park and played with him, got acquainted with him and built a cool relationship with him, after a while I would start asking how he felt about being from my gang of course at first they'll object, but good recruiters know how to talk and will use any and I mean any means necessary to recruit. Why you acting like you don't want to be in my gang and besides were suppose to be friends. There's plenty of people in my gang that wants to play with you , but you have to be from the hood because it's disrespecting to there image. Sometimes that all it takes I manipulated a dozen more people just like him the same way.

Who's at Risk:

Anybody can be influenced to become a gang member. I've recruited a person 25 years old and have seen older then that as well as young as seven or eight years old. The main target of gang recruiters as far as what type of people are your people, preferably between the ages of 9 and 15 years old. The older you are the more aware you become with your senses which make it harder to influence you even though it's not impossible gang recruiters favor easy ways of doing thing which makes 9 to 15 the easiest. The majority of young people follow crowds and the majority of young people follow the first crowd of people they can call real friends. When I recruit I go after young people who have family members already in gangs, young people who have had a relative killed in gang violence, dysfunctional families, single parents who are never at home or who never spend time with there children, loners and the ones that are curious. My reason is these kinds of youth are easily influenced when introduced to new activities and especially influenced when they see the materials I have such as money,drugs,guns not knowing the likely hood of them even reaching the stage I have is 10 to 1, they'll probably end up doing life, murdered before they make it half way, but I always can just recruit somebody else. I convince them that a gang can fill that emptiness they feel or take away the pain of there situations basically the answer to there problems. Most recruiters make it seem like an adventure that's fun and that nothings going to happen that was not suppose to happen already. Instead on informing the youth that it's a dangerous lifestyle that can get you murdered seriously hurt or in soo much trouble you'll never be able to get out. So we as gang recruiters know no young person is going to join anything that's gone to get them in that type of trouble.

Experienced Recruiter:

There's two types of youth that make up all the different types of potential victims of gang recruiters. They make up the population of this world and that's Followers and Leaders, so knowing that I along with a lot of experienced recruiters recruited a lot more people then we should have. I remember a while back before I was locked up I seen the influence of one of my now homies had on his friends. He was the model friend decision maker for them. Based on I recognized that there was no need to individually ask all of them did they want to join, I simply put the pressure on the leader once he gave in it was only a matter of days as I predicted it to be, for all his followers to follow his footsteps in becoming gang members. All experience recruiters have good eyes in seeing future killers, robbers, dope dealers, people to fill those jail cells, along the graves in the cemetery the definition of good eyes is no matter how strong how weak how scary or solid, any individual is, everybody can be utilized and participate is some sort of way in gang violence. If an experienced recruiter notices you're a weak link he will make you go and kill someone before you are jumped in so even if you don't kill again you already did your part in destroying our community.

The Ingredients:

There's three things that makes a gang stand: 1. Members without members there wouldn't be no gang. 2. Territory without a foundation or area to call the hood the gang wouldn't last because divided you fall and together you'll stand tall for example: There would be no use to own a house's perimeter with no house just like a gang, how can you say you have a gang with no territory. 3. Recruiters without new recruits to replace the gang members that are murdered, the ones that get life, abandon the gang, get paralyzed or any other reason that makes a gang member inactive. The gang would eventually get smaller until it vanishes due to no replacements. One of the most important things in a gang are the recruiters. With them you still see the other two ingredients that make a gang stand, fall into place.

"My Life"

My life was very hard growing up in Compton. It was a lot of gangs, drugs and girls. It was very bad for me and my family. I was not going to school because I was on the corner selling rocks so I could feed my family. My family was very poor. They do not have jobs. My pops is in jail for life so I had to watch over my little brother. My mom was on drugs. I was in and out of jail because of my gang. I joined a gang because they had a lot of money, cars, women and drugs. I joined a gang because of the money. I had to take care of my family because we did not have no money so I had to go out there and make some money so we could eat food every night and pay the bills.

"Two Directions"

My life, my ways, the struggle I face day by day, I often wish I could close my eyes and drift away. It seems like I'm stuck in a bad dream, brokenhearted from all I've experienced and all I've seen. Still young and green. Imagine a child locked in a prison scene. Lost hope for what tomorrow will bring, paying his dues for staying true to the game. If promised love, respect, money and fame, but in all reality all it gave was pain. It had him locked in a chain, time trying to corrupt his brain. Struggling to stay tame, hoping for a change, can't stop the adrenaline from flowing in his veins. Unable to ease his troubled mind, just reminiscing to go back in time. Lost so many partners in crime, very few homies left, sometimes it feels like I'm taking my last breath and if I die, I often wonder who will cry. Hypnotized gangsta with no comprehension, a never ending cycle, another dimension, where life only goes in two directions.

"White Crip from Long Beach"

My name is -------. I'm 18 years old and was Born November --, 198-. I was born in ********, California, but raised in Long Beach, California. Since the age of 9 1/2 -10 years old. I really started getting in trouble at the age of 8. I t started with getting into fights and getting kicked outa school. After so many (as in a couple) years of getting in trouble I was sent to Long Beach to live with my grand parents. This is where I started a whole new life.

Well the place I was living at, was not the appropriate environment that I should have been in. I was one of a very few white kids in the area. Well for that reason, I was involved in multiple fights to prove a point to where I knew that when I walked out the house I had to knuckle up and that's what I did until 199#. At that time, I was known around the community to the point that I would rarely have issues. Well at the end of 199# I was introduced to a gang called "------ Crip Gang". At that time I was jumped in and involved as well. I was called "---------" and this was a neighborhood known as one of the most hated, but well respected I was introduced to females (******) to be specific that were involved to the gang more than most females.

Well after a couple more years of doing what I did, I was finally known to my neighborhood as a keeper(200#) about this time I was locked up for 1st Degree Burglary, Discharge of a Fire Arm and Gang Related Home Invasions. It's now 200# and I'm still locked up in CYA hoping to get out in 200#."

"I'm a white boy that has white supremacist beliefs"

Music is an expression of my individualism. I feel that the types of music that attract me are the ones that represent the type of culture I grew up in and the one that I live in today. I am 20 years old and was raised predominantly in Fresno, California, and I'm a white boy that has white supremacist beliefs and tattoos and support every type of music that stays true to rock and roll. Punk and country and they're cultural backgrounds. Predominately I listen to new age metal and rock but have also been into alternative , punk and recently country due to a few of the roommates I've had while incarcerated in Chad since February of '03. Some of my favorite groups are Tool, Metallica, Marilyn Manson, Alice in Chains, Hate Breed, Korn, Mega Death and so on . Certain verses and quotes that have stood out in my head over the years that represent my frame of mind at times are: "Now is the time for me to rise to my feet, wipe your spit from face, wipe these tears from my eyes" (By:Hate Breed) " The world is an ashtray, we burn in side like cigarettes (By: Marilyn Manson). "Fu#% Authority, sound of majority, raise by the system, now it's time we rise against them."(By:Pennywise) I listen to a lot of classic rock too like Led Zeplin, The Eagles, Foreigner, and so on. In conclusion I hope to party and live like a rock star in the future!

Darkness imprisoning me all that I see absolute horror I cannot live, I cannot die .Landmines have taken my sight, taken my speck, taken my hair and taken my arms. Taken my legs left me with life in Hell" Metallica "One".

"Why Join a Gang?"
(From an Asian perspective)

There's many similar reasons why adolescents of all races, sex or religions join gangs. I can't speak for all, but I can certainly give a perspective from an Asian point of view, more specifically; from a group of Vietnamese known as "The Boat People" and from one that's been there and done that. For those that are not familiar with the phrase "The Boat People" allow me to clarify it for you. "The Boat People" are the products and or results following the Vietnam War. After the fall of Saigon and the American troops pulled out of South Vietnam the country fell to communism; but the idea of Democracy was harbored in a lot of

Vietnamese minds, which included lots of Northern Vietnamese who'd practiced in communism only as a necessity. From these minds came plots and attempts to escape the country. Countless perished in these attempts for a better life and those that made it out of the country were being hoarded for a gruesome journey in the refugee's camp. I've had firsthand experienced with the journey and for deeply personal reasons I don't care to get into any further.

Back to the main subject. Now in America, a considerable and majority amount of Vietnamese are the "Boat People". A lot these "boat people" had kids with them when they escaped from Vietnam. Here in America these kids became adolescent and those that can't handle the pressure of a cultural clash – this is where delinquency began. Take myself for example: All of my family members are over achievers so my family's expectation is very high. Being the youngest one of the siblings I felt the expectation was for me to surpass all of my brothers and sisters. I failed. I came from an old family heritage, so tradition and morals were very strict. I went to school and meet new friends and tried to be Americanized. I prevailed. You see, it felt good to curse, it felt good to put your leg on the table and smoke a cigarette. Of course, not in front of my parents yet... Yeah! I was feeling really Americanized, really grown up. At school I started hanging around a different group. Can you guess who? The "Boat People's" kids, that's right. It was instant bond, similar background, similar problems, and a huge understanding for each other. My new friends became my extended family and in time they took dominance. They were my priority. We didn't start out with extortions, prostitution, home invasion murders, etc.; we started out as rebels from our families. In a way, everyone rebels from their parents one time or another, it just the "Boat People" had a lot more factors to rebel from. This was my mind set at the time: I escaped from a country full of oppression – why should I come to America and follow so many house rules? Especially when so many kids at school are doing their own thing. I misinterpreted what being free is all about so kept moving in my ignorant ways. My friends and I started to cut school, come home late after school, smoke in front of our parents, and when our parents lost control to us, it was really on. It was like having a family that supported you for whatever you do, so you don't care what you do. See, in my country the value of human life is very cheap and respect and honor preside on the top of values. In almost all situations, killing your enemy because he's a threat to your family is more acceptable than stealing something. Thus, and when your family is a group of delinquents, there is gonna be a lot of killing. That's why you notice that the ratio of Asians being locked up is not a lot, but the ones that are locked up, a lot of them are in for serious crimes; home invasion, murders etc. In my country you are taught to hide, or even better, banish all of your emotions, while Americans teach you to express your feelings. That's one of the reasons that a Vietnamese kid that came here by way of the "Boat People" could kill you and hardly show any remorse in doing so. That's what happened with me. Although I've been a long way since I got locked up in the beginning of "9#". I've learned the value of life, remorse, empathy, expressing my feelings, etc.

I've also realized that it is not so bad to follow the road your parents pave for you because all they want is to protect you. Whatever hardship they went through or experienced they try to shelter you from it. So you see, when I said "I prevailed", what really happened is that "I lost."

"I am a White Separatist"

Some people say racism is a psychological disorder and will try to prescribe us a drug or others will say racism is born of ignorance and wants to "teach" us to abandon our "evil" ways. The public has been taught that we are all evil and hate filled people who just want to kill everybody and take over the world, this is not the truth at all.

I, myself am a racist and I can tell you I wish not harm on anybody just because he is an African , Mexican, Asian or any other race or ethnicity. I do not "hate" anybody because they are different than me. The American has a very warped sense of the word racism. Through centuries of psychological conditioning Americans, when they hear the word "racism" automatically they see a picture of Adolph Hitler killing Jews or some Klansmen burning a cross. This is not the case. Some of your friends and neighbors might be racist, the most prominent people in

American society are racist. It is not "bad" or "evil" to be racist.

What is racism? Webster's Dictionary defines racism as" discriminating based on the belief that some races are by nature superior." I tell you this is not true. Racism, as with any ism such as nationalism or patriotism, is being a advocate of and having an affinity for your own people. Nobody tells a Nationalist he is evil for wanting to do what is right for his own homeland. Nobody tells a patriot he should not love his country. By the same token we should not be prejudiced because we love and want only good for our people.

Before I expound more on what I believe I want to be aware that I am not a White Supremacist , I am a White Separatist. I believe that every race or culture was created with in born characteristics to aide in it's survival. I myself have studied the histories of many different cultures and there are admirable traits which they posses, but they are not my race.

The white race is a beautiful people who have risen out of time as a great nation of civilization builders. We matured out of harsh climate conditions and murderous wondering peoples hunting for our lives. We learned to love and respect the nature that kept us alive.

These are the laws which we must now once again rediscover. The laws or nature are the only immutable laws which never change and must be paid obedience. We must separate ourselves from these invading hordes. Throughout time when geographical barriers are broken down it leads to miscegenation and destruction of one or both of the races. In America, we have been brainwashed to believe that "multi-culturalism" is good. But, what is never said is that it is at the expense of white lives.

I don't believe that different cultures or races should be allowed into our country. Right now, our immigration policies allow about 900,000 people into our country each year, out of those 900,000 or so less than 10% come from European countries. This is not a good thing. Combine this with the standard of living forcing the women out of the home to make a living, rampant feminism causing women to feel that they are inadequate if they are "just house wives" or mothers, the rise of the gay movement, and being bombarded by a barrage of inter racial marriage propaganda, the white race is on a path for destruction.

We need to seal off our borders, get to the root of the problem and deal with it. We need to take back our media, our educational system and make our people, young and old, proud of who they are. Our people have shed precious blood to establish a home for us, we cannot let that all be for naught. It may be rough at first and it will probably get worse before it gets better, but we must be immovable in our position, indisputable in our beliefs, and we will prevail.

"A Day in CYA"

I wake up in the morning at 5:45 a.m. I brush my teeth make my bed and clean my room then I look out my window to see what kind of day it's gonna be. Then I go to my front window and I see three staff working. I then call for one of them to let me out for a shower but they say "let me take out my program and pass out breakfast and then I'll pull you out for your shower," so I eat breakfast and then they pull me out for my shower. I spend about 30 to 45 minutes in the shower, then I get dressed, come back to my room, and read my book for a couple of hours, but every time I hear a door open or close I go to my window to see who it is then I start reading again. Around 10:45 a.m. lunch comes: I eat, then I brush my teeth, reflect on the dream I had the night before, and go into fantasy land for about an hour: I make plans for when I get out and while I'm in here. I snap back to reality and start to write rap songs or love songs and sometimes I practice my freestyles. Every time I look out my room I see someone in shackles or handcuffs going to use the phone or going to shower or going to program or to a group. Sometimes I see people fight then I think " d**n do I want to live this way forever?" and I tell myself "I'm in a room by myself for 23 hours a day and I have to strip naked every time I come out of my room: I don't want to live like this forever," but then I pick up my book and start reading again or I start yelling for the mail bag or for program. When I go out to program I go into a cage by myself for one hour and if we get lucky, a little extra time. I've done spent four birthdays in this place; I have another one coming up in 11 days. May -- will be my last birthday locked up, then I'm done. Well, when I come back from program they pass out dinner bags, around 4:30 p.m. I get on my door and yell "Put the radio on Mega 100: oldies and R&B!" We listen to that for about 4 hours, and then someone yells, "put on the TV, there's a movie on Channel 40 'cause it's Friday night movies," so I roll up my bed and put it in front of my door so I could sit on it and watch TV. I get all my snacks that I've been saving all week just for Friday night movies. I eat my snacks and watch the movie until 10:00pm. Then the staff goes home and I unroll my bed, tie my sheets back on, and make my bed. Then I clean my room and wash my face and brush my teeth, then I lay down and go to sleep.

"Story of a Bulldog"

Well, it all started at age 8, when I first realized what my dad was doing. My dad was in and out of juvenile hall and then he went to Y.A. I heard he was doing good when he got out of Y.A., but I guess he got caught up for selling dope. So when my dad got caught he went to the pen, he did 2 years, got out on parole, 7 months later he was back in the pen for violating parole. He paroled 3 years later, he came home all tattooed down from head to feet. I looked at my mom and asked "who is that?", and my dad said, "It's me, your father." So this was when it all happened; when I first got jumped into Fresno ---- Bulldogs. I wanted to bang so I asked my dad to jump me into the Bulldogs. He looked at me, with a beer in his right hand and said to me, "So I been waiting for you to tell me that." I thought he was going to beat my little a*s up, but I guess he didn't, I was glad.

When I got jumped into my gang I was only 13 years old, and I was doing drugs at that age with my dad. My father always told me he wanted me to grow up just like him, and to be real with yourself. I wanted to be just like him, because everyone that knows him is scared of him. I learned my organizations history at a young age, so I was doing good.

I started getting locked up at age 13. The first charge I got was for having a gun, and then I got two charges of hit and run, and then for selling dope. I refused to get handcuffed, spit at a cop, and gave them false information.

I did a lot of stupid things that I wish I could go back and ask those people for forgiveness for. I got in trouble again for selling dope and went back to the hall. I was messed up. Then this lady named ------ came to my window and asked me if I was coming to Bible study that Monday. I said, "I don't know". I'd been going to Bible study for a long time and the Monday came. I was sleeping when they knocked on my door to tell me to go to bible study. I was too lazy to get up and I said, "I don't want to go today." I was going to try to go back to sleep, but I had a strong feeling that told me to go to Bible study, so I yelled out for staff and they came and asked me what I wanted. I said I wanted to go to Bible study if I still can go. They let me go to Bible study. We had 7 minutes to go back to our rooms, and I went to the lady and asked her if she can pray for me. So she put her hand on my forehead and started to pray, out of nowhere I hit the floor and then everything went black for a couple of seconds. Then I saw a bright light and walked to it. I couldn't see that good, but I know that I saw a cross and a man on that cross. I tried to go closer to see, and out of nowhere I started crying because I know what was on that cross it was God. So from that moment I looked at my homies and said you can call me a B***h or a Nac or Leva, but from this day I don't bang any more.

I still bang because I came to Y.A. and found out that my girl just had my baby, so I knew that I couldn't stop banging, because the people that I had hurt before will want to hurt my family and I don't want anything to happen to my little boy or my brothers or sisters or my mom and dad. I love them too much to get them hurt.

I don't want my little boy growing up like me; I want him to become someone in life. I will try my best for him not to grow up like his dad. When I'm at home with my dad and mom I get high with them. I spend almost all day with them because I love them, we go to the parks and get high, I drink beer with my dad.

But my mom don't drink, she don't like us drinking, but it's all right. Now I'm in Y.A. feeling sorry for myself. But in a way I'm glad I'm in Y.A., because I'm showing my father I ain't no punk, I could do Y.A and grow up just like my dad. Like I said, my dad wants me to be just like him. He writes me letters and tells me that I'm just like him and tells me that he gives me a lot of respect, because I show no weakness to him or anyone in Y.A., so all I have to do now is max out, then go to the pen, that's my goal. But I'm not going to let my kid follow my footsteps; I want my boy to be someone in life. I don't want him being like me.

Like I said, I'm in Y.A., I came to Y.A. December 200#, and I don't max out 'till 200#. To be real, if I knew my girlfriend was pregnant, I don't think I would have been in Y.A. I would have disappointed my father. Like I told you, I stopped banging and when I heard them say I was going to Y.A., I asked the homies if I could come back up, and they said I could come back up, but that wasn't the reason I wanted to bang again. I did it for my family and kid's protection. The reason I wrote this was because I don't want you kids or people to follow my footsteps, because all I do is watch my back. So remember what I said, and remember this if you're in Y.A. or the pen and you have a kid or a family out there. Remember the next time you step out of your room that it may be the last time you ever see them. My best advice from me to you is: don't bang and make the same mistakes I did in life.

VII.

What's Your Life All About?
The Demons of Thug Mentality

Many go through life aimlessly, never finding their God-given purpose. The average motivational speaker will tell you the purpose of life is to obtain your maximum potential and be the best humanitarian you can be. This is partially true; however, there are so many who have achieved their personal goals and still have a sense of emptiness. This leads them to set more challenging goals; yet still, they remain unsatisfied.

Goal setting, new relationships, exotic vacations, higher education, money, luxuries, religion, hobbies, thrill seeking – all these things can fill that void temporarily, but then empties away after a period of time. Countless individuals after going through numerous cycles in an attempt to fill their void become frustrated and depressed and drown out their void temporarily through substance abuse, sexual promiscuity, and other bizarre thrill seeking ventures.

They base their value or self worth on their material items, reputation, and performances. These people are continually seeking for the peace to fill that void, and seek it through worldly resources. This insane cycle can be repeated over and over in an individual's life until their life here on earth, eventually expires.

If you look at the human body, it is intelligently, uniquely and wonderfully designed. Every part of our body has a unique feature and design, different from anyone else on the planet. Every part has a specific purpose which benefits the other parts of the body in order to all work in perfect harmony towards our God given purpose.

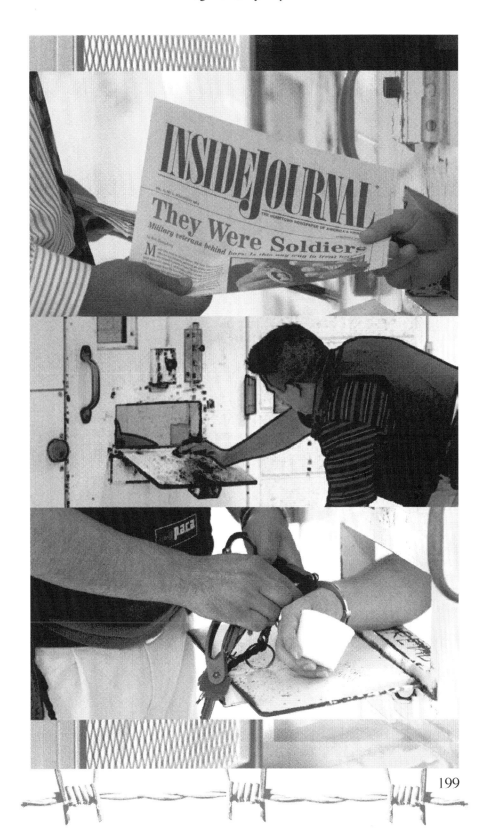

Our universe was fine-tuned and made specifically for us and it supplies all our needs. We can look at the beauty all around us, such as the ocean, mountains, trees, flowers, animals and tropical fish and know that it was designed for our pleasure in every way. Yet, many are born and go through life without ever giving real thought to their purpose of why they are here on earth.

It is like reporting to a new job at a big company and once your there, never attempting to contact your employer, but allowing co-workers and the work environment to dictate to you what your position, title, salary and job duties will be. Meanwhile, your employer is trying to contact you and tell you what your job title is, along with your duties. He has paged and sent you emails, but you have allowed yourself to get so busy by taking assignments from your co-workers or on your own agenda, that you don't even have time to check in. He has left you the company's job manual on your desk; however, you believe there is no time to read it due to all the tasks other people have given you.

As the weeks go by, you start to feel you should be doing something else, maybe in another part of the company. You notice that though you are working hard and at times being praised by your peers, your employer never appears to be satisfied with your work. You explain to him all the great things you have done. Yet, he informs you that you still have not done what he has assigned to you. He brings to your attention that you are working in the wrong department, under the wrong job title. He has been a kind and merciful employer and gives you another chance.

You look around in the company and you realize that those, who are the happiest and most fulfilled meet with the employer on a regular basis to ask questions, obtain advice and assignments from him. They attend all his training sessions, and are prepared to do a good job. These employees are also steadily receiving pay raises, bonuses, and promotions.

Many of us have checked into this world and behave like that new employee. God has placed you in his company called earth, to fulfill his purpose in your life, however many don't check in with him. They listen to their peers, media, themselves and latest trends for their purpose. God has given us all gifts and talents, which the world is eager to pay you for. The world, which Satan and his demons temporarily run wild in (resulting from the fall of Adam and Eve), is ready to prostitute your God-given talents in an attempt to get you away from developing a relationship with God, your creator and employer. He is prepared to give you bonuses and all the other perks in life, which he has created, as long as you work for his company and follow his job assignment and stay within his policy. Satan is always persistently advertising his job openings, but watch out! His perks always come with strings attached and are meant solely for your destruction.

Though I used this analogy of a company setting, Jesus referred to us as friends and children of God, so I like to look at God's kingdom as a family owned business.

How do we become good employees of this family owned business? By developing a strong relationship with God by reading His Word (Holy Bible), praying and being obedient. God cares for you and has talents and gifts for you that will give you great joy and fulfillment. To understand what they are, and how to use them, we must spend time with Him praying (communicating with God) and reading His Word. Understand that whatever the world gives you can and will be taken away. But what God gives you, no man can take away without His permission.

Every successful corporation has an operations and procedure manual. It is the same in life. God has given us His company policy, which contains His wisdom and the blueprint for our lives. It is called the "Holy Bible."

Though we will go through life with trials and tribulations, God has promised that if we abide by his manual, it will always work out to our good (Romans 8:28). Then when our life has come to an end here on earth, he has promised those who have called on His son's name Jesus Christ, and have accepted Him as their personal Lord and Savior, will go on to have eternal life in the spectacular, joyful and flawless city of Heaven. What a great company plan!

No Greater Love

Imagine a love that knew and cared about your every thought. A love that would give you direction and wisdom for a guaranteed solution for every challenge or problem you should ever encounter: A love that

would be willing to guide you 24-7 with counseling, friendship, and support.

God's love for you is far beyond all human understanding. He made the earth, universe and all that is contained in it, just for us. When you look at earth's beautiful landscape such as Yosemite National Forest and the Grand Canyon, the ocean and all its living wonders and the beauty of the sunset to the shining stars in the sky, it is evident that the awesome beauty that surrounds us was made for our enjoyment and to marvel at.

We don't even have to look that far, just look down at your hand and how purposely, and wonderfully it is designed. Our eyes, mouth, ears, nose and entire body are made for the purpose of utilizing and enjoying all the elements and sensations of this vast universe. When we look at all the wonderful food here on earth, such as the sweet and delicious taste of the strawberry and mango, and the large diverse selection of vegetables and poultry, it is evident that a nurturing and loving creator made these foods for our nourishment and enjoyment.

Yet, though he created all these marvelous wonders for us, God decided that was not good enough. The awesome God of this universe wanted to have a personal relationship with you and me. Yet, he gave us free will to make that choice on our own. However, man opted to take the solo route of sin. God did not want to make us robots – He loves us and wants us to love Him through our own will. I heard a pastor once say, "Love is not Love unless there is an option not to."

Though man opted to go his own way, God called us back into His family. In order for Him to have done that, He had to pay the price for man's sin. The price for our sin was death. However, there was not a sufficient sacrifice on earth to atone for our sins. Man was disqualified to atone for sin, due to the only sacrifice for sin had to be a sinless offering. God, the Father, out of his abundance of love gave His Son Jesus to pay for our sins, who was without sin. Jesus, out of His love for the Father and for us was willing to go to the cross on calvary.

Jesus lived a perfect life here on earth without sin, which qualified him to be a sacrifice for our sins. Jesus' life on earth was a perfect demonstration of how God the Father expects us to live our lives. The blood that Jesus shed for us on the cross was pure sinless blood; he was born from a virgin, by a seed planted by the Holy Spirit. This brought us mercy and grace and forgiveness for all our sins. In the Old Testament, or old covenant, sin could only be forgiven through the bloodshed of the innocent. That is why animals were used in sin sacrifices. Through Jesus' sacrifice, we can now come into the family of God and before God's throne, to petition our prayers. God the father has honored the blood of His son. We are now accepted into the family of God and called righteous and friends if we accept His son Jesus Christ as our Lord and Savior.

Once again, Jesus, God the Son was willing to give up the luxuries of the Kingdom of Heaven to become poor here on earth and suffer the most excruciating pain known to mankind. Out of pure love and humility, Jesus endured the crucifixion on the cross. Actor and producer Mel Gibson did a spectacular job portraying the crucifixion in the film "The Passion of the Christ." The film displays the most realistic depiction of Jesus' suffering. At any point, Jesus could have called on an army of angels to rescue Him, but He didn't. His surpassing, unselfish and compassionate love for us refused to retreat until the sacrifice was finished.

His perfect sacrifice took the cold gripping hands of death off us and gave us eternal life and life more abundantly (John 10:10). God the Father raised His son Jesus from the dead on the third day. The Bible tells us that Jesus now sits and reigns on the right hand side of God the Father's throne in Heaven, petitioning our prayers to the Father. Where death once reigned in our soul for man's sin, we now have been given the opportunity to fill our soul with Christ's eternal spirit, making us one with Christ and the Father and the Holy Spirit if we accept Jesus as Lord and Savior of our life.

Some more good news is that after Jesus resurrected from the grave, He did not leave us alone. He left us a comforter who would protect and guide us in His perfect will for our lives. This comforter would be God the Holy Spirit which is one with the Father and Son. This is the same spirit Jesus received from the Father when He was baptized by John the Baptist at the beginning of His ministry that was filled with miracles.

In describing the oneness of God in three, I like to give the analogy of the U.S. Government. You have three branches of government: The executive, which is the president; the legislative, which makes the laws; and the Judicial, which are the courts. All three have their own specific functions, yet they are all the U.S. Government. This is how the Holy Bible depicts God within the oneness of the Father, Son and the Holy Spirit.

1 John 5:7

7 For there are three that bear record in heaven, the Father, the Word, and the Holy Ghost: and these three are one

The Holy Spirit

God loves us so much that He sent His Holy Spirit to empower us so that we could overcome all the powers of our spiritual enemy the devil.

We become supernaturally empowered when we are filled with the Holy Spirit (Acts 1:8). The Holy Spirit gives us the power to overcome the obstacles and temptations of this world, in order for us to stay on course. Yet, we have a choice to allow the Holy Spirit to lead us or not. Satan is always utilizing worldly things and temptations to distract us from the Holy Spirit's voice which is why it is important to develop a close relationship with God so you know His voice when His Holy Spirit is speaking to you. The world is constantly throwing up a variety of flashy illusions like a Hollywood movie set in order to bait us and gear us off the course that God has set for us. Yet, God's word and spirit will give us warnings and instructions to overcome every one of them.

John 16:7-16

7 But I tell you the truth: It is for your good that I am going away. Unless I go away, the Counselor will not come to you; but if I go, I will send him to you. 8When he comes, he will convict the world of guilt in regard to sin and righteousness and judgment: 9in regard to sin, because men do not believe in me; 10in regard to righteousness, because I am going to the Father, where you can see me no longer; 11and in regard to judgment, because the prince of this world now stands condemned.

12 I have much more to say to you, more than you can now bear. 13But when he, the Spirit of truth, comes, he will guide you into all truth. He will not speak on his own; he will speak only what he hears, and he will tell you what is yet to come. 14He will bring glory to me by taking from what is mine and making it known to you. 15All that belongs to the Father is mine. That is why I said the Spirit will take from what is mine and make it known to you.

16 In a little while you will see me no more, and then after a little while you will see me.

The gifts of the Holy Spirit are many. There is the gift of tongues, healing, word of knowledge, wisdom, prophecy, faith, teaching and others. God gives them to us as He sees fit. The purpose for them are for His saints to use them to minister to the world, as a demonstration of God's power and love and for the building up of His Church which God refers to as the Body of Christ.

Gifts of Prophecy and Tongues

1 Corinthians 14:1-12

1 Follow the way of love and eagerly desire spiritual gifts, especially the gift of prophecy.

2For anyone who speaks in a tongue does not speak to men but to God. Indeed, no one understands him; he utters mysteries with his spirit.[1] 3But everyone who prophesies speaks to men for their strengthening, encouragement and comfort. 4He who speaks in a tongue edifies himself, but he who prophesies edifies the church. 5I would like every one of you to speak in tongues, but I would rather have you prophesy. He who prophesies is greater than one who speaks in tongues,unless he interprets, so that the church may be edified.

6Now, brothers, if I come to you and speak in tongues, what good will I be to you, unless I bring you some revelation or knowledge or prophecy or word of instruction? 7Even in the case of lifeless things that make sounds, such as the flute or harp, how will anyone know what tune is being played unless there is a distinction in the notes? 8Again, if the trumpet does not sound a clear call, who will get ready for battle? 9So it is with you. Unless you speak intelligible words with your tongue, how will anyone know what you are saying? You will just be speaking into the air. 10Undoubtedly there are all sorts of languages in the world, yet none of them is without meaning. 11If then I do not grasp the meaning of what someone is saying, I am a foreigner to the speaker, and he is a foreigner to me. 12So it is with you. Since you are eager to have spiritual gifts, try to excel in gifts that build up the church.

God created us and knows everything about us; He knows our likes and dislikes. His plan for our lives is better than any plan we could ever make up for ourselves. This is why we should pray and ask Him to give us our desires and talents for our lives, so we can be guaranteed that we are in His will. The terms in the psalms passage means a passion to do God's will, not to wait for a winning lottery ticket. You see, encoded in God's desires for us is our instructions for our lives. For example: After coming out of a prayer meeting, I have a desire to go visit a co-worker in the hospital. That desire came from God; this is the instruction He has given me.

The Bible tells us, delight yourself in the Lord and He will give you the desires of your heart (Psalm 37:14). I know many whom have given up on God because they feel they have served God, and their desires were not met. The problem here is not that God is not true to His Word, but that they expected God to bless them with their self-created desires. God's word says you ask and don't receive because your requests are selfish.

James 4:3
When you pray for things, you don't get them because you want them for the wrong reason—for your own pleasure.

Others come to God with pre-made plans that might appear honorable, yet their plans are not God's plans for their lives.

James 4:13-16
13 Now listen, you who say, "Today or tomorrow we will go to this or

that city, spend a year there, carry on business and make money." 14Why,
you do not even know what will happen tomorrow. What is your life? You
are a mist that appears for a little while and then vanishes. 15Instead, you
ought to say, "If it is the Lord's will, we will live and do this or that." 16As
it is, you boast and brag. All such boasting is evil.

I have heard a lot of Christians, including myself in the past, ignorantly "naming and claiming" things in the name of Jesus, such as specific jobs, cars, houses, even mates, validating the prayer by scriptures such as, *"Whatsoever you ask in prayer, believe you will receive and it will be yours"* (Mark 11:24).

This is why it's so important to be in tune with the Holy Spirit, so we can obtain God's big picture of His life plan for us. God is not our errand boy who is waiting to run and get whatever we plan and say. He is our Father, of whom we are first to ask what's best for us and wait for His answer and if approved, wait patiently for His delivery.

Many have lost their faith after praying for things and not getting it, believing that God failed on His Word. Yet all along God was waiting with something better, or was delaying while He was working out a character flaw in them that was hindering their walk with Him. God knew giving that blessing to them in their immature state, would distract them and take them further off the course He has planned for them.

The Armor of God

Putting on the armor of God is vital to winning the day-to-day battles over the enemy that we are faced with on a constant basis. To be an elite spiritual soldier you have to train; this takes developing a good work ethic by maintaining a consistent training program which I'll go over at the end of this segment.

In the United States military, soldiers first go through a rigorous training, called boot camp. Here, they get familiar with their weaponry and obtain physical and mental conditioning before they report to their assigned post. At boot camp, the soldiers minds' are conditioned to be ready for warfare. They go through extensive training to develop the habits of a superior soldier.

God's Word states in Romans 12:2: *Do not conform any longer to the pattern of this world, but be transformed by the renewing of your mind. Then you will be able to test and approve what God's will is—his good, pleasing and perfect will.* God instructs us to read His Word in order for us to be conditioned for spiritual warfare. A great place to start your conditioning is in the book of Ephesians:

Ephesians 6:10-20

The Armor of God

10 Finally, be strong in the Lord and in his mighty power. 11Put on the full armor of God so that you can take your stand against the devil's schemes. 12For our struggle is not against flesh and blood, but against the rulers, against the authorities, against the powers of this dark world and against the spiritual forces of evil in the heavenly realms. 13Therefore put on the full armor of God, so that when the day of evil comes, you may be able to stand your ground, and after you have done everything, to stand. 14Stand firm then, with the belt of truth buckled around your waist, with the breastplate of righteousness in place, 15and with your feet fitted with the readiness that comes from the gospel of peace. 16In addition to all this, take up the shield of faith, with which you can extinguish all the flaming arrows of the evil one. 17Take the helmet of salvation and the sword of the Spirit, which is the word of God. 18And pray in the Spirit on all occasions with all kinds of prayers and requests. With this in mind, be alert and always keep on praying for all the saints.

19Pray also for me, that whenever I open my mouth, words may be given me so that I will fearlessly make known the mystery of the gospel, 20for which I am an ambassador in chains. Pray that I may declare it fearlessly, as I should.

These are our instructions from our spiritual war training manual, the Holy Bible. Don't worry, God did not leave us to train for this ruthless spiritual war by ourselves, He gave us His superior trainer the Holy Spirit. The Holy Spirit is so essential to our Christian walk, that Jesus commanded his disciples before he ascended in heaven not to leave

Jerusalem to be witnesses without Him (Holy Spirit is a person).
Acts 1:1-9
Jesus Taken Up Into Heaven

1In my former book, Theophilus, I wrote about all that Jesus began to do and to teach 2until the day he was taken up to heaven, after giving instructions through the Holy Spirit to the apostles he had chosen. 3After his suffering, he showed himself to these men and gave many convincing proofs that he was alive. He appeared to them over a period of forty days and spoke about the kingdom of God. 4On one occasion, while he was eating with them, he gave them this command: "Do not leave Jerusalem, but wait for the gift my Father promised, which you have heard me speak about. 5For John baptized with water, but in a few days you will be baptized with the Holy Spirit."

6So when they met together, they asked him, "Lord, are you at this time going to restore the kingdom to Israel?"

7He said to them: "It is not for you to know the times or dates the Father has set by his own authority. 8But you will receive power when the Holy Spirit comes on you; and you will be my witnesses in Jerusalem, and in all Judea and Samaria, and to the ends of the earth."

9After he said this, he was taken up before their very eyes, and a cloud hid him from their sight.

I have to ask God daily to purge me from any selfish or unclean desires and to refresh his desires in me. He is a loving Heavenly Father and will give me exactly what I need (not always what I want). He sometimes guides me into tough circumstances, but it is always for my good, because it builds and strengthens my character and prepares me for life's tougher courses.

Nothing is wrong in asking for those things you desire, but when you pray you should make your request known, asking God if it is His desire. We know by faith if it is, we will obtain it. If it isn't, then we should rejoice also, because a wise individual doesn't want anything that God doesn't want for them. The Bible says a wise man's steps are ordered by the Lord (Proverbs 3:5-7).

5 Trust in the LORD with all your heart
and lean not on your own understanding;

6 in all your ways acknowledge him,
and he will make your paths straight.

7 Do not be wise in your own eyes;
fear the LORD and shun evil.

The Mechanics of the Body, Soul and Spirit

You are not just a body; you are Body, Soul and Spirit. The body is perishable, our soul and spirit is eternal. Let me give you a brief description of these three components in the order in which they operate.

Spirit:
Is a force either of sinful nature or Righteous nature through Jesus Christ that influences or governs the components of our soul (mind, emotions, will).

Soul:
This is the Mind, Emotions and Will (Our decisions).

Body:
This is the physical anatomy that houses our soul and spirit. The body is animated by the soul. To give you an example; the airwaves is the soul, the body is the television picture. In others words, you can't see the airwaves, until they are transmitted into the television set, which displays what the airwaves were carrying.

The Mechanics

There are two foundational spirits a human can possess, either what the Bible calls the spirit of the sinful nature or a righteous spirit, given when one confesses Jesus Christ as Lord and Savior, known as the "Born Again" experience.

The sinful nature is the spirit that every human inherited from the first couple on earth Adam and Eve when they sinned. This spirit cultivated by Satan (Eph 2:2) produces thoughts and desires in individuals to act out in ways which are contrary to God's commandments.

The spirit of righteousness which comes through the atonement of Jesus Christ does just the opposite. It cultivates desires to think and do acts of righteousness (Psalms 37:4).

These two spirits are at constant war with each other, struggling for control of our soul. Though it is our will which makes the final decision of which spirit gets control, this is preceded by both spirits attempting to draw us in through the other two components of the soul which are the mind and emotions.

The sinful nature attempts this through a baiting technique, which requires getting the mind and emotions stimulated, which is connected to the pleasure zones of our natural body, in order to get the body to act out the will of the sinful nature, which comes from the spirit of Satan.

For example:

A little boy wanders into a store with no money in his pocket. The sinful nature knows he likes candy bars and that he is also hungry. The sinful nature also knows that if he can get the boy to sin, then by God's spiritual law, it will open a door for him to inherit the curses of sin.

Deuteronomy 30:19

19 This day I call heaven and earth as witnesses against you that I have set before you life and death, blessings and curses. Now choose life, so that you and your children may live

Here is a step-by-step scenario of how spiritual warfare takes place everyday over our souls numerous times a day:

1. The sinful spirit places a picture thought in the little boy's mind of a candy bar. This brings forth the emotions of happiness and excitement.
2. The boy's emotions suddenly change to sadness when he realizes he has no money. The sinful nature puts a thought in the boy's mind that, "The store owners are rich, one candy bar off their shelf is no big deal and besides you have earned it, because you have been faithfully doing your chores at home and haven't received a raise in over a year. You should just reward yourself as soon as the store clerk goes in the back room, by just placing the candy bar in your jacket pocket when no ones looking.
3. The spirit of righteousness acting with the conscience immediately tells his mind that this is wrong, because stealing is sin, which produces an emotion of fear and guilt for the intention to convince and instruct the boy's will to make the body walk away from the temptation.

This is where the spiritual warfare really intensifies: *"Resist the devil and he will flee"* (James 4:7).

Words from Satan through the sinful nature and righteous words from God's Word (Eph. 6) through the righteous nature are formulated into thoughts as weapons against each other. Their purpose is to gain control over the prized soul.

The will which is the deciding factor will hear the arguments or statements from both opposing spirits. The spirit which is likely to win the majority custody of the soul is the one which is catered to the most.

Catering to the spirit is a way in which we feed the spirit. My brother-in-law had a sermon entitled, "Which ever you feed will lead." This is very true, because the stronger of the two will lead.

How can we strengthen our righteous spirit? God has given us the gift of His Holy Spirit when we are born again by accepting Christ into our hearts by becoming one with our spirit (John 17:11).

Getting Spiritually Fit

When someone is really serious about getting physically fit, they will seek out and obtain as much nutritional and workout information as they can. Some will go as far as hiring a personal trainer or nutritionist. From my own personal experience in conversing with personal trainers, I discovered that all of them said the following were vitally essential:

- Well balanced meals
- Consistent workout
- Rest

Doctors and fitness trainers will all agree that if you stay committed to all three of the above components that positive results are almost inevitable. It is easy for most to understand the importance of these three essential health tips; it basically goes under the category of common sense. Yet, unfortunately common sense is not that common. Many fail to do these three basic health principles for various excuses, and in the long run they pay the price with health issues such as: obesity, high blood pressure, fatigue, and other diseases.

Failing to abide by these principals is very detrimental to the physical body because continued improper maintenance of the human body will cause it not only to slow down and be less unproductive, but eventually it will cause it to shut down before it's time. Leaving any life goals left unfinished.

Our spirit, like our physical body, needs proper maintenance. Let me explain. We are made up of three components: body, soul, and spirit. As Christians, our spirit which was dead because of sin becomes alive in Christ after salvation.

The purpose of the Christian life is to have the new spirit of God within us, control our soul (mind, emotions, will) which will then control the body. When this order is out of alignment that is when sin takes over. The soul and body is left on its own and will be on a self seeking mission for immediate gratification, led by our old sinful nature (Galatians 5:19-25). Jesus said:

Matthew 4:4

4 Jesus answered, "It is written: 'Man does not live on bread alone, but on every word that comes from the mouth of God.'

How productive would you be in your everyday life if you went without water and food for a week?

There are Christians who go without God's Word for days, weeks and sometimes months. Many believe that a "pit stop" to a Sunday service or weekly bible study is all they need. Could you sustain your health by just eating one meal, two days out of the week?

As Christians, we are called to be soldiers for God's army. God has a mission for each and every one of us. We are going to need a healthy spiritual eating plan each day to have the strength to accomplish the many missions God has planned for us.

There are too many Christians who are spiritually out of shape. They wonder why their Christian life is like a roller coaster ride up and down. Why sin has them in a strapping headlock, which they can't get loose from. Their spirit has no strength; their sinful nature has taken control of their soul. They need to get their spirit in shape, so it can get their soul out of sin's viscous headlock, and send the sinful nature back into the spiritual grave where it belongs.

The Bible has a successful meal plan that will strengthen your spirit. I call it the Four Course Spiritual Meal (The following program is a recommendation I give to those starting their spiritual workout plan)

- Word: Make a commitment to read the Holy Bible in its entirety, from beginning to end, in order to understand God's Word in it's full context. Start with the 2-&-2 Plan, which is two chapters of the Old Testament, starting from the book of Genesis and two chapters of the New Testament, starting with book of Matthew. Take notes, and highlight key scriptures you want to memorize. Then after you have read your 2&2 go ahead and scan ahead or go back and review.

- Prayer: Pray at last 30-60 minutes a day minimum. Create and maintain a prayer list of family, friends, co-workers and the unsaved. The Holy Bible tells us to pray without ceasing. Remember, we can pray anywhere at all times, driving, walking, waiting in line and elsewhere.

- Praise: Set the atmosphere in your home, car and work (if possible) with Christian worship music. Take the music with you going to the gym or jogging. The Bible says sing a new song to the Lord. Make it a habit to spend more time thanking God rather than asking Him for things.

- Obedience & Spiritual Work: The Bible says God wants our obedience over sacrifice (1 Samuel 15:22). God did not just call us to be saved to sit around, be blessed and feel warm and fuzzy. He called us to save us from eternal damnation, and to commission us into His army to save the P.O.W's (Prisoners of war) in satan's prison camp. We accomplish this by learning how to witness, which is learning the skill of sharing the gospel to the lost. I recommend keeping Gospel tracks (Christian literature on salvation) and a pocket Bible with you at all times. These are your weapons to save the lost. Also, write down your testimony and memorize it. Be prepared to share it. This will be your most effective witness to the lost.

For all God has done for us, it is impossible to repay Him. All He asks is for us to accept Him as Lord and love him. We show our love for Him by following His commandments and loving others as He loves us.

Remember, the happiest, most fulfilling and safest place to be is in the will of God.

7 Steps in Developing a Strong Walk in God's Will:

1. Accept Jesus as your personal Lord and Savior and ask to receive his Holy Spirit.

"Lord Jesus, forgive me for all my sins. I believe that You died on the cross, were buried, and on the third day, God the Father raised you from the dead. Right now Lord Jesus, I open the door to my heart, and receive you and your Holy Spirit, into my heart, as my Lord and Savior! Amen"(Romans 10:9)!

2. Read and study the Bible daily.
3. Memorize and meditate on Scriptures and then apply it in your prayers and your everyday self talk (Hebrews 4:12).
4. Develop a consistent prayer life.
5. Find a Bible believing, spirit filled church and become a member and get involved.
6. Internalize the information in this book.
7. Share your Salvation on a regular basis.

Does God Still Do Miracles?

I know God still does miracles. I have seen miracles which many wouldn't believe. I can remember the first miracle I witnessed with my own eyes. This was about 15 years ago. An elderly lady at the beginning of a church revival service at Calvary Christian Center in Sacramento, California was hit with a large video camera, when the cameraman fell off a platform and the camera struck the woman in the center of her forehead. She was bleeding profusely as many around her went into a panic state. I was there on assignment as a photojournalist from the Observer Newspaper. As they took her out, church staff and members were frantically asking to see if a doctor or nurse was present. At this time, I remember seeing Pastor Phillip G. Goudeaux come out in a calm manner, move towards the woman and then lay hands on the lady's head, which was bleeding uncontrollably. He spoke out the word of God in prayer and the lady was healed instantly, the gash and bleeding gone. That was the first miracle I was truly able to confirm which by no explanation, I knew it had to be the working of God.

God showed me recently that He is still granting miracles. At the time, it had been nine years since I had entered the California Youth Authority Academy. While in the academy I contracted a toe fungus on my right big toe, which grew black and brown. It literally looked like a deformed piece of tree bark. After this, I always wore socks, because the sight of my discolored and deformed toe nail disgusted me.

About nine years after living with this diseased fungus, one morning I was watching a preacher on television (Pastor Greg Dickow) who stated that many Christians have gotten into the habit of praying faithless prayers. They pray out of routine, habit or obligation, not really expecting to receive anything.

That morning I thought hard about what the pastor had said and realized that the message was talking directly to me. I then felt compelled to look at my nasty toe. As I did, scriptures of healing started running through my mind. I had prayed countless times before using those same scriptures, yet to no prevail because though I prayed, I never could visualize my toe being healed.

As I began to pray, all of a sudden, I felt some faith arise in me as I began to meditate on those scriptures and I started to visualize my toe going though the stages of being healed. Then with great spiritual boldness I felt compelled by the Holy Spirit to speak to my toe in faith. I said, "Be healed in Jesus name, By Jesus' stripes I am healed" (1Peter 2:24). I got into the shower with my toe looking the same, but I knew something was different this time, and didn't think about it any more.

The next morning I was down stairs studying the Bible and it felt like I had a penny in my sock. I took my sock off and to my amazement my old crusty toe nail was hanging off. I looked closer and realized new healthy skin had grown on my toe and a new toe nail had already started growing. Today, my toe is totally restored back to normal. It was a miracle. God had listened to me because I believed in Him and spoke out a benefit that was entitled to me according to His Word the Holy Bible. This really taught me God's awesome love, it taught me that God even cares about our toes.

Matthew 8:17

17 This was to fulfill what was spoken through the prophet Isaiah: "He took up our infirmities and carried our diseases."

Mark 16:18

18 they will pick up snakes with their hands; and when they drink deadly poison, it will not hurt them at all; they will place their hands on sick people, and they will get well."

God's Word Works when You Work the Word

"God's Word works, when you work the Word," Pastor Phillip G. Goudeaux, of Calvary Christian Center in Sacramento, California used to drill in my head over and over, Sunday after Sunday. The Holy Spirit used this man to teach me that the Word of God is alive and active.

Hebrews 4:12

12 For the word of God is living and active. Sharper than any double-edged sword, it penetrates even to dividing soul and spirit, joints and marrow; it judges the thoughts and attitudes of the heart. 13Nothing in all creation is hidden from God's sight. Everything is uncovered and laid bare before the eyes of him to whom we must give account.

Saved for Real?

Being saved is not just about repeating a prayer and confessing your sins, or even confessing Jesus as Lord. It's about making Him Lord over every area of your life and having a clear understanding of what that means in your heart.

Many times Christians who witness believe that the confession, "Jesus is Lord" is enough. The Bible says that every living thing will eventually say that Jesus is Lord, including the devil and his army of demons, but that doesn't mean they will be going to heaven.

I ask gang members all the time when they tell me they used to be saved, "When you got saved, did you give up your gang and your gang banging lifestyle?" A long pause usually follows, followed by the excuses such as, "Well I slowed down, or I chilled out for a minute."

When we choose to stay and live in sin, we have not made Jesus the Lord over our lives.

1 John 2:4-6

4 The man who says, "I know him," but does not do what he commands is a liar, and the truth is not in him. 5But if anyone obeys his word, God's love is truly made complete in him. This is how we know we are in him: 6Whoever claims to live in him must walk as Jesus did.

Make no mistake, God is not requiring us to be perfect in order for us to be saved and He knows we are not going to be perfect after we are saved. However, he asks us at the time of our coming to be saved to willfully surrender our soul to Him, so He can begin His perfect work on our lives. He knows it's a process and he is patient with us.

God searches the heart; he knows whether we are sincere about whether we truly want Him to be Lord over our life, or whether we repeated the prayer for mere fire insurance, while we go on and live in idolatry by being lord over our own lives. This is the real struggle over being saved. No one wants to go to hell, but not everyone truly wants to stop being lord over their own life. This is why there are so many that attempt to poke holes in Christianity. They want the benefits from the Bible, but they want to do it their way, or do it by making Jesus co-Lord. They believe if they can find flaws, then they can rationalize their sins. They believe that if the Holy Bible has some flaws, then there are no absolutes.

When we surrender ourselves to Christ, the Bible says that He makes us a new creature. We become a spirit creature, desiring those things God has intended for us to desire, being fulfilled with true purpose and joy. However, we must strengthen our spirit through our obedience to Him or else our sinful nature will rise up and contaminate our soul again.

Many I talk to tell me living the Christian life is just too hard or say they don't want to miss out on all the fun of their youth. This is the great deception of Satan. What many don't understand is that anytime God has called someone to do His work in the Bible, He always planned to take them someplace better, as in the story of Moses, when God called for him to take the Israelites out of Egypt into the land of Canaan. God wants to take you to a better place; it starts with Salvation, by accepting Jesus Christ as Lord over your life.

I was talking to a white supremacist the other day that told me that he has been struggling with his beliefs of Christianity. In his cell, he had numerous books on various theologies and philosophers, some which presented a negative critique of the Bible. He told me that he had tried Christianity before, but it didn't work for him, and now he was after the "truth."

He said years ago he had accepted Christ as Lord, but admitted that he refused to give up his racial views and leave his racist gang. I find this very common, people wanting to customize their own salvation, bring their own sacrifices and expect God to bless it, and when He doesn't, they get angry, leave God and then slander His name.

Many don't want to make themselves a living sacrifice which is what God has called all of us to do (Romans 12:1). Christ made himself a living sacrifice through a horrible death on the cross so we could be reconciled with Him and obtain eternal life in paradise. He gave up the beauty and luxuries of heaven out of His love for us who were sinners going to hell. Jesus just asks that we love him back. "If you love me, you will follow my commands" (Jesus Speaking, John 14:15).

Hypocrite Theory

Many I have talked to make the excuse not to accept Jesus as their Lord and Savior by saying that they don't want to commit their life to Jesus, because they don't want to be a Hypocrite.

I respond to this reasoning by asking, "So you think becoming an enemy of God, promoting and doing everything that's contrary to his commandments is more respectable and makes it better for you in His eyes?"

1% Factor

What are you working and living for that's lasting? Not just for your lifetime, but the here after, better known as eternity. Think about eternity. I heard a minister once say that eternity is like having a small sparrow pick up one grain of sand from a beach in California and fly all the way to China with that one grain and repeat the process until every grain of sand on the beaches of California were totally sand free. At this point, eternity would just be beginning.

Our souls are eternal; our body is just the container, which houses our soul (soul=mind, will & emotions). Our soul is the real us, and it will live forever, whether in heaven or hell. When you look at our lives and equate the fraction of time we will spend our lives here on earth, it computes to less than 1%. The remainder of our lives will be spent elsewhere in eternity (Heaven or Hell), determined on how we live our short life here on earth.

So why are there so many stressing and working their fingers to the bone attempting to seek pleasure and wealth from this world? We often are told "you only got one life to live", which is true; however, many are unaware that our lives are but a vapor here on earth before they are sent into eternity. Look at it from this scenario: an eccentric wealthy family member gives you $1,000,000 on the contracted condition that you can never work for anyone else.

If you are wise, you will get a good tax attorney and financial planner and invest and budget your money wisely and watch it steadily grow. A foolish person on the other hand would squander their money on immediate gratification, buying expensive material items and on lavish vacations until eventually the money was depleted. Then after the depression sets in, the IRS would summon them to pay taxes on the $1,000,000, at which time they would be left in a bankrupt state and then incarcerated for a long prison term for tax evasion.

Our life represents that $1,000,000 in the above analogy. Like that individual who acted foolishly with his valuable gift, there are so many individuals when it comes to similar gifts of life. The gift of life here on earth is our limited term investment, which means after a period of time (death) we are forced to withdraw it. Sadly, there are many who refuse to accept the gift of eternal life through accepting Jesus Christ as their personal Lord and Savior. This leaves them spiritually bankrupt when their life expires here on earth.

God has given us His investment plan for our lives. He is our manufacturer and has full knowledge of our entire being, physically, financial, mentally and emotionally. His investment plan is guaranteed eternal life in Heaven's paradise, along with generous dividends paid to us during our temporary residency here on earth. The dividends on earth are insignificant to the dividends we will receive in heaven. The Holy Bible tells us while on earth we should focus more on building up our treasures in Heaven. *19"Do not store up for yourselves treasures on earth, where moth and rust destroy, and where thieves break in and steal. 20But store up for yourselves treasures in heaven, where moth and rust do not destroy, and where thieves do not break in and steal.*(Matthew 6:19-20).

Satan has an alternative plan; his dividends are paid to you quickly here on earth, which requires a deposit of your will to his allegiance. In other words, he requires for you to give him the authority to customize a path just for you. His offer is very tempting, in that a multitude of carnal pleasures are delivered quickly down this path. The downside is that his benefits are a limited time offer, and are laced with lies, destruction and eventually spiritual death.

Yet, many pay no attention to the fine print and are enamored by

Satan's glitzy presentation. He dresses up the sinful life like a Hollywood movie set. They are ignorant to the fact that Satan's investment plan gives him the deed to their souls.

Is there an alternative plan to these two? God in His Word tells us "no." There is only one path to eternal salvation in Heaven and that is through his Son Jesus Christ.

1 Timothy 2:5

5 For there is one God and one mediator between God and men, the man Christ Jesus.

Why Believe the Bible?

For centuries, the world has been warned over and over by preachers to repent because the rapture is coming. Jesus is coming back for His church (Christians) to take them to heaven before the lawless one (Antichrist) lets all hell loose on the world during the horrific tribulation period.

Much of the world has become desensitized to these warnings; some don't believe it at all. Well, is there any more reasons to believe and be concerned now than centuries before? Before I answer that, let me present my argument with as much clarity and simplicity as possible. This chapter is also written to help the believer defend their faith.

Biblical Prophecy:

We can trust and believe God's Word, because God has given the Holy Bible his authentic signature that is the fulfillment of His prophetic Word. Just as God gave his ambassador's (prophets) credibility in the Old Testament by giving them a prophetic word, which he validated by miracles, His word the Holy Bible is still alive today and still fulfilling prophecy, which was prophesied thousands of years ago.

Here are just a few prophesies that validate the truth of the Holy Bible:

In the Old Testament in Micah 3:11-12 it prophesies:

11 Her leaders judge for a bribe, her priests teach for a price, and her prophets tell fortunes for money. Yet they lean upon the LORD and say, "Is not the LORD among us? No disaster will come upon us."

12 Therefore because of you, Zion will be plowed like a field, Jerusalem will become a heap of rubble, the temple hill a mound overgrown with thickets.

This prophecy came true in 135 AD. Micah said that Jerusalem would be destroyed and that Zion (central part of Jerusalem) would be "plowed like a field". Jerusalem was destroyed in 586 BC, first by the Babylonians and then by the Romans in 70 AD. A collection of ancient Jewish writings called the Gemara, reports that the Romans ran a plow over Zion on the 9th day of the Jewish month of AB. There was even a Roman coin minted during that time that displays an image of a man using a plow.

Isaiah 35:1-2 makes this prophecy:

1 The desert and the parched land will be glad; the wilderness will rejoice and blossom. Like the crocus,

2 it will burst into bloom; it will rejoice greatly and shout for joy. The glory of Lebanon will be given to it, the splendor of Carmel and Sharon; they will see the glory of the LORD, the splendor of our God.

This prophecy came true in the early 1900's. The prophet said that Israel would become a barren land, but its desert would one day blossom again. This prophecy has been manifesting since the 1900's. A movement called Zionism started in the 1800's, the movement was all about the Jews moving back to their homeland Israel at which time was called Palestine. In 1917, it was reported that there was less than 25,000 Jews in the land. Today, the population is at 5 million and steadily growing. Millions of Jews have returned to Israel, and advanced farming technology has converted once barren dessert terrain into productive and thriving farmland. At this time, there are more than 200 million trees that have been planted in Israel since 1900(according to the Jewish National Fund).

This next prophecy got the world's attention to finally take notice that the Holy Bible is not just an ordinary book, but a truly supernatural book. Here, in the Book of Isaiah 66:7-8, the prophet prophesies the rebirth of Israel in one day, describing a woman giving birth that is metaphorically Israel. It also foretells that the birth pains of the country would come after the delivery.

Prophecy: Isaiah 66:7-8

7 Before she goes into labor, she gives birth; before the pains come upon her, she delivers a son.

8 Who has ever heard of such a thing? Who has ever seen such things? Can a country be born in a day or a nation be brought forth in a moment? Yet no sooner is Zion in labor than she gives birth to her children.

- This prophecy was revealed in 1948 when Israel was rebirthed.
- This accurately describes what happened on May 14, 1948 - when the Jews declared independence for Israel as a united and sovereign nation for the first time in 2900 years.

- The same day, the United States issued a statement recognizing Israel's sovereignty. And, only hours beforehand, a United Nations mandate expired, ending British control of the land.

- During a 24-hour period, foreign control of the land of Israel had formally ceased, and Israel had declared its independence, and its independence was acknowledged by other nations. Modern Israel was literally born in a single day.

About the birth pains after the delivery, within hours of the declaration of independence in 1948, Israel was attacked by the surrounding countries of Egypt, Jordan, Syria, Lebanon, Iraq and Saudi Arabia, but, as we see, Israel still stands.

God's Word prophesied that Israel would have divine, supernatural protection by God. Hear the words of Moses spoken around 1400 BC:

Leviticus 26:3-8

3 " 'If you follow my decrees and are careful to obey my commands, 4 I will send you rain in its season, and the ground will yield its crops and the trees of the field their fruit. 5 Your threshing will continue until grape harvest and the grape harvest will continue until planting, and you will eat all the food you want and live in safety in your land.

6 " 'I will grant peace in the land, and you will lie down and no one will make you afraid. I will remove savage beasts from the land, and the sword will not pass through your country. 7 You will pursue your enemies, and they will fall by the sword before you. 8 Five of you will chase a hundred, and a hundred of you will chase ten thousand, and your enemies will fall by the sword before you.

This Bible passage says that five people would be able to chase away 100 people, and that 100 would be able to chase away 10,000. Miraculously, it happened just the way it was described, in the following order:

- Within hours of Israel's declaration of independence in 1948, Egypt, Syria, Jordan, Iraq, and Lebanon invaded Israel. The combined population of those countries was at least 20 million at that time. Israel had fewer than 1 million Jews. Even so, the Jews won the war and expanded the size of Israel by 50 percent.

- During the War of 1967, Israel attacked the air force bases of the surrounding countries and took control of Jerusalem for the first time in about 2000 years. They also seized additional territory. That war lasted a mere 6 days.

- On Oct. 6, 1973, Israel was attacked by Egypt and Syria. Other countries later joined the attack. But, the Jews were able to push back the attacking armies and occupy land outside of Israel's border.

Matthew prophesies before the end of the world (the 2nd coming of Jesus Christ) that the Gospel (the New Testament books of Matthew, Mark, Luke and John) will be preached through out the whole world

Prophecy: Matthew 24:14

14 And this gospel of the kingdom will be preached in the whole world as a testimony to all nations, and then the end will come.

As of today, The Bible has been preached throughout the entire world, with the advancement of technology and worldwide availability of satellite television and the Internet. Daily, a multitude of lost souls are coming to the knowledge of Jesus Christ and are accepting him as Lord and Savior.

Another series of current events we can trace back to Biblical prophecy is from the New Testament book of Luke:

There will be signs in the sun, moon and stars. On the earth, nations will be in anguish and perplexity at the roaring and tossing of the sea (Luke 21: 25).

Most recently, we have seen this prophecy of Jesus, manifest through out the world. The South Asian Tsunami that killed countless thousands and the New Orleans "Katrina" not to mention the countless others.

The Bible has made many prophecies about the future of entire nations. For example, It prophesied that Egypt would never rule over other nations again. The prophet Ezekiel said:

Ezekiel 29:15

It will be the lowliest of kingdoms and will never again exalt itself above the other nations. I will make it so weak that it will never again rule over the nations.

Up until the time of Ezekiel, Egypt had been a world power for centuries, dominating many nations, including Israel. But for most of the past 2500 years, Egypt has been controlled by foreign powers, including the Romans, Ottomans and Europeans. Today, Egypt is an independent nation again. In 1948, 1967 and 1973, Egypt attempted to dominate Israel but failed each time, despite the fact that Egypt is 10 times larger than Israel. Egypt as we know is still in existence, however since the time of Ezekiel, it no longer rules over other nations.

How about some current Middle East prophetic news in the making? Look what the prophet Ezekiel tells us with remarkable accuracy in Chapters 38 and 39 of the Book of Ezekiel:

Ezekiel 38:1-23

1 The word of the LORD came to me: 2 "Son of man, set your face against Gog, of the land of Magog, the chief prince of Meshech and Tubal; prophesy against him 3 and say: 'This is what the Sovereign LORD says: I am against you, O Gog, chief prince of Meshech and Tubal. 4 I will turn you around, put hooks in your jaws and bring you out with your whole army—your horses, your horsemen fully armed, and a great horde with large and small shields, all of them brandishing their swords. 5 Persia (Iran), Cush (Ethiopia) and Put will be with them, all with shields and helmets, 6 also Gomer with all its troops, and Beth Togarmah (Turkey) from the far north with all its troops—the many nations with you.

7 'Get ready; be prepared, you and all the hordes gathered about you, and take command of them. 8 After many days you will be called to arms. In future years you will invade a land that has recovered from war, whose people were gathered from many nations to the mountains of Israel, which had long been desolate. They had been brought out from the nations, and now all of them live in safety. 9 You and all your troops and the many nations with you will go up, advancing like a storm; you will be like a cloud covering the land.

10 This is what the Sovereign LORD says: On that day thoughts will come into your mind and you will devise an evil scheme. 11 You will say, "I will invade a land of unwalled villages; I will attack a peaceful and unsuspecting people—all of them living without walls and without gates and bars. 12 I will plunder and loot and turn my hand against the resettled ruins and the people gathered from the nations, rich in livestock and goods, living at the center of the land." 13 Sheba and Dedan and the merchants of Tarshish and all her villages will say to you, "Have you come to plunder? Have you gathered your hordes to loot, to carry off silver and gold, to take away livestock and goods and to seize much plunder?

14 Therefore, son of man, prophesy and say to Gog: 'This is what the Sovereign LORD says: In that day, when my people Israel are living in safety, will you not take notice of it? 15 You will come from your place in the far north, you and many nations with you, all of them riding on horses, a great horde, a mighty army. 16 You will advance against my people Israel like a cloud that covers the land. In days to come, O Gog, I will bring you against my land, so that the nations may know me when I show myself holy through you before their eyes.

17 'This is what the Sovereign LORD says: Are you not the one I spoke of in former days by my servants the prophets of Israel? At that time they prophesied for years that I would bring you against them. 18 This is what will happen in that day: When Gog attacks the land of Israel, my hot anger will be aroused, declares the Sovereign LORD. 19 In my zeal and fiery wrath I declare that at that time there shall be a great earthquake in the land of Israel. 20 The fish of the sea, the birds of the air, the beasts of the field, every creature that moves along the ground, and all the people on the face of the earth will tremble at my presence. The mountains will be overturned, the cliffs will crumble and every wall will fall to the ground. 21 I will summon a sword against Gog on all my mountains, declares the Sovereign LORD. Every man's sword will be against his brother. 22 I will execute judgment upon him with plague and bloodshed; I will pour down torrents of rain, hailstones and burning sulfur on him and on his troops and on the many nations with him. 23 And so I will show my greatness and my holiness, and I will make myself known in the sight of many nations. Then they will know that I am the Lord.'

Ezekiel 39:1-16

1 Son of man, prophesy against Gog and say: 'This is what the Sovereign LORD says: I am against you, O Gog, chief prince of¹ Meshech and Tubal. 2 I will turn you around and drag you along. I will bring you from the far north and send you against the mountains of Israel. 3 Then I will strike your bow from your left hand and make your arrows drop from your right hand. 4 On the mountains of Israel you will fall, you and all your troops and the nations with you. I will give you as food to all kinds of carrion birds and to the wild animals. 5 You will fall in the open field, for I have spoken, declares the Sovereign LORD. 6 I will send fire on Magog and on those who live in safety in the coastlands, and they will know that I am the LORD.

7 'I will make known my holy name among my people Israel. I will no longer let my holy name be profaned, and the nations will know that I the LORD am the Holy One in Israel.

8 It is coming! It will surely take place, declares the Sovereign LORD. This is the day I have spoken of.

9 'Then those who live in the towns of Israel will go out and use the weapons for fuel and burn them up—the small and large shields, the bows and arrows, the war clubs and spears. For seven years they will use them for fuel. 10 They will not need to gather wood from the fields or cut it from the forests, because they will use the weapons for fuel. And they will plunder those who plundered them and loot those who looted them, declares the Sovereign LORD.

11 'On that day I will give Gog a burial place in Israel, in the valley of those who travel east toward¹ the Sea.¹ It will block the way of travelers, because Gog and all his hordes will be buried there. So it will be called the Valley of Hamon Gog. ¹

12 'For seven months the house of Israel will be burying them in order to cleanse the land. 13 All the people of the land will bury them, and the day I am glorified will be a memorable day for them, declares the Sovereign LORD.

14'Men will be regularly employed to cleanse the land. Some will go throughout the land and, in addition to them, others will bury those that remain on the ground. At the end of the seven months they will begin their search. 15 As they go through the land and one of them sees a human bone, he will set up a marker beside it until the gravediggers have buried it in the Valley of Hamon Gog. 16 (Also a town called Hamonah will be there.) And so they will cleanse the land.'

In Ezekiel 38-39, God foretells of a "latter day" invasion of Israel by a confederation of forces led by Russia. God states that several Arab nations will be part of the invading force. He states that these Arab nations will be: Persia (Iran), Cush (Ethiopia), Libya, and the House of Togarmah [Turkey].

This invasion will be coming at Israel from both the North and the South. Libya and Ethiopia will be invading from the West, marching through Egypt, and then up from the South. Russian forces, along with those of Iran and Turkey, will be coming from the North. Israel will be surrounded by hostile armies.

Let us now examine this prophecy in some depth (Ezekiel 38-39):

Verses 1-2: "And the word of the Lord came to me: 'Son of man, set your face against Gog, of the land of Magog, the prince of Rosh, of Meshech, and Tubal, and prophecy against him'…" [Parallel Bible, KJV/Amplified Bible Commentary]

This verse plainly identifies Russia as perpetrator of this invasion.

1. The word, "Rosh" is the old name for the country we now call "Russia".

2. The word, "Meshech" is the root form for the city, "Moscow"

3. The word, 'Tubal" is the name of one of the main rivers of Russia and the Ukraine.

A One-World Government

Prophecy in Progress: Russia would team up with an Arab Coalition to attack Israel.
Prophecy in Progress: 10 World Kingdoms

Daniel 7:2-8

2 Daniel spake and said, I saw in my vision by night, and, behold, the four winds of the heaven strove upon the great sea. 3 And four great beasts came up from the sea, diverse one from another. 4 The first was like a lion [England - the British Royal Family], and had eagle's wings [America]: I beheld till the wings thereof were plucked [USA - destroyed before NWO is fully setup], and it was lifted up from the earth, and made stand upon the feet as a man, and a man's heart was given to it. 5 And behold another beast, a second, like to a bear [Russia], and it raised up itself on one side, and it had three ribs in the mouth of it between the teeth of it: and they said thus unto it, Arise, devour much flesh. 6 After this I beheld, and lo another, like a leopard [European Union - Germany], which had upon the back of it four wings of a fowl; the beast had also four heads; and dominion was given to it. 7 After this I saw in the night visions, and behold a fourth beast [UN One World Government - New World Order], dreadful and terrible, and strong exceedingly; and it had great iron teeth: it devoured and brake in pieces, and stamped the residue with the feet of it: and it was diverse from all the beasts that were before it; and it had ten horns [Club of Rome - 10 Earth Regions]. 8 I considered the horns, and, behold, there came up among them another little horn [Beast - Antichrist], before whom there were three of the first horns plucked up by the roots: and, behold, in this horn were eyes like the eyes of man, and a mouth speaking great things...

Daniel 7:15-25

15 I Daniel was grieved in my spirit in the midst of my body, and the visions of my head troubled me. 16 I came near unto one of them that stood by, and asked him the truth of all this. So he told me, and made me know the interpretation of the things. 17 These great beasts, which are four, are four kings, which shall arise out of the earth. 18 But the saints of the most High shall take the kingdom, and possess the kingdom *for ever, even for ever and ever. 19 Then I would know the truth of the fourth beast, which was diverse from all the others, exceeding dreadful, whose teeth were of iron, and his nails of brass; which devoured, brake in pieces, and stamped the residue with his feet; 20 And of the <u>ten horns</u> that were in his head, and of the other which came up, and before whom three fell; even of that horn that had eyes, and a mouth that spake very great things, whose look was more stout than his fellows. 21 I beheld, and the same horn made war with the saints, and prevailed against them; 22 Until the Ancient of days came, and judgment was given to the saints of the most High; and the time came that the saints possessed the kingdom. 23 Thus he said, The fourth beast shall be the fourth kingdom upon earth, which shall be diverse from all kingdoms, and shall devour the whole earth, and shall tread it down, and break it in pieces. 24 And the <u>ten horns out of this kingdom are ten kings</u> that shall arise: and another shall rise after them; and he shall be diverse from the first, and he shall subdue three kings. 25 And he shall speak great words against the most High, and shall wear out the saints of the most High, and think to change times and laws: and they shall be given into his hand until a time and times and the dividing of time.*

Revelation 13:1-18

1 And I stood upon the sand of the sea, and saw a beast rise up out of the sea, having seven heads and ten horns, and upon his horns <u>ten crowns</u>, and upon his heads the name of blasphemy. 2 And the beast which I saw was like unto a leopard, and his feet were as the feet of a bear, and his mouth as the mouth of a lion: and the dragon gave him his power, and his seat, and great authority. 3 And I saw one of his heads as it were wounded to death; and his deadly wound was healed: and all the world wondered after the beast. 4 And they worshipped the dragon which gave power unto the beast: and they worshipped the beast, saying, Who is like unto the beast? who is able to make war with him? 5 And there was given unto him a mouth speaking great things and blasphemies; and power was given unto him to continue forty and two months. 6 And he opened his mouth in blasphemy against God, to blaspheme his name, and his tabernacle, and them that dwell in heaven. 7 And it was given unto him to make war with the saints, and to overcome them: and power was given him over all kindreds, and tongues, and nations. 8 And all that dwell upon the earth shall worship him, whose names are not *written in the book of life of the Lamb slain from the foundation of the world. 9 If any man have an ear, let him hear. 10 He that leadeth into captivity shall go into captivity: he that killeth with the sword must be killed with the sword. Here is the patience and the faith of the saints. 11 And I beheld another beast coming up out of the earth; and he had two horns like a lamb, and he spake as a dragon. 12 And he exerciseth all the power of the first beast before him, and causeth the earth and them which dwell therein to worship the first beast, whose deadly wound was healed. 13 And he doeth great wonders, so that he maketh fire come down from heaven on the earth in the sight of men, 14 And deceiveth them that dwell on the earth by the means of those miracles which he had power to do in the sight of the beast; saying to them that dwell on the earth, that they should make an image to the beast, which had the wound by a sword, and did live. 15 And he had power to give life unto the image of the beast, that the image of the beast should both speak, and cause that as many as would not worship the image of the beast should be killed. 16 And he causeth all, both small and great, rich and poor, free and bond, to receive a mark in their right hand, or in their foreheads: 17 And that no man might buy or sell, save he that had the mark, or the name of the beast, or the number of his name. 18 Here is wisdom. Let him that hath understanding count the number of the beast: for it is the number of a man; and his number is Six hundred threescore and six.*

Revelation 17:12-17

12 And the <u>ten horns which thou sawest are ten kings</u>, which have received no kingdom as yet; but receive power as kings one hour with the beast. 13 These have one mind, and shall give their power and strength unto the beast... 16 And the <u>ten horns</u> which thou sawest upon the beast, these shall hate the whore, and shall make her desolate and naked, and shall eat her flesh, and burn her with fire. 17 For God hath put in their hearts to fulfill his will, and to agree, and give their kingdom unto the beast, until the words of God shall be fulfilled.

The 10 Kingdoms of the One World Government

(Data gathered from:http://nwo-warning.tripod.com/ten-regions.html#10earthregions)

- The Club of Rome in its September 17, 1973, report,

235

presented to the world a Global World Government System. The Club of Rome is an organization whose members are economists, scientists, industrialists, and international government officials. This report is prophetically aligned with Daniel's prophecy in the book of Daniel (Information on the Club of Rome is available at: www.clubofrome.org).

Prophecy: Mark of the Beast

- In Revelation 13:16-18, the Bible says that there would come a time when a powerful leader would force people to receive a "mark" on or in their right hand or forehead, and that no one would be able to buy or sell unless they had that mark. When the book of Revelation was written about 1900 years ago, it would have been nearly impossible for a world leader to force everyone to receive such a mark. But, today, with modern technology, it would be much easier. Today we have advanced technology which can implant a microscopic bio-chip under a person's that could be used like a debit card. Currently corporations Verachip and Digital Angel are now selling this technology on the market.

God knew there would be skeptics concerning His Word; so His prophecy is His authentic encrypted password. No other religious book in the world can make this claim. Along with being accurately prophetic, the Holy Bible is also used as a creditable resource for archeologists, scientists and historians for its geographical, historical and scientific accuracy.

Scientists and meteorologists have marveled how there has been an increase of earthquakes and unusual weather patterns in recent years. However for Christians, this has been expected:
"And Jesus answered and said to them, 'See to it that no one misleads you. For many will come in My name, saying, 'I am the Christ,' and will mislead many. You will be hearing of wars and rumors of wars. See that you are not frightened, for those things must take place, but that is not

yet the end. For nation will rise against nation, and kingdom against kingdom, and in various places, there will be famines and <u>earthquakes</u>. But all these things are merely the beginning of birth pangs'" (Matt. 24:4-8).

Since the 1950's, earthquakes have continued to increase in frequency and power, just as the Bible predicts for the last days before the return of Christ. Look at the number of killer earthquakes since the 1950's, up until this time there was an average of two to four earthquakes a decade:

- In the 1950s, there were nine.
- In the 1960s, there were 13.
- In the 1970s, there were 51.
- In the 1980s, there were 86.
- From 1990 through 2000 there have been far more than 150.

When we look at the Tsunami which happened in December 26, 2004, which took over 150,000 lives, we can look at God's Word and see His warning in the book of Luke, for us who are living in the last days. Luke 21:25 reads:

"There will be signs in the sun, moon and stars. On the earth, nations will be in anguish and perplexity at the roaring and tossing of the sea." God tells us in 2 Peter 3:9: *"The Lord is not slow in keeping his promise, as some understand slowness. He is patient with you, not wanting anyone to perish, but everyone to come to repentance."*

First, let me say that though no atheist, skeptic or agnostic can logically dispute the past and current manifestations of biblical prophecy. There has been no time in history like the present where we have seen the rapid positioning of prophetic events for the premiere of the tribulation period as prophesied in both the Old and New Testament. The bible states that no one knows the day or the hour except for the father (Matthew 24:36). However, the Bible does warn us to pay close attention to the signs. What signs?

For starters, Daniel's prophecy in the Bible tells us that there would be four world governments before the tribulation events would unfold. God's Word shows us that the rapture will happen before the tribulation (Thessalonians 1:10). God promised to save his church (Christians) from the great wrath of judgment of the tribulation.

The first kingdom was Babylon, next was Medo-Persians, then the Greeks and last, Rome. In the prophecy, Rome was said to be made of iron. It is true Rome is no longer an empire, however it was Rome's government which shaped the foundation of almost all western nations. From the architecture of government buildings such as our Nations Capital to the Supreme Court building, to the creation of laws in the senate, it is evident that Europe and America's governments are extensions from Rome

According to biblical prophesy, the world stage is set for the coming of the one world government. In 1973, an organization that calls itself the "Club of Rome," made up of the world's elite leaders and scholars met for a meeting. The meeting that would take place was the planning of a one world government and right in line with the script of prophecy. Their blue print contained a world government divided into 10 kingdoms.

David prophetically writes that it will be the Antichrist who will rule over the 10 world kingdoms. A component to strengthen this one world government will be a one-world church. Believe it or not, this one world church concept is already growing in popularity.

Not too long ago, I was photographing an event for a newspaper at a church in Sacramento, called Christ Unity. It appeared on the surface to be a traditional Christian Church, however during the program I noticed that almost everyone who got up to minister whether in speech or song, conveyed the message, "There is one God and many ways to him."

At the end of the service, my curiosity got the best of me and I went to venture into their bookstore located on the premises. As I entered, I immediately obtained clarity to the church's interfaith doctrine. What I saw disturbed me. Inside this "so called" Christian bookstore were books, charms and ritual paraphernalia of numerous pagan religions, such as Hinduism, Taoism and Buddhism.

This new interfaith belief system is the primal top agenda item for a one world government planning commission. Why? Most government wars are rooted primarily by religious in differences. In creating a belief system that brings the world's religions in harmony with each other, it will securely strengthen the foundation of a one-world government. There are already inter-faith organizations on course of making this a reality at this time.

In 1986, the late Pope Paul II met with a 130 religious leaders from around the world at the *North American Interfaith Network (NAIN) Conference for World Peace* in Iccese, Italy. Hindus, Buddhists, Muslims, pantheists including the Dali Lama all who reject Jesus Christ as Lord and Savior participated in this conference. Pagan workshops were presented, rituals from various pagan beliefs were taught and believers of all faiths in attendance were encouraged to participate in them. These conferences are still on-going, and growing stronger and more influential every year.

> 1 Timothy 2:5 *"For there is one God and one mediator between God and men, the man Jesus Christ."*

> John 14:6, Jesus states: *"I am the way, the truth and the life; no one comes to the Father, but by me."*

> 1 Corinthians 10:21: *You cannot drink the cup of the Lord and the cup of demons too; you cannot have a part in both the Lord's table and the table of demons.*

> Revelations 17:2 -Prophecy of the one-world church, the wine represents the false teaching or doctrines of the Antichrist:
> *2With her the kings of the earth committed adultery and the inhabitants of the earth were intoxicated with the wine of her adulteries.*

Therefore, the interfaith concept of many paths to God is heresy or false doctrine according to Biblical scripture. Again, the stage is set for the second coming of Christ. Biblical prophecy and the world's current events are tracking in perfect unison.

Evolution Exposed

To follow-up on this evidence for Bible credibility, modern science is another forum that validates scripture. For example, science proves that the earth is not millions or trillions of years old as some scientific theories state, but between the age of 6,000 to 10,000 years old which parallels with the Holy Bible. They have discovered moon dust accumulates at a rate of 14.3 tons every year. After 4-5 billion years (evolutionist age of the earth), the moon's dust layer should have been 140 to 300 meters thick. Yet, today, the dust layer size is about 0.5-7.5 cm. thick . Now, who swept it away? Or why doesn't the scientific math add up to the rate of dust accumulating at 14.3 tons per year. Not only does the yearly moon dust pile not add up, but both the Bible and science can also validate the evidence of dinosaurs as a clue that the the Bible's word is truth.

In Job 40:15-24, God refers to a great creature called "behemoth." Some theologians believe this was a hippopotamus. Yet, one of the characteristics of this creature is that it had a tail the size of a large tree. Hippos have small tails like a small branch and thus could not be the creature the bible refers to. Dinosaurs and pre-historic man also help to illustrate the validity that the Holy Bible is a form of truth.

Evolution's "Nebraska Man" was created out of the discovery of one tooth, which later turned out to belong to an extinct pig. Peking Man was said to be 500,000 years old, although all evidence of his existence has mysteriously disappeared. Piltdown Man's jawbone was found to belong to a modern day ape. Also, the skeleton of the most famous Neanderthal Man was announced at the 1958 International Congress of Zoology to really belong to an old man who had suffered from arthritis(www. creationevidence.org).

"He hangs the earth upon nothing" (Job 26:7). It wasn't until 1650 that science discovered that earth hangs upon nothing. The Bible had already recorded this in early B.C.. The Bible also reveals the earth is round in Isaiah 40:22. The book of Isaiah was written between 740 and 680 B.C. It wasn't until 2000 years later that Christopher Columbus inspired by this scripture proved to the world without a doubt that the earth was round (www.creationevidence.org *Ray Comfort, Scientific Facts in the

Bible,2001,p.73-74).

DNA God's Software

Multi-Billionaire owner and founder of Microsoft, Bill Gates once stated "DNA is like a software program, only much more complex than anything we've ever devised."

Evolutionists and Atheists embrace the theory that there is no intelligent designer. They believe that all the spectacular and amazing creations in which we see and experience with all our five physical senses just happened by random chance, by a few chemicals meeting and exploding in a bang to make this wonderful fine tuned planet, which happens to house the right temperature, minerals, gases, plant life and all the other essentials to sustain human life.

Science continues to marvel at how DNA (deoxyribonucleic acid) with its six feet of software that's securely coiled inside every human body's one hundred trillion cells provides the genetic data necessary to build the uniqueness of our physical anatomy structure.

Let me break it down for you a little further. DNA has its own language or code made up of four chemicals called: adenine, guanine, cytosine and thymine. Scientists label them as A, G, C and T, because they operate as alphabetic characters in the genetic text. Each of us has our own unique code, which makes up who we are physically. Change just one letter out of its sequence and we are reprogrammed to be something else. From curly hair, straight hair, dimples, eye color, skeletal structure, short or tall, DNA is the software which makes us physically who we are. Atheists say this all happened to us by chance.

If someone told you that a high-definition video game with all its spectacular and intricate graphics and audio, had just evolved from an explosion in a software facility, would you believe it? Scientifically, I don't think you could come up with a mathematical equation for the odds of creation happening by accident. However, a theory with worse odds than this is being taught in our educational institutions. This course title is called "Evolution."

241

Just look at all the wonders around us in this vast complex universe. Our solar system keeps us rotating around the sun at precise speed and distance calibrated perfectly with our seasons and the temperature it radiates, which is conducive and safe for life to exist on Earth. Think about the moon which by gravity pull sets the earth at a precise tilt, which regulates our seasons, weather and ocean tides, and stirs up the minerals in the water that we need to sustain plants, animal and human life.

The sun also is an essential component that fine-tunes our planet. If the sun were moved just five percent in either way from the earth, scientists say that animal life would be impossible because the zone for animal life in our solar system is narrow. This is why the earth needs a circular orbit to keep the sun's movement in perfect rotation and zone to sustain life. In saying all this, my point is, if there is a design, then common sense says there is a designer. Just as every software program has a software programmer, the creation around us, points to an intelligent and loving designer and creator.

The elements in our solar system are far more complex than any design or program man could ever think about designing. I heard a minister put it this way, when referring to Evolution's Big Bang Theory. "Explosions don't bring things together; explosions scatter things about. Nothings better put together like our universe and us if you think about it."

All this talk of evolution reminds me of the story of two scientists in a laboratory; one a believer in creation, the other in the theory of evolution. One morning the evolutionist scientist walks in the lab and sees the creation scientist observing a spectacular, detailed model of the solar system. The evolutionist said, "That model is magnificent. I'm amazed at the design, color and detail. This must have taken months to create, who did this?" The creationist looks at the evolutionist and calmly responds, "Nobody. I believe that a lab rat got out of its cage last night and bumped into some of the chemicals in the tubes here on the counter, spilling and mixing them and this caused a chemical combustion, which somehow created this spectacular model of the solar system that we are both marveling at."

"You're crazy, you expect me to believe that insane story? Tell me, who created this?" The evolutionist said, losing his patience. After an awkward silence, the creationist said to his peer, "You find that hard to believe?" It was then that the evolutionist realized that the ridiculous story told by his colleague was parallel in theory to his own belief in evolution. How foolish, the evolutionist thought to himself, to live in a world with such beauty, balance and complex design, and yet to give its credit to aimless floating chemicals that by chance would collide together in space, creating a chemical combustion known as the "Big Bang."

Confessions of Evolution's Founder

Many people don't know that Evolution's founder, Charles Darwin (1809-1882), utilized the theory to justify racism (white supremacy) and immoral behavior. It is also not brought to the forefront about Darwin's confusion and doubt in his own theory. This side of Evolution is often hidden from our school textbooks, but is readily available at the library in Darwin's own writings. Here are some quotes from Darwin that teachers of Evolution wouldn't want you to read:

Racism

"At some future period, not very distant as measured by centuries, the civilized races of man will almost certainly exterminate, and replace, the savage races throughout the world" (Darwin, Descent, vol. I, 201).

"The more civilized so called Caucasian races have beaten the Turkish hollow in the struggle for existence. Looking to the world at no very distant date, what an endless number of the lower races will have been eliminated by the higher civilized races throughout the world" (Darwin, Life and Letters, p. 318).

Immoral Behavior

"A man who has no assured and ever present belief in the existence of a personal God, or of a future existence with retribution and reward, can have for his rule of life, as far as I can see, only to follow those impulses and instincts which are the strongest or which seem to him the best ones" (Darwin, The Morality of Evolution, Autobiography, Norton, p. 94, 1958).

Evolution Violates the Basic Rules of Science

"Often a cold shudder has run through me, and I have asked myself whether I may have not devoted myself to a fantasy" (Charles Darwin, Life and Letters, 1887, Vol. 2, p. 229).

"Evolution is unproved and unprovable. We believe it only because the only alternative is special creation which is unthinkable" (Keith, Arthur, forward to 100th anniversary edition of Charles Darwin's Origin of Species, 1959).

Evolution's Unanswered Questions

"When we descend to details we can prove that no one species has changed (i.e., we cannot prove that a single species has changed): nor can we prove that the supposed changes are beneficial, which is the groundwork of the theory. Nor can we explain why some species have changed and others have not. The latter case seems to me hardly more difficult to understand precisely and in detail than the former case of supposed change" (Darwin, 1863).

"I am quite conscious that my speculations run quite beyond the bounds of true science" (From a letter to Asa Gray, Harvard biology professor, cited in Charles Darwin and the Problem of Creation, N.C. Gillespie, p.2).

"To suppose that the eye, with all its inimitable contrivances for adjusting the focus to different distances, for admitting different amounts of light, and for the correction of spherical and chromatic aberration, could have been formed by natural selection, seems, I freely confess, absurd in the highest possible degree" (Charles Darwin, Origin of Species, 1st Ed., p. 186).

The Bible says, *"The fool says there is no God "*(Psalm 14:1). The evolutionist in the story got the point that he had been a fool.

In Romans 1:18-20, God's Word tells us:

The wrath of God is being revealed from heaven against all the godlessness and wickedness of men who suppress the truth by their wickedness. Since what may be known about God has made it plain to them. Since the creation of the world, God's invisible qualities-his eternal power and divine nature-have been clearly seen, being understood from what has been made so that men are without excuse.

"O' God"

Why is it easy for people to turn to the bible as it is for them to turn away from the bible. Do I personally believe in god? I'm not honestly sure, I do believe that something created all, but who? I don't know, there are so many gods, so many bibles, so many other religions?

Which one is right? only a few times in my life have I ever felt close to god, it's crazy how god demands for us all to follow his bible and to obey all of his laws. What the hell, what I see is war around me everyday, even if I wasn't in jail it's still there Ray, why does god allow us to hurt, hate and pain, when we where all given free choice that's cool, we make are own decisions, but why does he let people hurt the children!, also the counter diction in the bible, why wasn't the dinosaurs mentioned Ray? my mother is always talking to me to believe and pray, how come prayer ain't answered at all? There is so much hate and hurt and god allows it to continue, it to happen. He also is a jealous god who will send his people to hell for not following his path. People live good lives and don't believe in god, will they burn in hell for not being a faithful follower?

Also what about Job, that was f---'d up, he let the devil pump him up for failure, he hurt someone who willingly did good for god. God knew he killed Job's family. Whatever, he gave him everything back 10 fold, but they can't replace the love for a first born and the memories. Why didn't god take away

job's pain?
I don't understand how people can live there life by a book
man wrote, so many use god for benefits because they want
happiness, why doesn't god stop it? God helps those who help
themselves, why doesn't he answer prayer, why does he crush
dreams? It's gods will, it doesn't work for me at all, I want
to learn, but it's hard to explain to me, I believe, but I don't
know in what.

Is There a Spirit World and Heaven /Hell?

The Bible says in Ephesians 6:12: *"we fight not against flesh and
blood, but principalities and powers and rulers in high places."* The
Bible goes on to say that there is a battle going on in the spirit world for
our soul between good and evil.

There have been so many wards that I have counseled over the years
that have conveyed to me that they could bear witness that the spirit
world is real. Over and over, I have heard stories of encounters with
the spirit world. From demonic and celestial beings entering their cells
through walls and closed doors to come torment them, dead relatives and
friends appear in their room to re-cultivate a relationship or to chastise
them. Others tell their experience of strange voices that appear out of no
where which attempt to befriend, torment or tell them to hurt others and
themselves.

Are they insane? Or are these experiences real by them being in a
deeper spiritual realm which most others can't experience. Individuals
who report their so-called hallucinations to medical staff are almost
always prescribed medication for them. At the medical-secular level,
there are no clear answers why these wards have these experiences. The
creepy moving shadows, trees talking, walls breathing and demonic
manifestations, is the brain really that creative on it's own that it could
just some how construct these Hollywood special-effects on the canvas
of the mind, or is this a realm that truly exists. If you go to any drug
infested area in any city, you are likely to see a person rambling or talking
to himself or herself, sometimes yelling and screaming at the air. Most
pass them off as just crazy people who have done too many drugs or
drunk too much alcohol. But what if, what these individuals are seeing is
real? What if they unknowingly entered the door of a spirit world through

cultic rituals ,but the door never shut; now, they are seeing and hearing spiritual creatures mixed in with the natural world and cannot tell the difference? This happened to Professor John Forbes Nash Jr., a brilliant mathematician and Nobel Prize winner who was plagued by spiritual beings appearing in his life as real people, which he could not tell the difference between these spiritual creatures and the natural world ones. He was diagnosed as schizophrenic and insane, but was he really? This inspiring true story was turned into a motion picture called "*A Beautiful Mind.*"

Satan is always attempting to keep or pull us off the track that God has planned for us. He can accomplish this by tapping into the frequency of a person's soul (mind, emotions, will), but he needs an open portal. Drugs, sorcery, fornication, witchcraft, alcohol (drunkenness) and generation curses (curses passed down by family members who practices immoral behaviors) opens up the portals to ones soul. At this point once access is gained, Satan can use the individual's mind to be open to his theatrical visuals, which will stir the emotions, which will then prompt one's will to do his (Satan's) will or purpose.

A former satanist recently asked me the meaning about a dream he had where he looked in the mirror and saw numerous horrid holes in him which looked like pits which were opening and closing. Immediately, the Holy Spirit prompted me to tell him, that those were the open portals to his soul that he had opened up in the past due to cultic rituals. Demonic spirits were coming in and out of him controlling his soul like pilots. He already knew and felt that he was possessed by evil spirts, and expressed his desire to get free from them and accept Jesus Christ as his Lord and Savior. He expressed his frustration of wanting to do the right thing; however, he had an indescribable desire and passion to say and do evil things. I explained to him that the demons' mission is to come in through the open portals and install these sinful desires into the soul, to stir the mind and emotions to prompt the will. These desires are the instructions of Satan, for you to do his work. Why do people want to open the portals of their soul? Satan instructs his demons to make the rituals of opening the portals to have a feeling of ecstasy to one's flesh, so that people will continue to crave the visitations of these evil spirits inside them. The more they do, the more control Satan obtains over their souls.

If Satan can make people see and hear things that no one else can see, and make it so they can't tell the difference between the natural and the spiritual, then he can make the person act and feel insane and convince others to believe the same. This is how Satan is able to lower or mute God's frequency within a person's soul or conscience by redirecting a person off of God's path in their life, which is Satan's mission for all of us. Satan doesn't always send an illusion in an attempt to control souls, sometimes he will just plant thoughts into susceptible minds through various sources as I have discussed in this book so far.

At the end of this segment, I will tell you how an individual can close these portals to the soul. The natural and spirit world are interconnected, and God has made it that some natural remedies can cure some spiritual infirmities, if that natural remedy was instructed by God's wisdom, which is spirit. In others words, I believe God will at times give medical doctors divine spiritual wisdom to utilize medication, foods or even surgery to cure natural ailments which were caused from evil spirits, however there are situations when the evil spirit must be expelled so a person's mind or body can be restored to health. This is why it is so important to be on God's frequency so you can hear His voice. We pick up God's frequency in our soul by: studying His Word, praying, fasting, worship, obedience and doing his work. This opens the portals of our soul to receive God's desires and passions, which are His instructions for us, to direct us down the path he has for our lives. When God opens the portals to our soul and enters, Satan's will have to close. This means the so-called hallucinations stop and the sinful desires will start to die out as God's frequency increases.

Spiritual guidance is now advertised everywhere from astrology and tarot cards to psychic lines. Millions put their trust in these works of witchcraft on a daily basis, because they are amazed by some of the accuracy done in the readings and divinations they receive. What they don't know is that these so-called good spirits or angels are really demons masquerading around on Satan's orders, setting up scenarios to lure people's trust in them, in order to lead them into eternal damnation. Through divination or witchcraft, spiritists channel demons (usually masquerading as gods or angels) for fortune telling and to obtain secretive information. Demons are everywhere; many are amazed by psychics, when at times they give accurate information or readings. Again, they obtain this information through demons they have summoned, who are very familiar with the individual that the information is being requested about. This is all a plot to lure in the trust of naïve individuals, so Satan can lead them down a self-destructive path into eternal damnation.

There are also those who have never participated in cultic practices or substance abuse, but have experienced visual and auditory phenomenons. Some have had these experiences during a near death experience.

Dr. Maurice Rawlings, MD, a heart surgeon, has testimonies from patients in his own practice, who tell of their life after death experiences after flat-lining(dying) on the operating table, then coming back to life after being resuscitated. They came back from the dead testifying about a horrific fiery hell with demons while others came back telling about a beautiful and spectacular place called heaven. He has a movie you can see on- line at: www.amightywind.com/hell/testimonies. htm.

Demonic Encounters within the Correctional Facility

Early in my career, at N.A. Chaderjian Youth Correctional Facility, a ward called for my attention one evening to talk to me. This ward and his cell mate were hard-core Hispanic gang members "tatted" up to show their allegiance to their gang. Both had been involved in numerous riots and assaults since their incarceration. As I approached their cell door, the ward that summoned me made it known by the low tone of his voice, that he wanted our conversation to be confidential. He immediately pointed to a pentagram (satanic symbol used for rituals) in the middle of the cell's floor, then asked me if I could get him some paint or a Bible. He then leaned closer to the cell window and said, "All night demons fly out of the center of that pentagram and swarm all around tormenting me." After he said this, his roommate on the top bunk jumped down and came close to the window with an intense and frightened look, and concurred with his cell mate's story. They both at this time continued to urgently repeat their request of some paint to cover over the pentagram and a Bible. I will never forget the terror in their eyes during my conversation with them. Due to the late hour, I was able to obtain a Holy Bible for them, but no paint.

I can give countless other events during conversations with wards. On one of the unit's I worked, a ward that claimed to be a satanist, murdered and raped his cellmate in a satanic ritual manner. He told authorities he was instructed by the devil to do so. On another unit, eight wards on a cell block had got involved with a Quija board. Upon performing my routine cell checks, one of the wards involved flagged me down requesting to talk to me. The ward was in a state of fear during our conversation and requested to speak to me because he knew I was a Christian. I opened his cell door and immediately he explained the rituals that were involved with their make shift Ouija Board. He told me that they would wait until night then cut themselves on their arm to allow blood to spill onto the board for a sacrifice to Satan to answer their questions. He had thrown away the board a day before out of fear and conviction, but that it appeared back on his cell's desk the next morning. His cellmate confirmed his story. All of the wards had stated that as they asked the board questions, strange movements occurred and that owls would strangely appear in their cell window posted outside on the fence.

In another counseling session, a ward told me word for word how a demon was ridiculing me about the advice I was giving to him during a counseling session on his cell door. He vividly described what the demon looked like (said it looked like a normal man, with regular clothes) and what his body language was doing as I was talking with him.

The mental anguish and torment of the spiritual world is enough to make some individuals want to stop living. I remember talking to a satanic ward on suicide watch, who a couple days before, was restrained by unit staff, after he was observed choking the priest. When I asked him why he did it, he told me that he became angry when the priest denied his request to perform an exorcism on him. The ward told me that daily he is tormented by demons who spoke to him in screeching demonic tongues. He indicated to me that he was tired of the torment, and did not want to be a satanist any more. When I asked him, as a satanist, had he used drugs and performed any cultic rituals? He said "yes." He also stated he had witnessed human sacrifices and was baptized in blood as a young child.

The Lord gave me understanding in this area as to why these portals to the spiritual world stay open, even after heart wrenched repetitive prayers to God. Many of the wards stay in torment due to unforgivingness and unrepentant sin, meaning sin they refuse to turn away from, though they told God they were sorry. God showed me that if these tormented individuals would repent and forgive, He would close Satan's door to their soul and then will open His door, in order to reveal His perfect will for their life.

Demonic Desires

The thug culture opens up the portals of the soul for demonic influence and possession. The Bible calls demons unclean spirits. There is example after example in the New Testament on how Jesus dealt with these spirits. He even sent out 72 of his disciples (Luke 10:1-17) to cast demons out of people who were being tormented in the society and he still commands his followers to do like wise. Look at the great commission, Mark 16:17-18:

17 And these signs will accompany those who believe: In my name they will drive out demons; they will speak in new tongues; 18they will pick up snakes with their hands; and when they drink deadly poison, it will not hurt them at all; they will place their hands on sick people, and they will get well.

Satan is organized and ready for battle. The Bible says Satan has formed governments in which he has set rulers over them. His governments govern specific sins, cities and countries. The book of Daniel makes reference to this in the following passage:

Daniel 10:12

12 Then he continued, "Do not be afraid, Daniel. Since the first day that you set your mind to gain understanding and to humble yourself before your God, your words were heard, and I have come in response to them. 13 But the prince of the Persian kingdom resisted me twenty-one days. Then Michael, one of the chief princes, came to help me, because I was detained there with the king of Persia. 14 Now I have come to explain to you what will happen to your people in the future, for the vision concerns a time yet to come."

There is a Prince of Gangs, Drugs, Murder, and so on, and they utilize earthly resources to gain access to souls to do their bidding through various sources such as music, drugs, sex and anything else which they can utilize to draw the human heart from God.

Keys Demons utilize to open doors to the soul:

- Music
- Horror Movies
- Drugs/Alcohol
- Sexual Sin
- Tattoos
- Astrology/Horoscope
- Witchcraft (palm readers, mediums, tarot cards etc..)
- Cults (gangs, false religions)
- Idols (statues, lucky charms, occultist jewelry)
- Sorority's/Fraternity's (These give worship to Greek Gods. "Stepping" was a form of worship to the Greek Gods)
- Sin in general

Why Demons Enter

Demons want to enter our souls in order to carry out their destructive tasks for Satan. An unbeliever is an open target, due to Satan having spiritual ownership over their soul. He has a right to it, due to man's fall in the Garden of Eden. Satan carries out his destructive plans by assigning his demons to enter the souls of individuals who can be deceived by trickery.

The soul is our mind, emotions and will. The Bible states we are spirit, soul and body. However, when one is unsaved, their spirit is

dead from sin. The spirit is possessed with a carnal and sinful nature inherited from Adam and Eve. It is the person's spirit which influences the soul (mind, emotions & will), and it is the soul which then controls the body. So do you see why Satan attempts to send his demons into our body? By obtaining entrance into the body, Satan can get to the soul. Once he gains access to the soul, he can then mobilize people to do his sinful will.

Why does he want to make us sin? Well, sin is how he receives his praise and worship from us. That is why all the pagan (demon) deities which derived from Satan require sinful acts as their sacrifice. Sinful acts demonstrate obedience to Satan, and disobedience to God. Obedience is a form of worship to God, so sin is worship to Satan. God's word states that the price of sin is death (Romans 6:23), and that's exactly what Satan wants for all mankind.

However, if the believer willfully opens the door to sin, then the devil by spiritual law, has the right to enter into the believer. That is why God's Word tells us not to grieve the Holy Spirit. When an evil spirit enters the believer's soul legally, this spirit sets up an interference to the Holy Spirit and takes control over the soul. This influences the will to tell the body to commit sin, by giving it sinful desires.

Training for Battle

It is the believer's job to train to be a good soldier. In Ephesians 6, the passage tells us to equip ourselves with the armor of God. Many Christians are untrained and unaware of Satan's schemes. Therefore, Satan's demons enter these believers' souls by manipulating them to open the door, at which time they take control to do the will of Satan.

Many people associate the demon possessed as violent, insane individuals with saliva foam running down their mouths. Satan utilizes his army of demons very strategically in different forms and in different areas of an individual's soul. Here are just some of the demons that have been dispatched into countless souls:

Demons of:

- Anger
- Fear
- Insecurity
- Pride
- Importance (conceited)
- Religion
- Laziness
- Disorder
- Lust
- Culture
- Music
- Confusion
- Divorce
- Abortion
- Murder
- Theft
- Homosexuality
- Gangs
- Adultery
- Criticism
- Rebellion

The following is an example of how these demons organize and work together to create entire cultures. Why cultures? Cultures embed ritual habits into people and shape their beliefs. Satan wants sin to become our culture. Earlier I told you about the "Hyphy Movement", below is the story, from the same ward that gave his perspective on the movement and what it means to him. After he shared that with me, he gave me a little family background from his past. This ward told me that he actually feels and hears strange spirits come into him and out of him frequently. Many of those in his immediate family are deeply involved in voodoo. This ward conveyed to me that he was confused about whether to follow the spirits, or to follow Jesus Christ, who he once had a relationship with. He told me in his heart, he wanted to follow Jesus; however he greatly feared the visitations of these demons, which he felt overwhelmed by. He believed that it was certain family members through their witchcraft, which had induced much of what he was encountering. He expressed to me that in a way, he feels at peace being locked up, because the demonic visitations have lessened since he has been away from his family.

This is his story:

"So I Could See the Spirit Come In"

Let me start off like this. I'm or should I say, I was never the type of person to believe in ghosts or fairytales, and sh*% like that, but with some of the stuff that's happened with me there is no other way to explain it. I believe around 2001 some type of spell or hex was put on me by my family. It was my first cousin, yes she is a girl I think she is the one who did it but my grandmother had something to do with it. I don't know if it's true, but deep down inside I know it is. Plus my grandmother previous life included witchcraft. She came from Lake Charles Louisiana and I've heard a little about her and witch craft through other family. But it starts like this I had just met my first cousin. I don't want to say her name so I'll just call her DeDe through out my testimony. Well I had just met DeDe in 2001 and when we first met we was both damn near grown. I'm not even going to sugar coat it. It may have been wrong but we liked each other the way a man likes a women, you feel me. I thought that was both of our intention from the start. But I guess I was wrong. She had something else in mind for me. Well we started kicken it hanging out on the daily. She was pregnant at the time her baby daddy had left her, so it was like she was stuck with a unborn child by herself, until I came into the picture. She had the baby or what not and me being me I was there for her and her baby, even though I can't explain it in positive that she used her baby as part of her plot to seduce me. Well anyway it all started after she got me hooked on "crystal meth" At first me and her use to kick it smoke and drink. I didn't smoke meth at the time I just smoked weed and I would buy her, her drug of choice which was meth. So over time she got me using. I was on crystal meth some thing tough and I was all ways up under my cousin DeDe while on it.

Well I would like to give the reader some insight before I go on. Before I was really hooked on meth I had heard my grandmother tell my cousin DeDe some witch craft type stuff. She told her that if a female was to get a peace of a males hair and string that's the size of the male penis and wear it around their waist it would keep that male up under her, but yeah back to what I was saying. That's what I think my cousin DeDe did as well as some other stuff because I was all ways up under her and now when I think about it I was under her too much. It was like she had a hold on me. Well I can't really explain everything step by step because it's kind of hard to write about it but I'm going to give you straight up what happened over time. My cousin DeDe would come into my body not her body but her spirit. When she first did it I didn't know. I found out one day when I was listening to some music and I was dancing going dumb feeling myself and out the blue a voice in my head said, "that ain't you going dumb" and the voice was my cousin DeDe's voice. When I first heard it I thought I was tripin so I paid it no attention and kept dancing going dumb. Then I heard my cousin's voice again she said like I said nigga that ain't you, it's me. Then in the mix of me going dumb in mid dance she said see and I instantly starting dancing off beat and no matter how hard I tried to prove to myself that I was tripping and I couldn't get my rhyme back I was off beat. Then when she knew, I knew something was up she said I told you nigga. They stopped everything I was doing as realization hit. My fu#%'in cousin was inside me controlling me. Then I went through the stage to where I just thought I was tweaked off crystal meth and that my mind was playing tricks on me. I don't know exactly what my cousin DeDe did to me but I knew it was something because from the first time she let me know she was in me other people spirits could come in me to what I mean by this is say I was to go outside and walk by someone and there spirit would come inside me. I knew this because as I really started to see what was happening to me, it was like when a spirit would come into my body it was like the outer me was a body cast and I was inside the cast. So I could see the spirit come in. But I would only see it as it went in but once it was in it was like we was one, and the spirit would tell me something like let me ride with you, you won't go wrong and the reason I know different peoples spirits was going in and out of me is because I first noticed it with my family and you know as well as I do everybody knows a little something about there family members. Such as the things they do and say and the way they get down. Well when one of my family was in me I would hear there familiar voice asking me to let them drive and when they were fully in control. I would see myself doing and acting the way they do. I'm going to be honest most of my family that went in me would be nicer to me, meaning they would not torment me or have me running around like a chicken with his head cut off. Where to if a strangers spirit were in me a lot of them would be mean if I didn't give them full control. Like for example my cousin DeDe she was meaner than some of the strangers say when she would come in me and I didn't want her in she would not leave me alone she would torment me and while I 'm arguing with her in my head she would some kind of way inflick pain on me I would feel things poke me to where. I would really jump in real life and she would tell me inside me, see, let me in and no matter how hard I would fight her she would keep tormenting me until I gave into her. This is another way she would be cruel to me. There would be times when I would try to get away from her grasp and get away from her, meaning her body it's self, not her spirit and she would tell me in spirit while she was in me to don't even think about leaving and when I had it already made up that I was leaving no matter what. Say the radio or something was on no matter what it was it was always a subliminal telling me not to leave and if I did leave her spirit would travel with me so far, the whole time telling me things like if you past that tree I'm going to have some one beat your as# and it's been time to where she had people approach me while she jumped in them and when I gave in she jumped back in me and the people that approached me walked the other way, but yeah but say the closer I get to the tree she told me not to past I would really hear people that was out side saying thing like don't do it, or watch what happen and the things these people was saying they was talking to the respective people and not me but the things they said was fitting in the right place in the conversation I was having in my head. So yeah my cousin DeDe spirit was one of the ones that tried to torment me but I'm going to be honest at time she would be good to me it was like certain spirits would be my company. Because when all of the spirit stuff started happening to me I stopped hanging with friends. Well as for my dad's granny and uncles spirit was nicer may be because they knew I was family. Let me rephrase that I know they knew I was family. When on of their spirits would come in to me I would let them have full control. Because they would say something like ------(ward's name) you might as well let me drive we going to have some fun. I also remember my grandmother spirit would some time get in me and try to drive and when I didn't let her she would say ------- (ward's name) you not being fair you always let yo cousin DeDe in. And when me or yo uncles be in, we be blessin you with all kind of stuff (this is true) all that girl DeDe do is use you and if I wouldn't give her full control my granny would just leave me alone as well as my uncles and try later. Unlike strangers and my cousin DeDe they would just torment me and scare me until I gave in or go away from them. Stranger didn't really get full control over me because they weren't around me long enough to scare me because I don't be around people I don't know all day so the didn't really get to me like that because a person only encounter strangers. I can't lie I had familiar spirits that I would let in on a regular bases like my cousin I really had no choice she would be around me long enough to scare and torment the shi% out of me until I gave in, but like my grandmother uncles and different people I knew I would let in willing because all the people I just mentioned would ask to drive instead of trying to torment me. And even though all this happened to me I still tried to have doubt. I thought it was the drugs and thought maybe some one slipped me a "mickey" so I even turned myself into a mental hospital. Well when it was all said and done I still thought it was the drugs. Because I got locked up for about six months and I was not having any encounter with spirits so I thought I was back and had my mind right. So I must have got out of Juvenile Hall and when I got out so far so good I had no encounters with spirits or anything like that well that same night I was on my way to bed I was laying down comfortable ready to dose off when I felt someone blow on my neck I smelled the breath and everything and then I heard my cousins DeDe voice say yeah it's me "Lil Daddy" and I felt a feeling on my pe--- as if someone was sucking my pe--- and at that same moment someone knocked at the front door. I didn't know who it was until the person walked past the room I was in. well as the person walked by and looked me in the eye it was nobody but my cousin DeDe. She didn't say "Hi" or nothing and this was strange because I had just gotten out of jail. She just gave me a look like yeah it was me and walked in my grandmother's room. Well I done said enough you can think I'm crazy if you want to but I know all I said is the truth. All the spirits that come in out me no longer bother me I just let them do what ever because I would rather let them in then to be running around like I'm crazy. Like I was when it first started and now that I think about it they may come in my body but I get to be them so I don't see how I'm loosing, but I do refuse the bit%h as* spirits, the spirits got to have something I admire.

But yeah all that I have said is true. I don't usually tell people this because they will think I'm crazy or trying to play crazy.

But I'm not, this is all real.

Can Christians Be Demon Possessed?

Being possessed by a demon implies that a person is owned. A Christian is bought by the blood of Jesus which was shed on the cross of Calvary; they are owned by Jesus Christ. A Christian can not be demon possessed because they are owned by God, however a Christian can be subject to demonic influence where demonic spirits can actually hover or dwell in a Christian in order to oppress, influence and create a stronghold on their will. Yet, initially a door has to have been opened for this to occur. Ignorance is the main cause. Christians who naively involve themselves in cultic practices do not even realize it due to a lack of a disciplined prayer life and the studying of God's word. God tells us to be prayerful in all things and to obtain knowledge and understanding. Many Christians are too lazy to do any research on the activities or organizations they seek to be active in. They are moved by their own wisdom, emotions and self-will, not by God's. Therefore, they unknowingly open the doors of their soul to demonic influence.

The Bible says that our body is the temple of God, so the devil can't come in, right? No. Let's look at what our body contains. Humans as a whole are body, soul and spirit. The bible talks of Jesus referring to certain illnesses as spirits in the Gospels. Yet, I know many true and faithful Christians who have had their bodies ravished with sickness and disease, often by no fault of their own. But hold on! The body is God's temple, so why does God allow demonic spirits of sickness in His temple?

Do all Spirit filled Christians still sin? Yes, the Bible says those who say they are without sin are liars. In God's eyes, the sins of the Christian have been washed away by the blood of Jesus. Well, how is this, when the

Bible says a Christian's body is God's temple. How can we keep sinning? Because when a Christian entertains sin, they open the door to the temple to allow these evil spirits to defile God's temple. What about sickness and disease. The Bible states that the believer has the right to divine healing and to tell demons to go in the name of Jesus. In no way am I saying that all sickness is related to sin, sometimes we get attacked, but thank God as Christians, we can claim healing by the stripes Jesus suffered on his back (1 Peter 2:24).

The Bible states that Satan has blinded the eyes of unbelievers (2cor 4:4). Most don't understand that it is the spirit world, which we can't see influencing and controlling the natural world we do see. Ephesians 6:12 states: *we fight not against flesh and blood but with the demonic spiritual authorities and powers.* Ephesians 2:2 states: *Satan is the prince of the air, who operates in those whom are disobedient.* There are examples in the New Testament, where demons are always looking to inhabit a human body in order to carry out the will of Satan here in this earthly realm.

Expelling demons was the commandment of Jesus in the Gospel's "Great Commission." I asked myself, "Then why aren't there many churches doing it?" The Holy Spirit showed me that this was one of Satan's greatest deceptions: we won't fight what we can't see, understand or don't believe in. Many Christians don't deal with this area, because they believe or feel others will think that they're superstitious, or they don't want to offend people by telling them that they might have evil spirits oppressing or possessing them because of the stigma.

The Bible tells us that we should not be unaware of the devil's schemes (2 Corinthians 2:11). It also says, *"My people perish for a lack of knowledge"* (Hosea 4:6). It is a Christian duty to seek God's knowledge and understanding with all your soul.

Steps to Deliverance

1. Accept Jesus Christ as your Lord and Savior (John 3:16, Romans 10:9).
2. Repent for all your sins (John 1:9).
3. Forgive anyone that has done your wrong (Matthew 11:25-26)
4. Pray for Deliverance:

Lord Jesus Christ, I believe you died on the cross for my sins and rose again from the dead. You redeemed me by your blood and I belong to you, and I want to live for you. I confess all my sins-known and unknown-I'm sorry for them all. I renounce them all. I forgive all others, as I want you to forgive me. Forgive me now and cleanse me with your blood. I thank you for the blood of Jesus Christ, which cleanses me now from all sin. And I come to you now as my deliverer. You know my special needs-the thing that binds, that torments, that defiles: that evil spirit, that unclean spirit-I claim the promise of your word. "Whosoever that calleth on the name of Lord shall be delivered." I call upon you now. In the name of the Lord Jesus Christ, deliver me and set me free. Satan, I renounce you and all your works. I loose myself from you, in the name of Jesus, and I command you to leave me right now, in Jesus' name. Amen.

(This Prayer was used in the ministry of Dr. Derek Prince, from the book <u>Pigs in the Parlor</u> written by Frank and Ida Mae Hammond.)

Staying Delivered

Jesus said, *"When an evil spirit comes out of a man, it goes through arid places seeking rest and does not find it. Then it says, 'I will return to the house I left.' When it arrives, it finds the house unoccupied, swept clean and put in order. Then it goes and takes with it seven other spirits more wicked than itself, and they go in and live there. And the final condition of that man is worse than the first. That is how it will be with this wicked generation"* (Matthew 12:43-45).

The key to staying delivered from demonic influence is to protect the entrances of your soul from demonic invaders. The entrances of your soul are your ears, eyes, mouth, nose and your physical senses (touch, sexual organs). Whatever can impact your soul (mind, emotions and will) in an immoral way is a demonic attack. For example in Depression: Satan will often send an oppressive spirit to give individuals negative thoughts through the mind. Soon it negatively impacts their emotions, which then will compel the will to act out in a unhealthy and negative manner. This spirit can physically create an imbalance of chemicals in the brain. We see numerous times in scripture where physical elements were the cause of demonic spirits. The mind is our battlefield with the enemy. If Satan can control our mind, then he can have control over our will. This is why God's word says:

2 Corinthians 10:3-6

³For though we walk in the flesh, we do not war according to the flesh.⁴For the weapons of our warfare are *not carnal but mighty in God for pulling down strongholds,⁵casting down arguments and every high thing that exalts itself against the knowledge of God, bringing every thought into captivity to the obedience of Christ,⁶and being ready to punish all disobedience when your obedience is fulfilled.*

Because this is a spiritual battle, you must learn how to use God's spiritual weapons. When a sinful or negative thought comes to you, you must say, "I rebuke that thought in Jesus' name." Such demonic thoughts might persist, but you must not give in. The Holy Bible says *"resist the devil and the devil will flee"* (James 4:7).

God's Word is More Powerful than any Demon

The book of Ephesians is a good place to start to get your training. It addresses how we are to use the spiritual armor God has given us:

Ephesians 6:10-20

¹⁰Finally, my brethren, be strong in the Lord and in the power of His might.
¹¹Put on the whole armor of God, that you may be able to stand against the wiles of the devil.¹²For we do not wrestle against flesh and blood, but against principalities, against powers, against the rulers of the darkness of this age, against spiritual hosts *of wickedness in the heavenly* places.*¹³Therefore take up the whole armor of God, that you may be able to withstand in the evil day, and having done all, to stand.¹⁴Stand therefore, having girded your waist with truth, having put on the breastplate of righteousness,*
¹⁵and having shod your feet with the preparation of the gospel of

peace;[16]above all, taking the shield of faith with which you will be able to quench all the fiery darts of the wicked one.[17]And take the helmet of salvation, and the sword of the Spirit, which is the word of God;[18]praying always with all prayer and supplication in the Spirit, being watchful to this end with all perseverance and supplication for all the saints—[19]and for me, that utterance may be given to me, that I may open my mouth boldly to make known the mystery of the gospel,[20]for which I am an ambassador in chains; that in it I may speak boldly, as I ought to speak."

We must remember that God's Word is powerful and it is alive and active according to Hebrews 4:12. Many people are fearful about the spell or incantation made by a witch or satanist. They fear it, because they believe the words coming out their mouth has supernatural power behind it, and that it will accomplish what was said. However, when it comes to God's Words being spoken, many don't believe it or have very little faith in it. Spells or Incantations from a witch is incomparable to the power that God's Words possess. God's Word when spoken in faith will render any spell or incantation, null and void. That is why God's Word is referred to as a sword in scripture.

"Gang Leader"

How should we live in this life? That is a question I'm sure we all ask ourselves. Well today I'ma tell how it is to live a "GANGZSTA LIFE!" you see it all started out like this. Ever since the late 80's when I was born is the day I came into this life of evil. As I was growing up I seen people doing drugs, fighting, stabbing, and even sometimes shooting at each other, and as I got older I kept seeing all this and thought "Damn this is the life!!!"I seen how some people had more respect then others and how they got what ever they wanted and how many people were scared of those people. I said to myself, " I'ma be just like those people, but even better than them. So I started trying to kick it wit the older homiez on the block who are known as the "O" GZ (just so you know I was very young at about this time.) so yeah I would try to kick it wit the homiez, they would always tell me, " what do you want youngster?" I would always say, " I wanna kick it!" and they would just laugh and tell me to leave. That never stopped me I kept coming back every day just kicking it, well thinking I was, just standing around thinking I was cool, ya know?

Anyhow, one day I was like, "f@#% it" I told the homies, sup wit a "pisto"(beer) and their like, "give the lil homie a "pisto". That was it, ever since then I would go every day and always drink. As years went by it went from drinking beer to smoking some bomb(marijuana) now I felt like I was one of them. I was one of them! Years have gone by and now and I'm in my early teens and am now ready to make a name for myself. I started going on lil missions wit the homies. Sometimes we'd run into the "enemy" and I'd watch my homies f@#% them up then stab them, sometimes shoot them. I'd watch all this and sad to say .'I liked it!!!! Then the day came where I had to do something. We came across an "enemy" and I'd watch my homiez said," go f@#% him up! I said, shut the f*#@ up, I'ma do it my way, so now their trippin' I walked up to this guy and he's not even scared for the fact he's probably thinking "what's this lil foo ganna do?" With no feeling what's so ever I walk up to this fool and did my thang. Now I'm not ganna sit here and just lie to you cuz I'm not. I like what I did to that guy; I want to hurt that guy and I did. Likewise, I did what I did, and in the zone in trying to destroy this guy someone grabbed me and said let's go!!!!! If it wasn't for my homies I don't know what I would of have done to that guy. So the next day comes around and there's talk in the hood that some fool got shot the previous night so who ever did it better watch it cuz the cops are on it. To keep it real the cops were the least of my hoods worries cuz we were more worried about the "enemy." Lil did we know the guy that was shot was not a nobody and now people wanna know what happened. I kept my mouth shut for the fact that I had did some s@#% the night before and didn't want people thinking that I did it, ya know? Which it time was the talk in the hood, yup everyone thought it was me. Me? Sh#@! "I didn't care," to me it was like" you want some come get some" I didn't care, if they thought it was me then do something, feel me? I thought I was the s@#%. From that day on, is the day where my life is now in the life of a "gangzta" my life from there on out was not the way oneself would want it, but hey! I said I wanted that kind of life and I got it. I'd be walking down the street and all of a sudden bullets are flying by my head and come on! At a young age who would think that you'd have to be dodging bullets? Me, yup! That's right. I wanted be someone and now I was. Years went by and it was the same s@#% almost everyday. I'm now in my mid teens and I'm use to this s@#%, thinking what can get any worse than this? Oh! But lil did I know that was just the beginning. Everything is now how I always wanted it. Peoples fear me, respect me, and I got everything I wanted. Life was lovely, so I thought. Through this time I've had a girlfriend whom I'm wit till this day and also have a kid by. What am I getting to on this? I knew no one can harm me, but I didn't think that my "enemies" can harm the one's I love. One day my girlfriend, wit my kid was walking down the street and no one knows who she really is for the fact I never let her it kick it wit me anywhere, I didn't want people to know she was wit me, Anyhow, she's walking down the street and all of a sudden a car pulls up and some guys get out. The guy pulls out a gun and puts it to my girlfriends head and tells her where is ***** and she says, "I don't know where he is", he says, your lying and points the gun at my daughter' head and says, your lying to me, send your boyfriend a message for me and pulls the trigger. I don't know why and by the grace of god or something, but when he pulled the trigger the gun jammed or something. I don't know The guy got back in the car and took off. Now tell me, how you think I felt, I never knew what fear really was till my girlfriend told me what happened. Just the thoughts of losing my baby girl just 2 years old made me scared and realized that I am stoppable and can be hurt, "mentally" so yeah I was scared, but at the same time I only hated my "enemies" more than ever. I hated the world and wanted to hurt all that I came across. I thought "God" who is that?!!!!? Where he was when I almost lost the love of my life, there is no god! I was thinking all that but deep down I knew that is God who stopped that bullet from killing my girl, yet I refuse to believe that and just didn't care and didn't want to understand the truth. Why? To me what happened with my girl that was luck!!!! Nothing ever changed, but only got worse. Though out my time in this ganzta life of mine many bad things just kept happening. One day I was sitting on the porch with my homie and some car pulls up and me I'm not tripping cuz I'm up in my hood, ya feel? Nothing can happen to me. Anyway, this guy gets out and says, "Sup homie, remember me? I'm like, "who the fu@# are you fool" before I knew it, there's a Pop! Pop! Pop! And blood all over me, my homiez blood. I look to my right and I see that my best friend is missing a peace of his face. I couldn't feel anything. I just got up pulled out my hear gun and let loose on that b@#% as# fool, not knowing if I'm hitting him or not. God!!!! Like I said "who the f**k is that?"

I said before, what happened wit my daughter was just "luck" why would God let my homie die? After my homie died the only thing I wanted to do was find out who killed my homie. Not only did I have to watch out for my "enemies" I had to watch out for my own homiez for the fact there's someone who always wants to be #1. I couldn't trust anyone. I learned that people never respected me, no! They feared me for who I was, so yeah I couldn't trust anyone. I felt everyone was turning on me lil by lil and all "my" close homiez were dying. You see in this gangzta life your time will come to an end cuz really it's all just a game and in the end there's always ganna be a "game over", I ain't ganna lie it was "game over" for me and now it was my time to be the one who has to go. I thought I was the badest mathaf**#% and I was, but I made myself to known and not only in the end do I have to pay for it, no! All my homiez payed for it and now their dead, that's something I will have to live with for the rest of my life. You may be wondering .. Why are you still alive? Thinking about all this, hey! Maybe god has a plan for me I don't know and I really don't care. I still blame god for all that's happened to the ones that I love. Why couldn't it have been me, why? In the end I know it all wasn't worth it, but I ain't ganna lie. I'ma mathaf**% 'in gangzta and am still ganna live this gangzta life till I die cuz once you live that life there's no way out. There's people out there still this day that still want me, if they do I hope there ready cuz I'ma bring it as much as they will. Yeah I know I'm ignorant and should be trying to change, but I can't I can't till I'm resting six feet under. My mission is not complete till they take me out and the day I do leave this world I will take many wit me, why? Cuz I'ma "Gangzta---------."

"Devil told him come with me forget him you going to die anyways"

Back in 199- when I was like 9 or 10 years old I was walking at about 10:25 to 10:20 at night to a nearby store in --------- Sac, with my big brother --------- and two cousins and a friend. A truck goes by as it went by it came back around as it did I did not know what was going on, I hear gun shots near by, I don't know where it's coming from but as we were walking in the little driveway store my big brother fell to the ground. I did not know what was going on and he tried to get back up and I took him inside the store and called the ambulance. I was telling him "it's ok bro ; it's ok hang in there." As the ambulance came, everybody – my family, everybody – stared and was crying. I was just telling myself he is going to make it, I was hurt inside so when he was in the hospital I cared for him, months went by, he couldn't see at all but you got to be on the right side of him to talk to him and for him to see you. So it was a trip to look at my brother lying there alive. So then he went to another hospital he got well and in like 2 months he came home. See me and my dad and him are very close with one another, so he told me everything, my dad knew. So one day he came by the house, I went outside with him, we took a little walk, we was talking about little things. I was thinking, like man this can't be true that my brother is by my side. So he was like "let me tell you something little brother, he was like this, when I was in the coma I woke up and everything went blank. The door shut, he was just in the bed with nothing around, and everything went white, the whole room did he did not know what was going on. The window opened, as it did, he saw Jesus come in and stand by his right side and looked down on him for a minute and as the minute went by, he saw angels come in and was behind him, who do you want to go with?, who you want to go with?, everything went blank again but now the room changed to fire red all around him the room got red, the devil told him come with me, forget him. You going to die anyways, you broke, you sin already, you need me. So everything started to go red, white, red, white, so he was not thinking, what to pick, it was going back to back so he said, "Jesus, I want to go with you, take me now, as long as

269

I'm with you I don't care" so he did and boom, he came alive right at that minute everything went ok for him, he came out the coma alive and then he got out the bed, and started doing everything normal, I was thinking man, it can't be, it can't be. God helped my brother; I had to believe there is a God, had to be, as of right now he is doing everything like a normal human is doing. He got a kid, a wife and living a good life, I pray for him and his family and that Jesus help my brother stay alive in this world, I wish he can do that to a lot of people in this world. Well that is my story of my big brotha --------.

"It was like no one cared about females."

I saw all the dope dealers, hustlers and pimps, they had it all: from money and fame to power and women. I wanted to be like that. I picked up on what they did and tried to put it to use in my life. So I started hurting people and doing what I had to do to make sure I had what I wanted. That's why I joined -- MOB. I mean, look at what it stands for; --
thStreet, Money Over B#%@#'s. That's the kind of mentality that got me locked up. Not caring for anyone. Other than taking what I wanted, I tried to look out for my family. Those were the only people I cared for other than the people in my gang. Music was another thing that played a role in my thug mentality. Since I can remember I grew up listening to rap and a rapper calling females hoes and tricks – it was like no one cared about females – you hear them glorifying selling drugs or killing someone. Those are the two major things that come to mind when asked what played a role in my thug mentality."

"I wanted to be like the big homies"

I was born in the city of ----; my mother came from Mexico with my father when she was 16 years-old. She gave birth to me when she was 18. She moved to a low-income house otherwise known as the projects. In the ---- side of Fresno, in this area there was a gang known as --------. Slowly more and more of my family from Mexico started moving to Fresno. I had a lot of cousins and friends. By the age of 8 years old, I was already starting to understand that my area was a gang infused with Nortenos, I went to school with one of the head of ----(gang) little brothers, slowly we became friends. By the age of 9, I was asked to join their gang. By this time my father had left my mother and I had no father figures at home. So I was very hard to control. Once I joined the gang, I had to sell drugs for my older homies. There was a lot of hookers and drug addicts around the projects, my mother did not know English so I was influenced to sell drugs to help my family. As I got older the request got more serious, but I felt I could not refuse nor did I. I wanted to be like the big homies and I did everything I was asked. I began to steal cars, anything to make money even though I had no real use for it, all I wanted was to accepted and was. I felt loved and needed. Everything I tried so hard for was finally happening, my family was never in need. By 14, I had my own car and all the drugs I could sell. I was considered a well respected and high ranking person in my hood. Once I got locked up a lot changed. I learned why and how my organization came about, which motivated me even more to continue living this life style and it may cost me a couple years of my life, it is worth it. I believe that if I wasn't locked up I would have been killed by now. In my way I'm happy, but the better of me tells me I rather be free. I learned that I could be from my gang and not sell drugs or shoot people, but move forward with a positive state of mind but give to my organization what I can and forever my beliefs will stand firm in my heart and mind , but there is a lot more positive ways of going about how I can represent my gang. I hope you could understand my point of view. We are all different and come from different worlds as far as we were raised, but we are all human beings and all deserve to he healed with love and respect. Maybe one day I will leave my gang ties, but for now I don't see that happening no time soon.

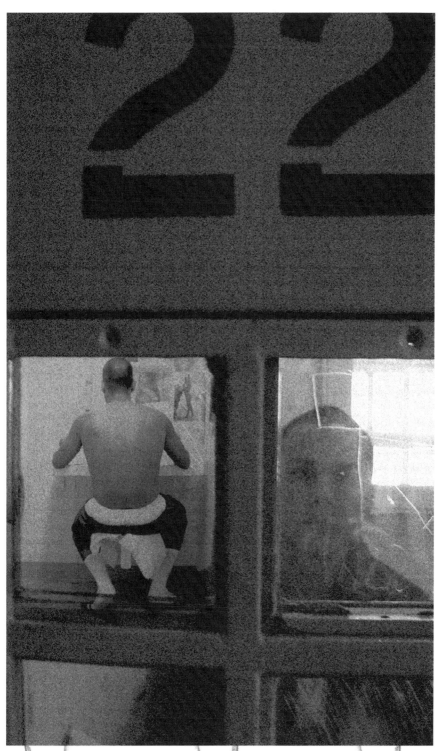

"Stronger Laws?"

In today's society it seems people believe they can get away with murder. This is partly because laws are not demanding. The respect they should have and partly because today's generation is not politically aware.

I feel that today people feel they can break the law as they wish, without having to, if you will, "pay the price." The reason for this newly developed mentality is because laws are becoming more lenient. I say this not because votes were taken and that's what the people want, but because I feel that our youth is getting "slaps on the hand" for what would be considered a serous crime if they were adults.

If the law was harsher on juveniles it may discourage the criminal life style at a young age before young minds are completely molded. By discouraging criminal behavior at a young age our percentage of criminally active adults will decrease in a large number.

Take my case for example. When I was in fourth grade I dropped out of school on my own will. By the time I was eleven I was using drugs and drinking habitually. At twelve I was involved in a strong armed robbery and sent to a group home 23 days before my thirteenth birthday. I stayed at this group home a little over three years due to my on going involvement in gang violence, drug use and all out rebellion.

After three years at this group home they realized I wasn't going to change so they decided to send me home just two months after I got two assaults with deadly weapons dropped due to lack of evidence. Just 15 days after being released from the group home I was sentenced to six months at Orin Allen Youth Correction Facility for vandalism on a police car.

While at Orin Allen I got kicked out 3 times, once just three hours upon returning for inciting a fight in which there was a black out and I hit a rival with a chair causing a riot. I easily turned that six months into nine in a half months. Yet, just three weeks after starting the riot I was still released due to the fact that my custody time was up. Only 25 days after being discharged from Orin Allen I was sentenced to CYA for a commitment of four years on which I have 13 months left.

I feel if the court system would have done more than a "slap my hand" while I was at the group home I would have been discouraged to continue down the path I was headed. Now that I have had serious and valuable time taken from me I now have the thirst for a change for the better , but have a small fear that it may be to late.

From experience, I developed the belief that laws should be strict on juveniles to prevent adult crime. "Develop character while still maturing, and the mature product will be of fined essence" said Mark A. Thomas , author of Mans Unconquerable Mind.

"Gang Banging ain't like it was in the eighties. "

When I was about thirteen I thought it was cool to go around and victimize other people just because they weren't from the same part of town as I was. As I got older I slowly started to realize how stupid I was: I used to always look up to older homeboys and my uncles. I had a lot of clout when I was out because of who my family was. I got roughed up a lot when I was a little kid. My mom would always make me fight with the older kids in my neighborhood. She said if I don't kick their as#, she would kick my as*, I made sure I didn't lose, but if I did, my mom would make me fight him again. Some of them would get so tired of fighting me, they would let me win. I realized that being in a gang ain't what people really expect it to be. Back in the days, my whole barrio (neighborhood) used to get along, now I hear that they're out there shooting each other and fighting and sh*t. Gang Banging ain't like it was in the eighties. I guess it's because they're too many youngsters trying to earn their respect. I'm glad I'm locked up and not out there having to deal with all that bullsh*t."

Finding God's Mission for Your Life

Goal Planning

If someone asked you to get in your car and just to start driving on the highway and didn't give you a destination, saying "Lets just drive and see if we can find something exciting," would you waste the gas and wear and tear on your car on a frivolous exploit like that? I know it sounds like a dumb question, but statistically this is how the majority of society lives their lives. Statistics state that only 3% of society sets specific goals. The majority just live their lives day-by-day, paycheck-to-paycheck.

The majority of society lives reactive, not proactive lives. They respond to things as they come, instead of before they come. They let circumstances and their emotions dictate and shape their lives, instead of preparing and planning their lives to their God given heart's desires. Thus, they make their lives stressful, unstable and unfulfilled.

Imagine working for an employer who did not appreciate or reward anyone for doing an outstanding job. The employees' moral would be low. Many of the employees would be moody, calling in sick, and some would quit, because of the lack of incentive to work. Unfortunately, many individuals treat themselves identical to the example above. They work, but have little or no incentives for their life. Therefore, their life becomes unmotivated, boring, and unhappy. From time to time, they experience immediate gratification that they indulge in, but soon after they are left with an insatiable emptiness.

This is like playing soccer without scoring a goal or playing golf without a hole. The game would become monotonous and unfulfilled. Many people go through life on a day-to-day basis, not having any idea where they're going or where they want to go in life. What a scary, frustrating, and depressing way to live, especially when we were given the God-given gift to plan and live our lives according to the desires He has placed in our hearts (or wants to place in hearts during our prayer time with Him). God has given us all talents and gifts that he has custom designed to fulfill our every desire and to meet His purpose, at the same time giving us great peace, fulfillment and joy in our lives.

Sadly, many individuals pass up this right for various reasons, such as low self-esteem, fear of failure or laziness. Many have aborted their dreams because what someone told them: "You're not smart enough to go to college", "They don't hire your race in that industry", "You're too short", "No one is going to give you a job; you have a criminal record."

As a result, they end up living a life someone else has shaped for them, because they have accepted someone else's belief about themselves. This is the lie that so many individuals live with. This is where the bad attitudes, depression and stress come from. Individuals, whom live their lives with this mentality day by day, can't handle stress well when something goes wrong, because their lives appear so frustrating, hopeless and meaningless already.

It is important when traveling through your life journey to have the right road map. You can only get that through prayer, reading and studying God's Word. However, you must expect problems and difficulties. God warns us in His Word to be prepared for troubles and difficulties and commands us not to give up. God uses the trials and tribulations in our lives, while traveling on His path, to develop our character and to strengthen us (James 1: 2-5).

Greatness takes time; successful people aren't born overnight. They are developed over time, after being tested and tried through trials and tribulations. I remember getting frustrated as I landscaped my yard one day, my wise old neighbor would often encourage me, by saying, "Ray, Rome wasn't built in a day."

A woman who is pregnant anticipates having much discomfort, sickness, and pain for a period of several months. She has weighed the pros and cons, and has assured herself that without a doubt, a precious baby is well worth the wait and the pain. It is human nature to gravitate to what is easy, pleasurable, and comfortable. Yet, the truth is, what is easy, comfortable, and pleasurable is not always good for us. Stuffing yourself with junk food, reclining back in a lazy boy, lighting up a cigarette and going to sleep, can be easy, comfortable, and pleasurable for some people, but I can guarantee that 5 out 5 doctors (sand doctors that is) will tell you that it can be very detrimental to your health.

Others have set goals, but are too lazy to organize their goals in a detailed written plan. It sounds impressive when they tell others; however, they have taken no effort to research, study, and chart out how and when they will meet their objectives. It is like a man walking into a bank asking for a loan to start up a business, without having a business plan or a foreman telling his crew to build a skyscraper with just materials and no blueprint. This sounds illogical and foolish, yet it is how many people live their lives, never having a specific plan.

How do we get started in planning our lives? A good starting point is to pray. God says in the Holy Bible that if we delight ourselves in Him, he will give us the desires of our hearts (Psalms 37:4). He will place desires in our heart that glorify Him and bring us joy, purpose and blessings. I personally ask God daily to purge out of me anything in my heart and mind he does not want me to have. This way I can be sure that I am always in His will. I used to be scared to do this, thinking that by doing that, God would extract all the fun out of my life. I have learned that this is untrue, as a matter of fact, it's just the opposite.

God tells us in the book of Jeremiah: *"For I know the plans I have for you, declares the Lord, plans to prosper you and not to harm you, plans to give you hope and a future. Then you will call upon me and come and pray to me, and I will listen to you. You will seek me and find me, when you seek me with all your heart. I will be found by you"* (Jeremiah 29:13).

God will give us the wisdom to be realistic when setting goals; otherwise we will end up frustrated and unhappy in our pursuit. If you have a laser focus of being a NBA basketball star and you've been cut by your high school team for the last three years, maybe you should focus on another career you would enjoy and are good at and plan to entertain your love of basketball by joining a city or church league. We have to be mature in our goal setting and that means to thoroughly identify and evaluate our God-given talents and desires. When selecting a goal, it should be exciting and rewarding. Don't over-analyze your wishes, dreams, and desires, just write them down. Many people talk themselves out of their dreams by immediately building a case against them.

At the correctional institution where I counsel a multitude of youth with low self-esteem, I often start the topic of goal setting by asking the following question, "If someone came to your cell door and told you that they had approval to take you to work at a job in the free world, any job you wanted, but you would work for free, what job would you choose?"

The purpose of the question is to prompt the individual to start envisioning themselves in a career and environment that they would find exciting, stimulating, fun, and fulfilling. Many of the individuals after asking this question still will say, "I don't know" because many of them feel they are not smart enough, or unqualified. I then will follow up with the following questions: what magazines and books do you like to read? What types of television shows do you watch? What do you like to talk about? These questions are geared in a way to get the individual to start thinking about what things are interesting to them. Once you have zeroed in on your interests, now you have a foundational base to work from.

When an individual is placed in a career or lifestyle that is not interesting to them, you will find a bored, unhappy, and frustrated human being. With all the freedom we have in the United States, many enslave themselves in careers and lifestyles that they hate. The following are some common reasons:

- Fear of failure

- Immediate gratification
- Low self-esteem
- Laziness
- Procrastination

How does one get the confidence and motivation to start setting goals? First, there must be a sincere desire to change. To stimulate the desire to change, we must strategically place ourselves around people, places and things that will help to promote a positive change towards our goals.

When I decided to become a freelance photographer, I hung out with photographers, I read books about photography, and I studied other photographers' work in publications and in galleries. Many aspects of my life evolved around photography. I internalized the goal I had set; the goal of becoming a professional photographer. I envisioned myself vividly, taking photos at celebrity, sporting and news events. As I continued to keep this vision, I was also acquiring knowledge in the field, which was adding confidence and faith to the pursuit of my goal. Every day I was feeding my goal with positive stimulants and self talk which in turn was giving me more and more momentum to accomplish my goal at a rapid rate. Within three years, I had won first place in two national photography contests and had obtained a job as a photojournalist for a local newspaper, which gave me press credentials for many professional sporting and celebrity events.

This dream started at a very young age, when my friends and I would catch the bus downtown and purchase posters of our favorite professional football and baseball players. We used to talk on the bus on the way to the shop, how cool it would be to be a photographer on the field, taking photos of our favorite athletes. That thought gave birth to a desire that gave birth to a goal, which in turn with the proper nurturing gave birth to its reality. I grew up having a low self-esteem relating to education. I performed poorly in school up until the 10th grade, mainly because I felt school was boring and I had no realistic exciting plan of what I wanted to do with my life.

When I developed my love for photography, it changed everything. I started envisioning myself owning a successful photography business.

I was enlightened that school now had a purpose. I then started to diligently study and practice the art of photography along with the other courses; rapidly, my low self esteem dissipated away. I started believing that I was creative and smart. As I started to embrace this new thought process, my grades started improving, and so did my creativity. The key is once you make the decision to visualize your goals, you must immediately act on them.

Proverbs 29:18 (King James Version)

18 Where there is no vision, the people perish: but he that keepeth the law, happy is he.

You must make it a habit to visualize your goals, write them down, get photos that pertain to your goals and hang them up around the house and take them with you in a folder or binder. Search for advice and mentors who can help guide you with your vision. Volunteer for organizations that are related to your goal. This is the best way to find out if your desires are accurate. It is also a good way to feed your vision with faith.

The more vivid the vision becomes, the more confident you will become. Remember, if your goal does not motivate or excite you, you won't stick with it too long. If you do, you will live an unhappy life. Continuous focus on a rewarding exciting goal will keep you motivated. A wise man once said, "That if your mind can believe it and your heart can receive it, then you can achieve it."

The Bible says, "*Faith without works is dead*" (James 2:26). I can believe my car will take me to point A to point B, but if I don't act on it by turning the key, what good is my belief? Many times a goal can seem too overwhelming to obtain, but we must learn to attack our goals piece by piece, and not all at once. Henry Ford, the founder of Ford Automotive, said, "Anything is easy, when you break it up into small parts."

Goal setting is not just for careers; we must learn the skill of setting goals for every area of our life. This includes our behaviors, social life, health, family, spiritual, recreation and other personal areas. It is paramount that we develop and maintain a well-balanced lifestyle. The true meaning to success is maintaining a happy well-balanced life style under God's supervision. Many individuals have flourished in one or more areas, while they have sacrificed other areas, which in turn infected their flourishing areas.

There are many actors and entertainers in the Hollywood spotlight who appear successful when you look at all the money and fame they have; yet, their personal lives are in turmoil because of drugs, affairs, depression, irrational spending sprees, and hostile behaviors. Their lives are out of control, and they know not what direction they are going in; their lives are in utter chaos. They did not plan or set appropriate goals for a well-balanced life, which will eventually lead them to failure.

Below is a method to avoid this downfall. Once you have decided on your goals, I advise you to follow these steps precisely:

Goal Action Plan

1. Write out your goals, as well as a detailed plan on how you will obtain them
2. Write out the values (rules) you will commit to live by.
3. Include detailed goals such as: career, family, behaviors, financial, recreation, etc…make it vivid.
4. Make 2 columns, one for your goal, and the other for how you will obtain it.
5. Structure your goals as follows:
   Daily, Weekly, 1 month, 6 month, 1 year, 3 year, 5 year, 10 year.
6. Pray about it.

SUCCESS PLAN

S -   SELECT A POSITIVE GOAL

U -   UNLOCK ALL NEGATIVE THINKING

C -   CHART YOUR COURSE

C -   COMMIT YOURSELF

E -   EXPECT PROBLEMS AND DIFFICULTIES

S -   SACRIFICE

S -   STICK TO THE PLAN

There are so many proven strategies to obtain success. Yet, though we might have the ingredients to a winning plan, many forget that we must obtain the self-discipline to accompany the plan or else the plan is meaningless. Self-discipline is the key ingredient for success to any winning plan. Procrastination is the archenemy of self-discipline. I heard one pastor put it this way: "procrastination turns a problem into a crisis." To win the battle over procrastination, we must learn to concentrate on the gain and not the pain.

Building Success Habits

The motor behind positive change is in our habits. The will to initiate the process of developing positive habits is the barometer in which one can use to tell if an individual is sincere about change. At work, I have individuals all the time telling me they are willing to change, however when I give them an assignment and they don't do it, this informs me they are still unwilling to make the commitment for change. When an individual truly wants something, they will make changes in their schedule to allow themselves to obtain it. The issue is that most people don't have a strong enough desire to change. One successful business man put it this way, "successful people just do what unsuccessful people don't want to do." It takes a 100% non-compromise commitment. This chapter will assist you in creating a winning strategy.

Setting the Atmosphere for Success

When a man wants to impress a woman he likes on a first date, he will likely take her to a romantic place where there is soft music so she can feel relaxed for a good conversation. He might meet her at the door with flowers to convey to her that he feels she is a special person. He will carefully decide what outfit he will wear, get a fresh haircut and carefully select what cologne to put on. He will clean and wax his car and then determine what radio station or CD he will play and the volume of the tone, making sure it's not too loud where it will annoy her, but not too low that it doesn't alter the atmosphere. He is taking time in planning the atmosphere, and setting the mood for a successful date.

The place where we are in life today, whether positive or negative, is a reflection of the atmosphere we have surrounded ourselves with. Successful individuals prioritize settings and maintaining a positive atmosphere. Unsuccessful people set forth a negative atmosphere; most are unaware they are doing so.

Here are some of the components of our atmosphere which either positively or negatively affects our beliefs which affects our attitudes, and helps dictate our actions/behaviors:

- Peers
- Reading Material
- TV/Video
- Music
- Appearance
- Environment Setting (clean, dirty, organized, disorganized)
- Body Language
- Voice Tone
- Diet

If you're always negative and angry, one or more of the above components is setting your mood. Remember that association brings along similarities. In other words, what or whom you associate with is what you're similar to, and the experts say you will be the average of whom you are hanging out with. A wise person once told me that if you want to fly like an eagle, you can't run with chickens. If we want to be successful, we must strategically place ourselves around the components which successful people utilize. If you want to be unsuccessful, do the opposite. It is simple; successful people just do what unsuccessful people don't want to do.

Here are some steps to get you started in setting an atmosphere for success:

- Evaluate all the components of your atmosphere and identify the negative and positive ones. Then take the initiative to replace the negative with the positive.
- Set some positive, exciting and realistic goals for yourself to keep you motivated and positive about life.
- Smile more. It is a scientific fact that people who _will_ themselves to smile, even during stressful situations, have a better attitude along with reduced stress. Besides, it takes fewer muscles to smile than to frown.
- Look in the mirror and analyze your body language, such as your facial expressions. Ask yourself, "Do I look approachable or unapproachable?" Negative body language can poison a positive atmosphere.
- Watch the voice tone. The experts say that it is only 10% of what you say and 90% how you say it.
- Most importantly nothing sets the atmosphere better than prayer, reading God's Word and praising God for all he has done for us. You might believe you have nothing to be grateful for.

There is a book by David Smith, If the World Were a Village, where he explains if the world was a village of a 100 people:

- Only 26 would have to eat regularly.
- 31 of the 38 school aged children would go to school. Most of the girls would not.
- 76 villagers would have electricity. There would be just 24 televisions and no more than seven computers.

When we look at our lives from this perspective, I believe most of us can be thankful for what we do have.

Change your Life, by Changing your Mind

I often hear: "I act like this because I was born this way"…"I'm from this hood"… "It's because of my color" or "I'm just like my dad or like my mom; it runs in our family." We are financially, physically, emotionally, and spiritually based on our beliefs. Every behavior we have ever done first started with a belief. We all have negative and positive beliefs, which give birth to negative and positive behaviors. Our beliefs, after a period of time, become our reflexes which respond instantaneously once we are faced with encounters that trigger our ingrained beliefs. For example, I know gang members on my unit that will on reflex assault anyone who disrespects their gang regardless of whether they are close to going home or not, because they were taught and conditioned by their gang to have that belief, to the point where it developed into a reflex. However, many of them regret later that they responded this way, due to the fact that they get "time-adds," and other consequences that make their incarceration even more uncomfortable and dangerous. They often say the following after thinking about their actions, "I just flashed," or " I blanked out." In other words, they acted on instinct during an encounter that triggered their belief process. Drug addicts, alcoholics, insecure, depressed, abusive and emotionally unstable individuals suffer from this same epidemic. They are prisoners of their own belief process. Many feel that a new environment, relationship, or career is the answer, but the truth remains unseen. Their problem is their beliefs and no physical or environmental change is going to necessarily make a change until they make a change in their thinking. For example, a laptop computer, no matter where you travel with it, will work the same. It will only work different, if you change the software not the location.

If an individual believes that he is a no-good, mean-spirited loser, just like his deadbeat father, because his mother told him this, his behaviors will dictate his belief. He will behave irresponsibly, unconfident, possibly abusive and will most likely ignore his parenting responsibilities. This belief was given to him by his mother, and he decided to believe it, because though he might have not have had a good relationship with her, he instinctively trusted her judgment as a parent. Sadly, this is the case with many individuals in society. They have believed others' beliefs about themselves that were not healthy and for the most part untrue. We live in a society today where individuals unknowingly program themselves with negative beliefs through their selection of friends, music, television programs, movies, publications etc... There are rich kids in rich neighborhoods that have never stepped in or driven through a gang-related neighborhood, however, they talk and behave in mannerisms that would make you think that they grew up on some of the meanest streets of South Central Los Angeles. These beliefs and mannerisms came to them through the gangster entertainment industry. They have identified with something they admired from these gangster icons, the hardcore image: power, respect and invincibility they deceptively portray in their videos. They assume that replicating the artist's beliefs, which they hear and see in their music and videos, will produce the same results in their life. These beliefs are meditated on and chanted over and over by the youth and are locked into their subconscious part of the mind, because it's cool, has rhythmic beats and talented vocal delivery by the artists. As I said previously, these musical messages have the power to bypass the conscious state in the left hemisphere of the brain and enter the subconscious on the right hemisphere of the brain, which then unknowingly transfers it back to the left, which influences a person's beliefs, emotions and behavior without the individual's permission. The medical profession has discovered that violent music in rock and rap, triggers the "fight or flight" chemical of the brain, which unconsciously creates violent and rebellious behavior in individuals. Is it any surprise that crime is at an all time high in this country? More and more of society have come to tolerate thug mentality and others to embrace it due to its entertainment value and the emotional high they receive from it.

Many youth are adopting these artists' lyrics as their own self-talk, thus living out the artists' fantasies in their own virtual reality world. Yet, we still wonder why so many members in our society are so rebellious and disobedient. On the flip side, there are many who are thriving with success because they have developed positive beliefs. Many of them have come from very challenging upbringings, yet they made a commitment to believe only the positives about themselves and their situations, no matter what they encounter. I have spent an extensive amount of time studying and reading about exceptional individuals like these. Much of my reading has come from studying biblical characters. It was an awesome revelation for me when I discovered that just by changing my belief, I could change my life. All of us have some beliefs we can change for the better. Below is a simple module on how are thought process works:

I use the Acronym B.E.A.R. which is:
Beliefs +Emotions +Actions=Results.

Negative:

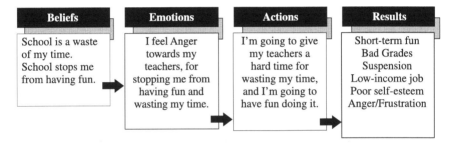

Beliefs	Emotions	Actions	Results
School is a waste of my time. School stops me from having fun.	I feel Anger towards my teachers, for stopping me from having fun and wasting my time.	I'm going to give my teachers a hard time for wasting my time, and I'm going to have fun doing it.	Short-term fun Bad Grades Suspension Low-income job Poor self-esteem Anger/Frustration

Positive:

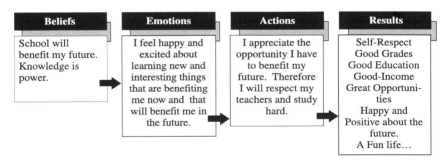

Beliefs	Emotions	Actions	Results
School will benefit my future. Knowledge is power.	I feel happy and excited about learning new and interesting things that are benefiting me now and that will benefit me in the future.	I appreciate the opportunity I have to benefit my future. Therefore I will respect my teachers and study hard.	Self-Respect Good Grades Good Education Good-Income Great Opportunities Happy and Positive about the future. A Fun life…

Developing a Positive Thought Process

1. First, evaluate your current beliefs- positive and negative ones. This means look at the patterns in your life. There is a belief

attached to our every emotion and action. The easiest way is to identify the results from your actions and keep working backwards until you get to the core belief. The brainstorming questionnaire below, will assist you in this (use a scratch piece of paper for this exercise):

<u>Belief Questionnaire</u>
- My belief is:
- I was_____ years-old when accepted this belief.
- My belief comes from:
- The significant events and influences behind me accepting this belief are:
- I believed my belief to be true because:
- My belief is true because:
- My belief is false because:
- My belief is positive because:
- My belief is negative because:
- My belief gives me the following feelings:
- After my beliefs give me these feelings I act out or behave in the following way:
- I want to change this belief because:
- I don't want to change by belief because:

2. Write out your beliefs in a simple sentence. The positive and negative ones.

3. Think about where the beliefs came from, and if they are true or not. Write this out in detail. Relax and look at the list of your core beliefs and think back at where they came from. Did they come from your family, friends, music, books, religion, television or a past experience? Look at your beliefs from all angles, not just from your perspective, but also from the perspective of others. Then make two columns on a piece of paper, listing the good and the bad points of your beliefs. For example: in the negative example above, the individual believed going to school was "a waste of time", but the results proved that their belief was untrue. They also believed school stopped them from having fun. This was only true because they believed that learning was not fun, however

in the positive example, the individual believed learning new and exciting things was fun. The results for having this positive belief opened up an exciting and fulfilling life for that individual.

4. Make a commitment to replace your negative/untrue beliefs, with positive/true beliefs: remember good values produce good results; bad values produce bad results. Good values are those which align with your God given conscience. If you violate your conscience you have violated your self-respect. A good place to get good beliefs which align perfectly and peacefully with my conscience is the Holy Bible. The Bible, God's Word, has positive beliefs to fit every area of our lives. It not only fits every area of our life, but it produces great results too. For example, this is a belief the Bible has about how to respond when we are disrespected:

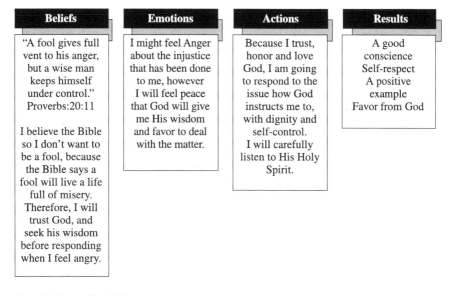

Beliefs	Emotions	Actions	Results
"A fool gives full vent to his anger, but a wise man keeps himself under control." Proverbs:20:11 I believe the Bible so I don't want to be a fool, because the Bible says a fool will live a life full of misery. Therefore, I will trust God, and seek his wisdom before responding when I feel angry.	I might feel Anger about the injustice that has been done to me, however I will feel peace that God will give me His wisdom and favor to deal with the matter.	Because I trust, honor and love God, I am going to respond to the issue how God instructs me to, with dignity and self-control. I will carefully listen to His Holy Spirit.	A good conscience Self-respect A positive example Favor from God

Good Tact, Bad Tact

Many people go through life clueless of why it is so hard for them to make friends and maintain stable relationships and employment. They have the mentality that it is them against the world and that people in general are out to get them. They live their whole life from one crisis to another. They believe that most people are too sensitive, have no sense of humor and don't like them. Therefore, they walk around in life with a "chip" on their shoulder, being very defensive and unpleasant. They believe if everyone and everything changed to their liking that their life would fall into place. They are oblivious to the fact that it is their own behavior which is creating their problems.

To condense the above paragraph into two words, they have "bad tact." They have poor communication skills which equal poor relationships, and brings forth ongoing problems.

A successful salesperson once said to me, "Communication is only 10% of what you say and 90% of how you say it." Individuals with bad tact are like a bull walking into a china shop attempting to deliver a message. They may succeed in delivering the message; however the bull will break up a lot of merchandise in the process. These individuals are reckless with their words, not caring about another's feelings; their only goal is getting their message across to their satisfaction or amusement.

The following are examples of statements that people with bad tact make:

- "Is that gray I see? You're getting old, huh"
- "Are you gaining weight?"
- "You're too skinny"
- "I didn't recognize you without your makeup"
- "You're losing your hair, huh?"
- "I like your car, <u>but</u> you should see John's"
- "Your nose is pretty big"
- "I didn't know your ears were that big until your haircut"
- "What's that spot on your face, is that your birthmark?"

You would be surprised how many individuals spend countless hours, worrying and distressed about their physical insecurities. They don't need us to remind them of it, even in a joking manner. They might laugh at the joke, but many times it's just a mask to cover up how they were hurt by a reckless comment. It's okay to have a sense of humor and to joke, but be responsible. Joke with people about appropriate subjects that won't offend them or damage their self-esteem. We all have our

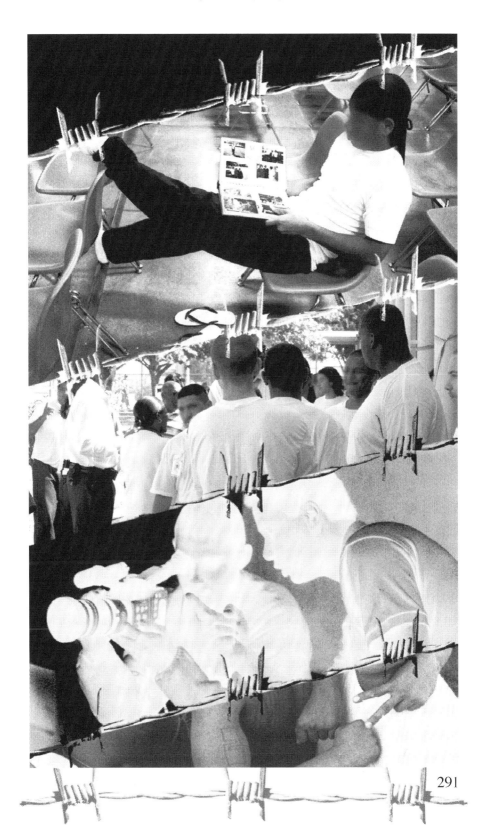

own insecurities; think how embarrassed you felt when people have gone out their way to comment on yours.

Karen Carpenter was a well renowned female singer in the 80's who heard a reporter referring to her as "chubby." Her self-esteem was so hurt by that comment that she became obsessed with losing weight. It developed into anorexia which she soon died from. Proverbs says, *"Life and death are in the power of the tongue."*

Dampening Someone's Glory

- "That's nothing, I caught a fish this big"
- "That's good, but my grade point average in high school was 3.8"
- "That's all? I made over $50,000 last year"
- "You did a good job, but that's easy"
- "Your car is nice, but I would have waited and got the newer model."

Think how good it feels when you accomplish or win something that you have worked hard at. Now, do you need someone to put a dark cloud over your achievement by minimizing it? Of course not! So don't do it to somebody else. Be humble and happy for others' accomplishments. Don't rush to try to compare and challenge yours with theirs; they won't appreciate it and neither would you.

Proverbs 3:34

34 He mocks proud mockers but gives grace to the humble.

Speaking the Mind

Many individuals boast about being a "straight shooter" or "telling it how it is." They take great pride that they're bold enough to say just what's on their mind, without sending it through their cognitive editing room. In essence, they don't care what others think or feel, just as long as the missile from their mouth hits the target. They say what they say with emotion, and conviction. Some use profanity, and when they're done, they feel the satisfaction of a housewife who has completed her spring-cleaning. They don't care about the damage or casualties they caused at the time, again, as long as they hit their target. Yet, when others return fire on them, by recklessly speaking their mind, they are appalled, offended and sometimes deeply hurt. Motivational speaker John Maxwell had some great advice about confronting others. He explains you must sincerely care about them, and you must demonstrate it in your mannerisms when you're confronting them. People respond better to constructive criticism when they know that the person doing it truly cares for them.

Proverbs 29:11 (King James Version)

11 A fool uttereth all his mind: but a wise man keepeth it in till afterwards.

James 1:19 (King James Version)

19 Wherefore, my beloved brethren, let every man be swift to hear, slow to speak, slow to wrath:

Active Listening Skills

Learning to listen attentively before speaking is a good habit. Nothing is more annoying than having someone interrupt your sentence to give a comment. This leaves them with the feeling that they're not important or not interesting enough to be heard by that individual talking over them.

Basic Manners

Basic manners is learning to say "Thank you" and "You're welcome," to anyone who consents a kind act towards you. Most individuals do not mind assisting others, as long as the person demonstrates appreciation. Nobody wants to feel used and unappreciated. Make it a habit to demonstrate appreciation, even in the small things. Next time someone offers or gives you something, give them a big smile and a "thank you" or a "no, thank you." Never take anyone's kindness for granted or for weakness.

Using Profanity

There is a proverb that says, and rightly so, that "Profanity makes ignorance audible." Many individuals use profanity as adjectives, conjunctions, and nouns. Many believe that using profanity gets their point across stronger or makes their joke funnier, and it is usually because there is an audience that believes the same thing. Why? Most could not even give you an answer.

The profanity they are using makes no literal sense in their sentence structure. This is ignorance, because they are using words out of habit without even knowing or acknowledging their meaning. These words inappropriately describe obscene and sexual elements of our society, and are immoral, disrespectful, and inappropriate in our communication with others. The use of profanity is a clear sign that one needs to expand one's vocabulary and do a check-up and clean up of their personal morals and values.

Attire

Attire comes down to common sense. I remember working at a group home and coming on shift after about four of our residents had come back from a job search. They came into the house discouraged, claiming they were the victims of racial profiling. Granted, these teenagers had their hats tilted, braided hair, pants sagging, with their shirt out, walking like a "gangster mob." They didn't understand that when walking into someone's business establishment, asking for a job, they must display to the employer that they can fit the characteristics, attire and grooming standards required for a position in their establishment. Remember when you go for a job interview, you're asking to work for them, so don't expect for them to change a policy or standard for you. I told them that when you start your own business, you can wear the clothes and hair however you want, but when you ask to work for someone else, you must sometimes humbly conform to their policies if you want employment (unless it's immoral).

In Summary:

Good tact is the key to successful communication, even with those who are difficult to get along with. "Treat others as you want to be treated" is the key. We accomplish this by putting ourselves in the shoes of the person we are communicating with. Visualize things from their perspective and not just our own. Practicing this will give you a deeper understanding and knowledge about people and life in general. You will obtain respect from others and some long lasting friendships to go along with it.

The Bible says that "you reap what you sow," (Galatians 6:7) meaning that if you plant seeds of hostility, you will get a harvest of hostility. If you plant seeds of kindness, you will get back a harvest of kindness.

Here are 12 Key Points of "Good Tact":

1. Be humble; don't brag and praise yourself.
2. Be sincerely happy about others' successes; don't compete with or attempt to minimize them.
3. It's not just what you say; it's how you say it (Watch your tone, facial expressions and body language).
4. Do not gossip and use profanity.
5. Do not point out other's insecurities, unless you can sincerely help them.
6. "Edit" your thoughts before talking
7. Go out of your way to sincerely compliment and help others.
8. Listen to others as you want to be listened to (Make yourself see it from their perspective).
9. Remember that attitudes are contagious.
10. Remember the rule "you reap what you sow." Talk and treat others as you wanted to be treated.
11. Attempt to find and see the good qualities in everyone (It helps give you a more positive outlook on life).
12. Make it a habit to be nice, polite and appreciative, even over the smallest things.

Problem Solving

The root to life's frustrations are problems. Problems come in two categories, which are the uncontrollable and the controllable. Being able to properly identify which category your problem falls into will alleviate a lot of the frustration and distress.

The Uncontrollable Problem

The uncontrollable problem can be identified as an issue controlled by nature, such as weather or aging, or something that is in total control of another person or organization.

In these instances, stressing and complaining is useless and unproductive. This is when our interventions come in, exhibiting our levels of maturity. Below are some good examples of intervention and coping methods:

- Identify the Problem.
- Find the positive side of the problem. Look at your problems as challenges.
- Realize that all successful people in life have faced the uncontrollable; however, they utilized problems as strength builders.
- Do an honest examination of yourself. Could it be your attitude, or action that caused the problem? Many times I have discovered that a change in my attitude or change of habit has diminished many of my problems. It's a humbling experience, yet with great rewards.
- Relax and maintain your self-control and integrity. When relaxed, we think clearer and more creative, which is a key ingredient to problem solving. Keep your integrity under the most severe trials, tribulations, and persecution. Integrity is a great confidence booster. Make it a rule to treat others as you want to be treated, regardless how they act. Spewing out insults and hostility is a quick fix, however it leaves a long lasting bitter taste, which can also trail long-term consequences. Do

not let others' stupidity towards you become your own.

I have seen how the contrast between integrity and immorality will expose the wrong or ignorance of the immoral, often bringing forth repentance or a rally of support to the one operating in integrity, verses the one operating in immorality. Regardless of the outcome, integrity will leave you with an unexplained inner peace, confidence, and joy that no person or circumstance can take away.

The Controllable Problem

Unfortunately, some individuals place many controllable problems in the uncontrollable category as soon as the problem raises its ugly head. Anger and stress can handicap us mentally and disable our problem solving and creative abilities, thus creating a bigger problem.

The following is an effective strategy that I personally use to solve problems, which I have learned from studying the testimonials of well-balanced successful individuals. All of these concepts I have discovered have come from Biblical principals.

- Get the Big Picture of the problem. Examine it from all angles, not just your own. Try to see the problem just as clear from the opposition as from your side. Weigh the pros and cons to each potential decision. After you have done this, write down the problem in detail. The majority of the time our creative imagination creates the illusion of the problem being 10 times larger than it really is. The imagination makes the problem grow bigger by feeding it "what ifs?" Writing down the problem almost always reduces it, alleviating most of the stress. Keep writing throughout the entire problem solving process.

- Examine your attitude, actions, habits and values. Again not just from your perspective, but from the oppositions. A few minor changes to ourselves might diminish the problem all together or make the problem solving a whole lot easier.

- Identify your resources. Below are a list of some helpful resources. Remember we shouldn't attempt to utilize others as resources, until we know clearly we are incapable of doing it ourselves. Using people to do what you can do yourself will leave a bitter feeling by others towards you and will "burn bridges." No one likes to be exploited, but they won't always tell you that.

- Evaluate own abilities and potential
- Counselor/teachers
- Library
- Internet
- Non Profit organizations/Businesses
- School
- Church
- Letter writing/email

Strategy/ Action Plan

After you have obtained the needed resources, it is time to plan a strategy. We must look at our resources as pieces to life's chess game. It is also a must that we see the big picture, not just the today but 1,5,10 and even 20 more years down the road. A great chess player views the entire board and examines not only every one of his potential moves, but those of their opponent.

7 Steps for Problem Solving

1. Relax and make sure your decision is based on common sense and integrity and not from pure emotions or feelings. Make it a rule to never make a decision which goes outside the parameters of your values. Again, this is operating in integrity. Remember, one bad decision could delay you from reaching your goals, sometimes prevent you from ever obtaining your goal.
2. See the big picture and write down the problem in detail.
3. Examine your plan by weighing the pros and cons. Pray and go to the Holy Bible, to see what God has to say about your

problem. Use the index, to find your problems subject for quick reference. Memorize faith scriptures that address your issue, and make it part of your self-talk. If you're still unsure what to do, and if time permits, obtain wise counsel from a parent, church counselor, minister, mentor or friend. Make sure it's a resource with Godly wisdom. After you have received counsel, pray and make sure God had given you a peace within about the situation. If you don't have peace, seek counsel until you get it.

4. Write out your plan in detail. Rehearse it in your mind to perfection. Have a plan for what could go wrong, so you're not caught off guard.

5. Implement your plan.

6. Review the outcome of your decision. Ask God to show you, how you got into the predicament in the first place. Try to identify if it could have been avoided. If you find out that you could have prevented it, then pray and study God's Word for a wise strategy from preventing it from happening again. Remember good habits will prevent many of life's problems and will strengthen and sustain you for those uncontrollable ones. A good sports team reviews tapes after a game for a critique in order to make the necessary changes from their mistakes and to hone in on the successes. We must learn to do the same in order to fine tune are problem solving skills. Remember that experience is one of life's best teachers.

7. Continue to pray for wisdom and understanding.

Building an Exciting Life Model

When I was growing up, I remember being thrilled going to the department store to look for a "cool" looking model to build. I would spend long periods of time pacing back and forth down the isle scanning the shelves and the photos on the front of the boxes for the perfect model to take home and build. There were always a wide variety of model planes, cars, and aircraft carriers and so on to choose from. The decision was which one? After I cautiously had made my selection, I would have to choose what color to paint it. I would carefully hold up different colors to the model, trying to use my imagination to get the perfect color to fit my model.

If someone would just have given me a model to build that I didn't like, let's say for my birthday or Christmas, though I would be grateful, I probably wouldn't have been motivated to build it. Building a model is no quick project if you plan to do it right. You have to spend long periods of time carefully reading the instructions and methodically applying the information in putting intricate pieces together to bring harmony to the vision. One piece out of place or missing can ruin the image of the model. Building a model is a long tedious task. Who would want to waste their time building something they know their not going to like?

Our life is a model. This is where the term "role model" comes from. A positive role model is an individual who has built a successful balanced lifestyle by following the right values and instructions. A negative "role model" has built their life following immoral values and instructions.

Sadly, many never take the awesome opportunity and privilege of selecting the perfect life model for themselves. They just go through life building useless model trinkets. It's fun while their building, however the let down comes when it is finished and it comes apart on them as the satisfaction dissipates away.

For example, some are lured to the "gang model." The picture on that visual box looks exciting and adventurous. The "riches" and "street prestige" look very appealing. Yet, many have opened this box, and followed the instructions to a "T", just to find out that what they built does not look at all like the front of the box. What they really built was a life full misery and a deadly trap for themselves and their loved ones.

Many have chosen to build life models given to them by others for the purpose to appease others. For example, a father tells his son, "I am an accountant, and our family comes from a long line of accountants. It would be disappointing to me if you would be the first to break this tradition." The son now feels an obligation to build the life model of an accountant; however, the young man really has a strong desire to be a fireman. He hates math, and the idea of sitting in an office from 9 to 5 makes him nauseous.

The son graduates from college and becomes an accountant at a respected firm; however, he is unhappy. He dreads going to work and only lives for the weekends. He feels unproductive, often dreaming how his life could have turned out, if he would of put his foot down and pursued a firefighter career. Constantly thinking about it, he goes into a deep depression, which leads him into drinking and doing drugs to escape the pressures of reality. If things couldn't get worse, excessive missed days of work brought on by his depression results in him being fired and his father's disappointment.

Unfortunately, there are countless stories just like the above two, where people go through life building models they don't like. The successful, happy and fulfilled person is the individual who takes the time to dream, pray and research what the perfect life model for them is. Then once they envision what they want on the visual box (which are exciting and interesting things) of their model life, they open it up by taking action and then proceed to get wise Godly instructions.

They discover that studying and applying instructions is exciting. School and reading books become interesting and exciting. They see that as they apply the knowledge and wisdom from their instructions, their dream model is steadily becoming a reality. What does your life model look like? Is it boring or exciting?

Here are 3 steps to building a rewarding and exciting life model for yourself:

1. Visualize what the picture looks like on your front of your life model box. If it is not attractive, exciting and rewarding, you probably won't have the motivation to complete it and why would you? Plan your life model to be interesting, fun, exciting and rewarding. Get a visual picture in your mind and then write it down. Find pictures in magazines or newspapers related to your life model and make a "Vision Book" that you will look at daily to keep motivated. In planning, ask yourself:

- Where would I work for free?
- Who would I like to help?
- What are my deep interests and hobbies?
- Where and how would I like to live?

- What are my values and is it God's will for my life?
- What do I want my income to be?
- Do I want to get married, and what type of person would I want to marry?
- Am I the type of person someone would want to marry? And if not, what must I do to become that type of person?
- Do I want a family?

2. <u>Get wise Instructions.</u>
- Education
- Books
- Mentors
- Seminars
- Prayer
- Church
- Counselors
- Individuals in your field of interest.
- Non-profit organizations

3. <u>Don't Quit!</u>

It is Our Responsibility

Role modeling is the most awesome responsibility an individual will ever take on. The reason why is because role modeling shapes the characteristics of impressionable minds, either for the good or bad.

We should all have it in our hearts to be positive role models. In order to become an effective and positive role model, we need the tools to do so. The most important tools are the values of our character. Our values are our beliefs and it is our beliefs that dictate our behaviors. When we are role modeling with negative values, we are infecting young, impressionable minds that observe us. We are encouraging them to act out these negative beliefs with negative behaviors. When we role model with positive values, we can clone positive beliefs and behaviors.

There are some athletes and entertainers who have said, "I'm not a role model." What they fail to realize is that role models are chosen, not self-appointed. Role models never know specifically who they are acting as a role model to. There is a huge market in today's society for role models. There are a lot of youth from broken, abusive, and neglectful homes who are searching for a hero to give them some direction: someone to trust in, admire, and pattern their habits and behaviors after; someone who can demonstrate how to get their needs and desires met. For example, a young boy watches his father beat his wife into submission, so the boy has learned he must threaten or beat others in order to get his way. That same boy observes his father verbally disrespect and cheat on his mother and cover up and justify his affairs with lies. This boy has now learned to disrespect women and to lie to get his lustful needs met.

A young girl hears her father bragging about how he cheated a little on his taxes to get a huge refund check and then later overhears her mother on the phone telling her friend how her flirtation with the head supervisor got her a profitable promotion. The girl has learned that lying is profitable and that she doesn't need a diligent work ethic to get what she wants. She has learned that by flirting with men she will get her needs and desires met.

Another boy watches his older brother sell dope on the corner then takes his profits and gives some to his mother for groceries; the remainder he spends on some stylish clothes and on his beautiful girlfriend. The young boy has now learned that it is okay to sell dope if you help your family out and that beautiful women are attracted to dope dealers because they have the latest style clothes and plenty of cash. These images have been reinforced by the music videos he watches over and over which display young entertainers with stylish clothes, expensive jewelry, and material items as they boast about their criminal activities as beautiful women throw themselves at them and their enemies creep away in fear. The boy has learned from his role models that violence and crime will meet his needs and desires in a quick, exciting and pleasurable way. However, he has not been truthfully informed by his role models about the harsh and possibly fatal consequences that await him if he chooses such risky endeavors.

Much of society is under the false assumption that our youth choose only role models that they like. The fact is that our youth are choosing role models who are demonstrating to them how to get their needs and wants. It is not whether they like the particular role model or not. If you are stranded and about to die of thirst in the desert and an individual you dislike drives up and offers you a ride in an air-conditioned vehicle, stocked with a chest of ice cold bottled water, are you going to pass it up? This is many of the youth's perspective in today's society. If the youth are not taught other options on how to meet their needs and desires, they will often in desperation use the first option they observe that is appealing and that appears realistic and successful.

Are you showing someone how to get his or her needs and wants met in a positive or negative way? We have to remember that people are watching and observing us all the time, even when we don't know it and don't want them too. Often young people choose role models even if they don't like or respect them. I see this all the time as a youth correctional counselor. A young offender who hates his abusive father, but yet has imitated his father's behaviors due to the fact that it met his needs. His father got him to do what he wanted by abusing him and now the son makes others do what he wants by abusing or threatening to abuse them.

Sadly, the role modeling for youth and adults is coming from the entertainment industry. Some of these entertainers have developed and cultivated worldwide thug cultures through the power of music. This music has installed thug values and beliefs, which have produced the popularity and glorification of thug behaviors. They have successfully role modeled to millions that thug behavior can meet all your needs and desires. This is role modeled by their flashy music videos and magazines in which they show off all their lavish "riches" in their "gangsta paradise."

I remember having a conversation with some gang members during their recreation program about some of their favorite gangster rap artists and why they liked them. I also talked to them about why they liked staying in their gang. They would reply with words of praise for these rap artists and talk about their insight and street wisdom and how they admired their keen entrepreneurial skills these entertainers utilized to build their financial empires. They talked proudly about how their gang was a tight knit family that took care of each other and about the pride they had in representing their "organization." When I brought to their attention the immoral things that their favorite rap artists and gang promoted and embraced, they quickly rationalized and minimized it with a barrage of excuses.

Yet, my next set of questions caught them off guard. I began to ask them one by one, questions like, "Knowing what your favorite rap artist talks about in their music, how they boast about their mistreatment of women and the criminal activities that they are involved in, would you want or allow your daughter or sister to date one of these gangster rap artists?" One by one, reluctantly these individuals gave me the answer "no", often followed by a long explanation. Then I asked, "Do you, or if you had a son would you raise them in love?" "Yes" was the overall response. I then followed up and asked, "Would you want or allow your son to join your gang or want him to hang around your favorite gangster rap artists, knowing the violent atmosphere they cultivate with their words and actions?" Again, an overwhelming majority said "no."

I began to close the discussion by asking, "why would you praise, participate and attempt to emulate a lifestyle or person that you would not even want your son or daughter to associate with? Isn't that hypocritical?"

I remember letting a caseload of mine who was an Asian gang member make a phone call in the parole agent's office. During the call, he was speaking in his foreign tongue; he appeared stressed, and looked as if he was fighting back tears. When the phone call ended, he sat down tensely in the chair directly across from me, and started shaking his head, turning his head from me, side to side, as if to distract me from seeing his eyes, which at any moment appeared ready to release a river of tears. He finally told me that his younger cousin was killed in a gang-related shooting. **"I feel it's my fault"**, he kept telling me. He explained that when his cousin was about in junior high, he started becoming rebellious to his parents. His cousin wanted to hang with him and his gang, because it appeared they were having all the fun. He explained to me that his younger cousin looked up to him, and would have listened to him if he told him to obey his parents. But instead of

305

directing him down the right path, he allowed his cousin to hang out with him. After the ward was incarcerated, his younger cousin became more entrenched in the gang lifestyle with his older cousin's associates, and his gang affiliation eventually cost him his life. The ward was now afraid to be released, knowing that his parents, and other family members, would blame him for the death of his cousin.

We have the power and responsibility to make our family, community, and world a better place or we can assist to make it a miserable place. Yet, it starts by us as an individual taking up the awesome responsibility of becoming a positive role model.

We must live and act according to life's big picture, understanding the chain reaction of our every action. Let's ask ourselves, "What are the pros and cons of my actions and how do they effect and reflect on my family, my society and me?"

"Fatherly Advice from DMX"

DMX Interview/Sister 2 Sister Magazine Interview
October 2006 Issue:
Jamie Foster Brown (Interviewer): "How do the kids deal with it when things are in the paper about their father?"

DMX: They're used to it by now. My son is about 5'8, 5'9, 13 years-old, yeah so you know, I ask him just to see what's going on, how much sh#t he's got to deal with. He's like, "Nah, ain't nobody saying nothing," Then I was like, a'ight, first time somebody opens their f#@king mouth, you take their face off. He already knows that.

The Success Action Plan
"Plan your work and work your plan."

Oftentimes, I talk to and counsel wards who display a sincere desire to change. They might have obtained their GED or High School Diploma, learned a marketable vocational trade, and successfully completed all their required Board-ordered requirements. I was talking to an individual like this the other day that did a good program during his incarceration and was paroled, but was brought back due to a violation of his parole for associating with his former gang peers. For that four-month period that he was out on parole, he had obtained a job, enrolled in college, and had even made his college football team. Yet, he had tainted his success strategy by allowing himself to go to a party with old friends, many of whom were gang members. That one negative decision that night infected the positive routine and goals he was diligently working toward. Basic math will tell us that positive times negative= negative.

Our decisions in life are like a chess game, with earth being the game board. When we move to a place on the board just because it looks good, enamored by all the glitz and glamour or just by mere convenience, we handicap ourselves. A wise chess player looks at the whole board and the opposition's pieces, and attempts to formulate speculations of the opponent's strategy. A bad strategy will inevitably get us check-mated and taken off the board. This happens, over and over, to those who return back to our facility after violating parole; they have been taken off the board and placed in the penalty box. It is obvious they need a better life management strategy.

God is the master chess player because He has the aerial view of earth's chessboard and has the guaranteed winning strategy. He knows our opponent's strategy (our opponent being the devil) before the opponent knows it. Though we might on our own move into a checkmate position, he is able to bring us out every time with His wise and miraculous working power. We must learn how to hear from God, the great chess strategist, in order for us to obtain our plan, purpose, and strategy to bring forth His perfect will in our lives.

We also must be aware of the distractions the enemy, the devil, will deploy on our soul in order for us to lose God's reception and pick up his. His weapons of destruction are packaged in music, visual imagery such as TV, movies, videos, and publications, all of which are utilized by him (Satan) to formulate the trends and culture of our society.

God's Word is the weapon to discern and annihilate the demonic elements from Satan's arsenal. Again, these demonic weapons are formed to sabotage the frequency of God's transmission to us in an attempt to replace God's strategy for our lives with his (devil).

When we're walking in God's perfect will, He will open and close doors for us. You won't even have to turn the knob once you have made that connection with the Father. It will be as if you made the connection with your foot on the matt in front of the grocery store door; it will open up automatically. I'm talking about doors which will lead you to being blessed in every aspect of your life. The safest, most fulfilling and joyful experience in the world is following God's strategy for your life, which is His perfect will.

God's strategy is to set us up in an environment of positive peer pressure, not negative peer pressure. Setting ourselves in a negative peer pressure setting, no matter how positive we are, is like swimming upstream; eventually, we will tire out fighting the temptations and will then flow back with the fast rushing current of carnality and sin.

We can look in His Word and find great leaders such as Abraham, Noah, David, and more who sought out God's strategy through prayer and obedience. Then we see those who later went away from God's strategy on their own, only to meet tragedy such as, King Saul, Solomon, and the many other kings of Judah and Israel.

In order for us to obtain His strategy, we must first hear His voice, which comes only through praying, reading, and obeying His Word. Only then can we enter the peace, joy and fulfillment of being in His perfect will.

Thug Money

"Quick, fast and in a hurry" is the motto by which the thug mentality lives by. The "gangster paradise" is an attractive dream, because it is presented with a "get rich quick" theme. And unlike earning wealth the traditional way, through hard work and education, it is believed to be by many, a pleasurable, fun and exciting venture. However, the dilemma that arises for many is that if they believe they cannot be a pro athlete or rapper, the only alternative some believe they have is to obtain their dreams of wealth through criminal methods. Before I go on, I will tell you that this chapter will present legal creative ways on how almost anyone can make a lucrative income, without a college degree. I am not discounting the value of a college degree, because I know it opens up many doors, but to present to you an alternative way of thinking, which I learned from successful individuals.

Hollywood has assisted in providing graphic and visual images of the benefits the thug life can get someone in just a brief period of time. The majority of the wards I work with tell me that the lust for wealth will be their biggest temptation when they hit the streets. Hollywood's messages convey to society that if we muster up the courage and confidence to act like a thug who lives their life care free and recklessly, then we too can reap these luxurious rewards. The business industry knows selling this destructive dream is a big money maker. The sad part about this is that there are so many who believe the lie and go out and try to achieve it. Many have left our institution and were killed behind the thug philosophy of: "I'm going to get rich, or die trying." This phrase or belief came from a song by the rap artist, DMX. I have had many wards who have indicated to me that this is the core value in their life.

The mentality often teaches that going to school, steady employment and living with moral values is for "squares" and some will say you're a sell-out for living this way. This idea creates negative peer pressure on youth, in which some have developed inferiority complexes: often because they have obtained good grades or come from a family that holds on to good values. Everyone wanting to be portrayed as a thug wants to act and look hard, and wants everyone to believe that they grew up hard. They believe it lends them "street" credibility.

Making Cash Creatively & Legally

The other day I was informally counseling a very angry and frustrated ward at his cell door. During the conversation, which started off about me confronting him about his escalating hostile behavior, he blurted in an angry but desperate tone, "I have nowhere to go!" He then proceeded to vent very heatedly that he "didn't care" and that he was going to get out and "gang bang" to the fullest. The ward that recently came from a lock-up program had an extensive history of violence within the institution. Besides having nowhere to go, he had little to no family support which was emotionally weighing on him heavily, which resulted in him lashing out on others with verbal and physical abuse. He was a hardcore gang member with tattoos draped all over his body, including his face. His core belief was that society would reject him, therefore his only alternative was to go back to the gang who would accept and support him. Yet through the emotional pain I discerned in his voice, I knew that this was not truly what he really wanted.

That week I held a small group entitled, "Making Money Legally" where we discussed how to start a small business on a shoestring budget. During the group, the ward told us about a witty invention he had thought of a few months back; it was actually a great and realistic invention (which I promised not to mention). There were about four in my group, and they became really enthused about the invention, and we spent most of the group talking about a marketing plan for the product. Great creative ideas were being tossed back and forth during the session with excitement. Another expressed his interest in the vending machine concept I had mentioned. He conveyed to me with deep conviction "I'm going to do that!" When we came out of the group, that individual with the great invention who had been negative and frustrated the day before, came out enthusiastic and confident. He requested me to get some information off the internet relating to his invention, than he asked to use the phone, in order to instruct his brother to patent his idea before those who were in the group steal it.

Many of these wards feel that based upon their criminal record and tattoos, it is unlikely they will be able get a good paying job or no job at all. I was presenting to them a realistic alternative called self-employment. That is, if no one else hires you, hire yourself. Many of them were self-employed on the streets, however their business activities were illegal and immoral which brought them to prison. Yet, some I talk to at the prison, admit that they are still ready and willing to step out for another opportunity for success at their illegal business ventures, this time believing they are smarter and craftier enough to stay under law enforcement's radar. Though it is true that there have been some thugs or crime lords who went to their graves old and grey, and were able to duck under the law enforcement's radar during their stay here on earth, there is a higher law enforcement that they didn't escape. It is called the Kingdom of Heaven where God reigns as King and Judge over the entire universe. Listen to what God the almighty Judge has to say about those who break his laws:

Proverbs 15:6

6 The house of the righteous contains great treasure, but the income of the wicked brings them trouble.

Proverbs 13:11

11 Dishonest money dwindles away but he who gathers money little by little makes it grow.

Proverbs 15:27

27 A greedy man brings trouble to his family, but he who hates bribes will live.
Proverbs 22:8

8 He who sows wickedness reaps trouble, and the rod of his fury will be destroyed.

Deuteronomy 28:15-28

(What God said through a prophet to Israel after he brought them out of slavery in Egypt.)
Curses for Disobedience

15 However, if you do not obey the LORD your God and do not carefully follow all his commands and decrees I am giving you today, all these curses will come upon you and overtake you:

16 You will be cursed in the city and cursed in the country.

17 Your basket and your kneading trough will be cursed.

18 The fruit of your womb will be cursed, and the crops of your land, and the calves of your herds and the lambs of your flocks.

19 You will be cursed when you come in and cursed when you go out.

20 The LORD will send on you curses, confusion and rebuke in everything you put your hand to, until you are destroyed and come to sudden ruin because of the evil you have done in forsaking him.[1] 21 The LORD will plague you with diseases until he has destroyed you from the land you are entering to possess. 22 The LORD will strike you with wasting disease, with fever and inflammation, with scorching heat and drought, with blight and mildew, which will plague you until you perish. 23 The sky over your head will be bronze, the ground beneath you iron. 24 The LORD will turn the rain of your country into dust and powder; it will come down from the skies until you are destroyed.

25 The LORD will cause you to be defeated before your enemies. You will come at them from one direction but flee from them in seven, and you will become a thing of horror to all the kingdoms on earth. 26 Your carcasses will be food for all the birds of the air and the beasts of the earth, and there will be no one to frighten them away. 27 The LORD will afflict you with the boils of Egypt and with tumors, festering sores and the itch, from which you cannot be cured. 28 The LORD will afflict you with madness, blindness and confusion of mind. 29 At midday you will grope about like a blind man in the dark. You will be unsuccessful in everything you do; day after day you will be oppressed and robbed, with no one to rescue you.

A little later in this chapter I will present some of the self-employed concepts and life skill resources I share in my groups.

I was raised to never rely on just a job, because I was told a job can be taken away from you at any time. I was taught by mentors to build equity in yourself by learning a trade or starting a small business, marketing a needed product or service. It is a gift to be able to start and operate a part-time or full-time business in something that is your passion. I believe that an individual should always have a moral, legal plan to earn a living with or without a job. A job provides you fish; a business makes you the fisherman.

Along with being a Youth Correctional Counselor for the California Department of Corrections and Rehabilitation (formerly, the California Youth Authority), I also own and manage a photography business, a network marketing business and co-own and operate some rental units. My father was entrepreneur-minded, and he imparted that same mentality into me. He also had a habit of reading motivational books. I still read those success books from his collection, and they still continue to bless and motivate me.

I remember the satisfaction my friends and I had in grade school when we would go from street to street washing cars. We would feel so proud counting our money; then we would go out right after and blow it on pizza and video games. Though all the money vaporized away in fun, the experience and the lessons stayed with me for a lifetime.

Just out of my teens, I came across a young successful black businessman named Michael Bolden who owned a financial planning company. He held weekly free classes on financial planning. In the class, he discussed goal planning and duplicating the habits of successful people. At the end of every class, he would go over the following formula /acronym for success:

S- Select a Positive Goal
U- Unlock All Negative Thinking
C- Chart Your Course
C- Commit Yourself
E- Expect Problems and Difficulties
S- Sacrifice
S- Stick to the Plan

At this time, I was also faithfully attending Calvary Christian Center, a church with a solid youth ministry which helped teach me the Word of God, and blessed me in every area of my life. I was busy, no time to get into trouble. A mentor once told me, "Too much idle time, turns into evil time." I was strategically placing myself in and around positive and motivational people, places and things. I was learning the meaning of the proverb, "Association brings about similarities." I had learned after a few hard knocks that it's a lot easier to be successful in life, when you place your self in an environment of positive peer pressure, rather than the negative. This is a concept I'm always teaching and emphasizing to my caseload at the correctional facility.

I currently have a few financial mentors, some who are millionaires, others who are self-employed and making six figure-plus incomes. These are not all relationships in which I waited for these individuals to come to me: I was proactive and initiated an encounter with them. Stop waiting for a mentor or program to come to you; get proactive and go to the mentor or program.

They taught me how a small business can transform itself into a corporation and obtain significant tax advantages. They also taught me how to develop a financial team to form partnerships, to obtain investment property, and why it is important to have a lawyer, accountant, or tax attorney along with a financial planner in accompanying your business strategies.

Through these teachings, I have learned how to set up a profitable small home business for under $300.00. They have taught me their successful business habits, told me which books to read, and have given me a lot of constructive criticism. My association with them has brought about blessings in my personal life (For more information about business resources, you can log on to my website at www.thugexposed.com.

Below is a brief summary of business ideas, some which I have had some success in utilizing. Remember, before taking action on a business venture, contact your local city hall about information about obtaining a business license, permit and registering a business name. It's also a good idea to go to the library or bookstore and get a book on how to start and operate a small business.

- Wholesaler: Purchase items off the internet wholesale, and resale them at retail at: swap meets, auctioning sites such as Ebay, or to local retail stores on consignment (stocking your products in a retailer's store, and then split the profits with them.).
- Vending Machines: While working a regular job, discipline yourself to save up about $2,000. I was told by a very successful businessman in the industry, that on the average, a soft drink vending machine can profit approximately $300.00 a month (he stated this is on the low end). You can purchase a used vending machine for about $1,100 or less: look for deals in the classifieds, Internet and the yellow pages. Next you need to find a discount wholesaler to purchase your sodas. You can start with discount stores such as Costco, Sam's Club and others, also check the Internet. Many businesses will let you place your machine in their business for free, in that you are providing a service for their customers. You can negotiate this yourself, or there are companies who will negotiate the contract for you, at about a price of $200.00. Figure in about $200.00 or less to stock your sodas. Not including the price of your business license and permits, which are usually low expenses depending on your city or county, your start up cost is about $1,500. With the remainder $500.00, you can purchase business supplies and place the remainder in the bank. Being conservative, you can speculate a $300.00 profit a month on your business. Remember, your still working your regular job. Put all the profits in the bank. In five months you will have another $1,500: duplicate the process and now you are profiting $600 a month. In three months duplicate it again, and you are making a $900.00 profit a month. Keep duplicating – I think you got the picture (A millionaire in this business shared with me this system).
- Network Marketing: Find a reputable company –Many will have a low out-of-pocket investment, in which you

can make a substantial amount of money in a short period of time while working a regular job, doing the business on the side. I have a friend who made a little over $14,000 last month, through his multi-level marketing business. He has only been in the company for four years, but he now does his business full time. The advantages of multi-level marketing, is that it teaches you leadership, accounting, people and marketing skills, along with a host of other successful habits, which you can utilize in every aspect of your life. There are many rich and successful individuals who endorse multi-level marketing, despite all the critics. It teaches individuals the skills and mind-set to be company owners, rather than company employees.

- Photography: Learn the skill of photography. Show up at community events and say that you would like to give them a special offer, which is to take photographs for no charge, but that you will have the photos available for viewing and purchasing if they like them. Pass out your business cards, set an appointment to come back for a viewing and ordering session or return promptly back the same day with the photos from a 1 hour photo lab, or digital prints from a computer. Keep the originals for viewing on a large piece of construction board, album, and collect orders for duplicates and enlargements. There are many good books on photography and on the business of photography. Many photographers, such as me, use a website to post photos and collect orders after photographing an event. Do some research and talk to other photographers before you decide to get started.

- Real-estate Investing: Get a job and maintain it, meanwhile apply for a secured credit card at a bank. Certain banks will open a line of credit for you for as little as a $500 deposit. They will give you $500 of credit, which is at no risk to them, and on your end, you will earn interest for your deposit. After you have developed a consistent history of making your payments on time, you will develop a good credit history, which you will need for the purchase of your first property. Discipline yourself to save at least 20% of your pay check. I read that most individuals in

Japan practice this principal (no wonder why they have the money to come here and buy up some of America's top companies). Get four of your friends or trustworthy investors (check the internet for investment clubs) who are financially stable to do all of the above, until you all collectively save up about $10,000 (this is an estimate; the amount you will need will vary on your location). The concept here is that many people don't have enough money to qualify for a home loan by themselves, but with a small team of individuals, they can qualify. Get a lawyer and form a partnership: open up a business banking account. You and your financial team can purchase a duplex, which has two units that you can rent out. Pay your mortgage (loan payment) on the property, and put the profits back in the bank, to save up for your next property. I and a few business partners bought a duplex years ago which had a mortgage of about $500. One side of the duplex paid for our mortgage, the other part we put back into our bank account. You and your financial team can make a commitment to each invest a portion of your income back into the business from your current paycheck from your job. In my group, our investment amount was about $180.00 a month each (you can ratio this out depending on the portion of each investor). Continue on, until you have enough to invest in another property, and then just continue to duplicate the process. Do your research by talking to realtors, investors, bankers and reading books on real-estate investing and developing partnerships.

- Website: Learn web design by reading books and taking classes or find someone who has that skill, and create a website that will draw the attention of the public, or a particular interest group (keep it moral), and has content that will keep them coming back. I use photos that I have taken from current events on my website, which keeps people coming back to see what other photos I will have on my site next week / month. You can then sell advertising space on your site. To Host a site can cost less that $30.00 a month, leaving you a huge profit margin if you can get enough visitors to your site. The current average advertising rate on websites is about $20.00 per thousand visitors; meaning that if you can get content that is exciting enough to bring a least 500 visitors a month to your site, then you can charge a business $100 a month, to have their banner ad on your website.

- Offer a Service to a Non-Profit Organization: If you have a talent, service or trade, you can offer it as community service through a non-profit organization. For example: an individual who is a good artist might offer their services to a senior citizen home teaching the residents water painting, or an individual trained in landscaping may offer their services to maintain the yards of disabled people. Income would come through grants or donations from various institutions and corporations. I have done this myself in teaching photography to inmates and youth in inner city programs. I would write a formal proposal, which would include per project or annual budget operating costs along with my fee for my services. Instead of starting my own non-profit organization, I contracted my services under the umbrella of an existing non-profit group, which was in line with my mission and services. Doing it this way also saved me from a lot of "red tape and paperwork." The best thing about this concept is that you get to create your own job, along with offering free services to people in need within the community. The library is the best place to get information on writing proposals and getting funding to service non-profit organizations.

• Invest in the Stock Market: You can buy books and attend seminars on investing in the stock market. Many people don't do it because they think they need thousands of dollars to get started. You can now get started on-line for under $50.00. Go to www.sharebuilder.com for more information.

Getting Started on Your Own

Here is a basic 7-step system I recommend in getting started on your own. I created this system based off information given to me by my personal mentors, books, and a lot of trial and error. This is just a base system; I advise that you customize it to fit your needs and goals. This is what I give to wards preparing for parole:

1. Set Short and Long-term Goals: Starting without a goal is like starting off on a treasure hunt without a map. It's difficult to stay motivated and on course if you don't have a clear destination.

2. Obtain Wise Counsel: Set a counseling appointment at a junior college, church or non-profit resource center with a counselor. Explain to them your entire situation, along with your goals. They are set up to assist you in many other areas besides school. They often network with employment, housing and financial aid agencies. They can assist you in charting out a plan to achieve your goals, along with referring and providing to you many helpful resources. They can refer you to classes and workshops in your community to help you with the following topics: employability skills, vocational training, cooking, paying bills, budget planning, relationships, parenting skills and more.

3. Housing: Depending on your situation, whether your coming out of high school or college or being released from a correctional facility, it is important that your first priority is to set up an atmosphere for success. The following are some options you might consider:

•   Get a Roommate: A roommate can be a blessing or a nightmare. You want to get a roommate that is responsible and has good values. The benefits of having a roommate is that rent and utilities can be cut in half, which leaves you more money to put into savings for your future. I have had roommates where we agreed to buy food in bulk and split the grocery bill. This created a great savings in my living expenses, which helped me to utilize the extra money to put into my side business of photography. Where can you find a good roommate? The bulletin board at a local college or church, where they also might have posted, room's for rent. The classifieds in your daily newspaper, and there are roommate service agencies in the phone book and on the Internet. Make sure you do thorough interviews with the candidates you are considering.

- Studio Apartment: This is an inexpensive apartment, in which all the appliances except for the bathroom are in one room.
- Non-Profit- Rehab/Transitional programs: Many churches have these programs, which assists individuals by providing housing to those who been released from prison, are homeless or who have a substance abuse addiction. They also provide counseling, employment training and assistance, along with other helpful resources. The best way to get in contact with these types of programs is to attend a counseling session at your local community college, church or community outreach program, they network with some of these programs on a regular basis. These agencies will also lead you to financial assistance, which might provide you emergency money to stay in a hotel or other placement, if there is a waiting list for the program.

4. Employment: Prepare a solid foundation for your long-term goal. Remember it is important to choose a career or business that you will enjoy. If you don't, you might make a lot of money; yet, you will be a miserable wealthy person. Do not forget the majority of society spends most of their time at work, so doing what you enjoy, will improve the quality of your life. It is wise to look at every job (that is a moral job), no matter how little the pay, as stepping-stones to your goals. These jobs will provide you invaluable training and experience for the next step in your goal process.

- Education/Vocational Training: I have discovered in my own life, that when you have an exciting goal, it's a lot easier to stay focused in school. This leads to you knowing why your going to school and the value in it. The following are some inexpensive ways to obtain training:

  - Volunteering: Find a business or organization that utilizes the skills that pertain to the field you are working towards, and find out if they have a volunteer program. If not, put in a request to volunteer. For example, if you want to be a youth counselor, request to volunteer at the Boys and Girls Club. If you're an aspiring artist, volunteer to create some public service posters for an anti-gang and drug campaigns. If you want to be a fireman, many fire stations have an apprentice or volunteer program. Most jobs ask for experience. Volunteering gives an individual not only experience, but training, which makes them a lot more marketable. Always ask for a letter of recommendation from the agency you have volunteered with. This will give your resume a big boost.

- Junior Colleges: This is one of the least inexpensive ways to get solid training in your career or business field, along with a certificate or degree.
- R.O.P. (Regional Occupational Program): This is a program I utilized in high school to learn the trade of photography. They also offer it to adults as well. This program trains high school and college students in a variety of career and business fields then provides them an opportunity to gain real life experience in an actual business.
- Labor Union/ Unemployment Office: These are both agencies which provide employment and training in various work fields. Check your phone book for listings.
- Interviewing: You must look, act and be the part of the business establishment you're requesting to be employed at. This means you must fit the employee profile of the company or organization. For example: if an individual is going for a job interview at United Parcel Service, it would not be a good idea to walk into the interview chewing gum, using profanity, sagging pants and tattooed down. Why? Because U.P.S. is a professional business establishment, that deals with professional individuals and businesses. They want to hire individuals who display themselves in a professional manner. They want to hire individuals that will appropriately represent their company. Therefore realistically, if an individual wants a job with U.P.S., they should attend the job interview in professional attire, with professional mannerisms. I recommend for those who have visual tattoos to get them removed. If you

can't afford to, there are many non-profit organizations that provide grants to have them removed for free. Study the business or organization you are applying for, and observe how their employees dress, their mannerisms and job duties. Know the history of the company, their mission statement and their operational procedures; this will help you greatly in the interview process.

5. <u>Investments/Savings:</u> It's not how much you make; it is what you do with what you make. A wise investor looks at the money from their employment as seeds and knows if they want a good harvest they can't eat all their seeds. A good rule of thumb for savings is to save 10 percent for long-term (Money Market Account/Stocks/Real-estate) and save 5 percent for an emergency fund. The experts say to have six months of savings in the bank in case of a hardship. The most important investment is in the Kingdom of God. Due to God owning everything, He only asks for 10% of our income which is called a tithe (Which is God's in the first place.). An offering is money given beyond the tithe (This is the seed for financial increase). The greatest investment one can make is into the Kingdom of God, which its business is to provide and minister to the needy and to gather and save lost souls from entering eternal damnation. We should all give without the intention of getting something back. God promises in His Word if we give with a right heart that He will give a greater blessing back to us. God rewards His servants for being good stewards over His money. God wants servants that He can trust with His money and resources, so he can use them as instruments to bless others. In other words, God doesn't mind giving to someone, who He can get it back from. This is how God accomplishes His Kingdom Work here on earth.

Malachi 3:8-11
8 "Should people cheat God? Yet you have cheated me!
  "But you ask, 'What do you mean? When did we ever cheat you?'
  "You have cheated me of the tithes and offerings due to me. 9 You are under a curse, for your whole nation has been cheating me. 10 Bring all the tithes into the storehouse so there will be enough food in my

Temple. If you do," says the Lord of Heaven's Armies, "I will open the windows of heaven for you. I will pour out a blessing so great you won't have enough room to take it in! Try it! Put me to the test! 11 Your crops will be abundant, for I will guard them from insects and disease. Your grapes will not fall from the vine before they are ripe," says the Lord of Heaven's Armies. 12 "Then all nations will call you blessed, for your land will be such a delight," says the Lord of Heaven's Armies.

6. <u>Free time/Recreation:</u> "Too much idle time leads to evil time", a wise mentor once told me. Make everyday as productive as possible. To keep your lifestyle healthy and balanced, each week incorporate the following: physical workout (gym/athletics), education (reading), hobbies (photography, fishing, pets), spiritual (church, Bible study, prayer), community outreach/volunteering (volunteer in the soup kitchen, visit the elderly, or be a mentor or big brother to an at-risk youth), personal development (if you are an artist, work on your craft during your free-time, take classes, enter contests and exhibits), entertainment (movies, bowling, fishing).

Read and gain a deeper appreciation about the world and the Holy Bible by educating yourself about what's going on in your community, country and world. Reading will help you become a better conversationalist and improve your I.Q according to the experts. I have a friend who is extremely knowledgeable about current events going on in this country and through out the world. He utilizes his wealth of knowledge in his investing because he has profited well off the stock market. His reading habits have given him the advantage of having a global view of the world market. One day he gave me some wise sound advice. He told me one of the secrets of his in-depth knowledge; he reads three magazines faithfully: the Economist, Keplingers and National Geographic, along with listening to news on public radio. He was right. In a short period, my knowledge increased rapidly, and during the process I obtained more in-depth knowledge, faith and appreciation for the Holy Bible. I was now able to gain a fresher perspective and clearer picture on the various beliefs, cultures and prophecies described in the Bible through out the world. At the same time, I also have been utilizing my new global knowledge as an aid in my investing in the stock market.

7. Peer Association: Over and over, I will continue to say, association brings similarities. If you want to be the right person, associate with the right people. The experts say you will be the average of the individuals you hang around. Take a good look at who you hang around, and then ask yourself, "Is this the average I want to be?" If the answer is "no", then take the initiative to create a new positive peer group, which will encourage you to go in a positive direction. You can find a lot of these positive peers during your free-time activities. A wise person creates an environment where there is positive peer pressure and avoids environments where there is negative peer pressure like the plague.

Here is an anointed prayer I received from a ward, given to him by his mother, from her church. This daily prayer has truly blessed me. I believe it will do the same for you (I have modified this prayer a little).

God Bless,

Rayford L. Johnson

Daily Prayer

Heavenly Father, I will now pray in the power of your Holy Spirit, by the authority of your written Word and in the name of your Son Jesus Christ, our Anointed Savior.

I bind, rebuke and bring to no effect: All fear and fear-related spirits, doubts and unbelief's, pride, arrogance, complacency, selfishness, division, discord, disunity, rebellion and witchcraft spirits, disobedience, confusion, disorder, envy, jealousy, gossip, slander, evil speaking and filthy communications out of people's mouths, lying, scorning delaying spirits, slothfulness, lust, gluttony, poverty, greed, the fear of lack, harassing and tormenting spirits, addicting spirits, thieving spirits, obscene spirits , seducing spirits, false teachings and gifts, manifestations of lying signs and wonders, spirits of the Anti-christ , and all occults.

I break all curses that have been placed and break the power of negative words and attitudes going out of the mouths of the people. In the name of Jesus, I destroy all generational curses and diseases. I render useless all prayers not inspired by the Holy Spirit, whether psychic, soul force, witchcraft, counterfeit tongues, or prayers out of ignorance that have been placed against me.

I loose God's will in my life and, His blessings of prosperity, deliverance, healing and salvation, in the name of Jesus. My steps are ordered by the Lord. The Holy Spirit leads me into all truth. I discern between the righteous and the wicked, between those that serve God and those that don't.

I take authority over this day, in Jesus name, that it is prosperous for my soul, body, spirit and finances. I plead the blood of Jesus over every area of my life. Let me walk in your love and show forth your glory. I thank you Lord for your righteousness. I thank you Lord that I have a God kind of faith an ever increasing, limitless faith.

I pray for the ministry you have called me to be a part of and to walk in. I thank you for the financial support to do the work unhindered by lack. I thank you for help to assist in the work. For intercessors to hold the ministry up in prayer at all times, we stand firm untied in spirit and purpose, working side by side, centering in on the Gospel work. We follow after righteousness, godliness, faith, love, patience, meekness and long suffering.

I put on the full armor of God according to Ephesians 6:14-17. " No spirits of retaliation can come against my family, my possessions, my investments, nor me. When trouble comes, it will not see me, my family or those on my prayer list, for we are hidden in the shadow of God's wings and covered with the blood of the Lamb."

In Jesus name, Amen...

"Father as a Pastor"

I have six older siblings, two sisters and four brothers, two of which are from my father's side to whom I've never met. Reason is my mother killed my biological father when I was three years old. My father was a very abusive man and from what I've been told was somewhat a drug addict. Anyway my mother killed (stabbing him three times) because he threatened to kill us (me and my brother) and her if she did not agree to his ways. See my father was a control freak and didn't want my mother to socialize and have friends. Basically never to leave the house and my mother wasn't having that. She was up until the day he threatened to kill us and the attempt to come through with his threat, which cost him his life. I wish things didn't end up that way, but unfortunately they did, and my father died and my mother was given 12 months for manslaughter on the account of self defense. During the time of my mothers incarceration, there was an issue of who would have custody of me and my older brother. Me and my brother have different fathers it really wasn't a question of who would take care of us seeing that his father was still alive and a pastor, well deacon at that time or maybe minister, well something like that. Well after me and my brother testified as good as we could on my mother's behalf, my brother's father was given custody of me who then was known to me as my surrogate grand father, but quickly came to be my father. Life with my brother's father was somewhat boring. See my "popa" was a very, very religious man in Christ, who believed without any doubt in God and the truth and tried his hardest to persuade or shall I say force me and my brother to believe and accept Jesus, at a young age, which was his biggest mistake, because it caused both of us to rebel or rather stay away from church at the end.

Let me explain. My pop had an obsession with church that is the only way I can describe it. Me and my brother went to school Monday Friday in church. The same church we attended Monday Friday night as well as Saturday revival and Sunday's service. This was an on going daily thing until my mother returned home from jail. I loved pops and never hold that against him cause I know he did it out of love, the good thing is almost every church in the Bay Area and some in Sac knew me from when I was young and my brother and pops. So that's cool, not to mention when ever I do go to a church that he has preached in I get some weird type of attention especially from the females around my age. Anyway when my momma came home I was gratefully given back in her custody as well as my brother. My mom tried to get us to church at least every other Sunday, but eventually stop trying. Growing up with my mom I hate to say, " made me extremely rebellious as a teenager. See me and mother are exactly alike and that's not a very good thing. She thought that what she did was alright and I thought she was a pain in the a*s, but I loved her to death and extremely grateful for her life (believe it or not) any way, I started getting into an abundance of trouble so fast it finally added up and after my second visit to the hall I was introduced to CYA. Shortly after my pops passed my brother never really was a troublemaker and is the good boy out of us all. He took his father's death harder than I did. Forgive me for not grieving. I actually look at it as a blessing, he was sick and is in the place he knew he would always be. A place for sure without any doubt that his soul resides, Heaven. See even though I didn't remain a church go er, I am still very Christian. I just choose not to accept the knowledge that I have, because I am not ready to see the "truth" of the whole matter, it frightens me. Did I make myself clear when I stated the "truth". I know what exists and what is the truth. But, I cannot and will not accept it in till I am fully ready to dedicate. All I can do is wait and ask God for patience and hopefully it just won't be too late.

"It's not easy to change"

I do not consider myself to be a gang member. When I was younger there was a group of people I hung out with. We did do some crimes together, but we didn't have a certain group who was our enemy, so we never set out to hurt people. We shared the same views and basically hung out together. I did not get my beliefs from these people, but they did support them. I grew up around my own race and established my views from my family as I was growing up. And since I grew up around my own race these views became stronger. I started going to jail from an early age and learning the jail house mentality, which contributed to these views even more. So basically what it comes down to is I was taught to think a certain way all my life and it's not easy to change something like that, especially in this type of setting. I have, however, matured a lot and have learned to not let my views affect other people. I give respect where it is due and I have an open mind to others views.

"The Life of a Miscreant"

We are juvenile delinquents, hoodlums, gang bangers, drug dealers. We come from various backgrounds ranging from rich to poor, functional and dysfunctional families. We are black , white, brown and yellow. Some of us were raised in a world of religion: Catholic, Christian, Muslim, Buddhist, Baptist or Methodist and some of us were raised atheist. Yet we all have one thing in common: at some point in our life we broke the law and were caught. Some of us were convicted of felonies and sent to CYA, some were let go on probation are back in society portraying the same behavior prior to getting arrested. What are the reasons for these immoral acts? Why continue living life as a criminal? You will soon have your answer.

You see, we are young when we develop our "bad habits". Most of us had no guidance or sense of direction in our lives. So therefore, it is inevitable that we acquire a life of misconduct. We simply followed the examples given to us by those unforgiving streets. But this alone doesn't justify our actions, does it? Oh, no, it goes deeper than this. Some of it has to do with peer pressure. Some can even say it's hereditary. Within the last decade and a half, scientists have conducted research to ascertain if criminal and violent behavior are passed on through generations of family members. Whether their theories are accurate or irrelevant, they many be true in a sense, but not likely.

Juvenile miscreants, like me, totally demolish their theory that criminal and violent behaviors are hereditary. I myself came from a middle class family. Although I wasn't raised by

my parents, my grandparents instilled in me a sense of direction and taught me right from wrong, polite and impolite, moral and immoral. They introduced me to religion, which was supposed to be a frame of reference to show me the ideal lifestyle and set me on the path of "righteousness". They worked hard to show me that there are rewards from being kind and considerate. They stressed the importance of education. Never pushing too hard but keeping a firm grip on my activities. They supported me at my football games and wrestling matches, and they came to my school concerts to watch me play the drums. I was not spoiled with materialistic stuff, I was spoiled with love and attention. Their affection for me was obvious. So how did I go wrong?

The reason a kid like me gets into trouble is merely curiosity and the rush of adrenaline. Who hasn't gotten into trouble as a child? I guess some kids perpetuate their lifestyles as criminals a bit more than others. Our indulgence in crime becomes addictive. We begin as thieves, stealing candy and toys. Then some of us get introduced to drugs and figure we need money to buy materialistic things. Better clothes, jewelry and more drugs. Why more drugs? To sell of course. It beats robbing people, so we think it all ties in. You meet the wrong people, join a gang and that's where your old world ends and new one begins.

At this point, we are uncontrollable. Family begins to wonder why you stay out so late. You begin lying to them. You stop caring how much you are loved because you have your homies who you think love you. You want to prove yourself not only as "down for the homies" but your importance as a young man. In school you pick fights, get suspended, then stop going to school altogether. You hang out, do drugs, drink beer, go out at night and shoot off a gun your homie stole from his dad and at this point you think you're invincible until you end up drawing the last straw with the police.

So now you're locked up. This isn't your usual 1 night, 1 week, 1 month stay. You go before a judge and he gives you 4 years! You think to yourself", are you serious?". But eventually you begin to accept it. You still have your homies who got locked up before and after you. But now you can't party any more. Can't steal, can't do drugs together. What do you do? The only thing you can do, gang bang and fight for a reputation as a tough guy.

By this time some type of hatred has been embedded inside you. You tell yourself it wasn't your fault that you got locked up and begin pointing the finger. Barely a week into your commitment you start to become anxious at what you might do for the next 3 yrs. 11 months and 3 weeks. You began to stress out. All of a sudden you miss being home when at the time you spent your whole days roaming the streets. You think you're the only one who has a right to be mad at the world. But unfortunately, every single inmate feels the same way. No one is capable of adjusting to each others emotional tribulations. You become very irritated over little things. He keeps staring at me; he scuffed my shoe; he bumped into me without apologizing. Next thing you know you lash out and fire(assault) on the next guy who said the wrong thing.

The funny thing about fighting is that for most inmates, it's like a drug. Violence brings adrenaline; adrenaline brings you the release from reality. It's an escape route you take so you don't have to confront the issues you were sent to jail for like stealing, gang bangin, doing drugs, and the like. And now people notice you ain't no "sucker fish" and began to respect your mind." Now all you care about is maintaining your image. The abusive talk and fighting never stops. But little by little you start to realize it's only a temporary escape, on the spot pleasure. Staff start to confront your ill behavior, now staff is the enemy for trying to do their job. But you don't see it that way.

It takes about 3 years to realize you need to change your act and then it takes about another year and a half to actually do something about it. This is if you have a conscience. You began to realize that it's you who has to adjust not the staff, not your family. You find other things to do to occupy yourself other than fighting. I workout, read, and do school work to cope with time. Every now and then you write your family. You set goals to obtain for when you get out. Regardless under

the circumstances of confinement, you have to put up with daily occurrences: strip searches, one hour out of your room, lack of food you get, people talking trash to you because they had a bad day.

Now the only difference is that you've developed some self control. You have values all of a sudden. You realize how important your family is, how important your freedom is. You think of ways to keep you from getting locked up again, and what got you locked up in the first place. By this time you realize you're a young adult and hold more responsibilities when you get out. Now all of a sudden right when your time is up, you decide you want to change your life, be the person your family wanted you to be. But more importantly, you want to be the person you wanted to be which is anything you want, as long as it's not illegal, and won't get you into trouble. It's never too late. The first step toward a positive change is realizing you have issues that need to be altered. And although you are confined physically, your soul is released and runs free. This is the life of a miscreant.

"I learned to hate them for that."

Let's start this essay off by saying that it's evident that I've got a problem being told what to do, especially when I feel that they are telling me to do it because they have authority over me.

Also before I can get to the root of the problem, which would be my problems with authority figures. Since I was small I've had a problem with police and officers of any sort, because they seem to think that they are invincible because of their badge and status that they hold above me and certain groups of people.

Since I was small I've had to deal with authority figures only doing things I didn't like. For example; taking my family and friends to jail or even myself. I learned to hate them for that. You had your gang vs. police shoot outs and when the police shoot my family or homies on top of taking all of us to jail, I gained fear of authority figures. So it's human nature to hate what you fear and can't concur.

Now that I'm in jail, I'm always being told what to do by staff, sometimes teachers and I don't like it and have a hard time accepting it and that causes an NFI (not following instruction behavior report) or other things that staff label not doing what you are told.

"Dogs with dreams"

It's amazing how you people say dogs don't have any dreams. We'll first of all I'm a dog and I have many goals to become someone in life and give birth to many souls..

So I ain't much different from you, in fact we're all the same human beings. It's just that I'm out to do a job and that job is to claim fame.

So don't criticize us because we weren't fed with a silver spoon in our mouth, it's amazing how you people could judge us dogs and still find it hard to realize that we are all the same human beings .it's just that we make decisions in life that lead to mistakes but we get up and try again, and ask for God's sake so remind yourself before you judge a book by its cover to look in side and don't say dogs don't have any dreams, because mine are full of pride.

"I was always with it."

The gang lifestyle was never forced upon me nor was it glamorized in my eyes. The gang lifestyle surrounded me and after a while consumed my whole physical being. The store clerk gangbanged, some of the security at school gangbanged, everyone in my projects gangbanged. We as people are a reflection of our community, a mirror of our environment — for the most part.

I never sought acceptance. I was naturally accepted, so by me getting jumped in or on my hood was just saying, "I've always been from here, but now I'm officially down for the set". After that nothing really changed. I was always 'with it' so I just stayed with the business.

I was looking through immature eyes. Now that I've grown, I've matured in my understanding, but still hold firm to my beliefs. From being locc(d)ed up I have submitted to the "prison politics" in here and although I have matured, I still choose to push my organization and my hood because I do believe in both although it holds ignorance, there is also wisdom.

If I had a chance to leave it all right now, I would decline based on we all have a turning point in our lives and 'we" are the ones, the only ones that can make that change. When my turning point comes then I will consider it, then until that point in my life comes I am a dedicated soulja to the cause and loyal to my homies.
Mad A#% Cripin'

"Why I'm in?"

Coming from a one parent family I turned to the streets for what you'd call a father figure. Therefore "gangstas" and "thugs" became my role models; they took me in without a hesitation. They taught me what I needed to learn in order to survive in the ghetto streets. I continue to strive because it's all too familiar to me; it's what I know best. In some odd form the streets are "homey" to me. I was once taken in by "my people" when I asked for guidance and now it's my turn to do the same to those in need.

"In a way, this YA saved my life"

I didn't have nobody at the house putting pressure on my back talking about you better go to school. My mom was doing her own thang. The only person that was trying to get me on the right track was my daddy, but based on he didn't stay with us it was kind of hard to keep up with me, but until this day, I still remember him coming to the house when I'm not at school and trying to wash my mouth out, like that was gonna really do something.

I remember being young and seeing one of the neighborhood drug dealers counting his money sitting on a clean as# car surrounded by hell of females, that's when I told myself I want to be just like him. That was fifteen years ago, now looks where I'm at.

The environment I live in, it's hard to make it without doing something negative, based on you ain't seeing too many people waking up early to go to work, I'm surrounded by dope fiends and bums and high school drop outs and ex convicts. In a way this YA saved my life.

I look at it like this, why should I work 9 to 5 and only get $300 to $400 dollars a week when I can make that in two or three hours. I knew I was doing wrong and one day I would get caught but that's life. Everything you do in this world is taking chances.

Most people out there that do criminal stuff don't have to do that. They just want to do it for the f*#k of it. Sometimes it makes you feel good when you take something from a person when you have a gun cause somebody took something from you with a gun so it's like a favor for a favor.

Everybody wants to have a family a nice car and house but do you have a nice paying job for all that cause drug money can't do it. You might get it all but soon as you get caught and everything is in your name, the police gone take it. I know based on I seen it happen to a couple of my uncles.

"I didn't come up in a dysfunctional home"

I'm a nineteen year old Mexican that grew up in Southern California. I lived in a middleclass neighborhood in the city of Santa Ana. I didn't come up in a dysfunctional home, my parents or none of my family members are gang members. I began to like gang members at a very early age. My house was across from a park so when I came out of school I went home. Both of my parents held fulltime employment so then I would go to the park and hang around my older homies, I liked their style they would always have drugs, guns, money and people were scared of them, so as time passed I knew a few of them pretty good. I learned how to play handball so my interactions with them grew, I got older and they gave me a nickname. I began dressing like them and sometimes they would give me beer. Then later on I got jumped in and I was one of them. I felt comfortable being around all the homeboys, I did a lot of things and gained my respect.

"I felt like I was part of the family that I didn't have at home"

I was born to parents who were gang members in 1975. My first memory of being exposed to gangs was when I was about 4 years old, I can remember being at a park in Sacramento with my mother, father, and some of their friends. While we were about to leave, a diesel truck drove through the parking lot. The driver of the truck said something out of his window to my father. My father responded by jumping on the truck and pulling the driver out and started to beat the driver in the middle of the parking lot along with some of my father's friends. After they pulled the driver from the truck some guys jumped into the truck and drove off in it.

Since that incident I can remember many more like it. Growing up I began to look up to other people who did negative things like victimizing people. I first joined a gang in 9'. Once I joined the gang I felt like I was part of a family that I didn't have at home. My mother was into drugs and my father was locked up in prison almost all of my life. My father being locked up left me and my brother without any type of positive role model in the household. In order to fill that void I looked towards gangs and other older gang members for role models.

While I was in the gang, I was exposed to more negative behaviors like drugs, sex and doing time. Back when I was in the gang, our idea of having a good time was to get high and look for trouble. At the time, I didn't realize that self destruction was the only road I was headed for by choosing to involve myself in the gang lifestyle. Being in the Youth Authority and participating in treatment groups has shown me that being a gang member and choosing to live that lifestyle leads to nothing but negative consequences like being a drug addict, locked up in prison or worse.

"Who Cares?"

Who cares out there? I'm not sure anyone cares what happens to someone with the mentality of a thug truly, to every person out there do you care? Not to disrespect anybody because some do care, but with the eyes of pain in these insane times I see more hate than love. Because, I'm not wanting nor willing to change. Some of the aspects of myself.

I see mamas out there leaving their babies behind so they can kick it with us thugs. Some of us just don't care whether these mamas get back to their babies to give them love and care: But aren't we the ones that created these lil' ones just yesterday?

It seemed I was living-n- a lonely place; but sooner or later I realized that these bullets will dissipate and all that will be left is my children with rage, filled with colors that are war paint. Filling their daddy's shoes, singing the county blues that they give us unlikely to survive past the age of twenty five because we have the attitude to "ride or die", and stay high, while we try to survive.

But why? In the beginning I asked who cares out there, but who cares in here? Inside my here temple seems like a black hole that sucks up love from somewhere above, but it keeps being replanted to satisfy my trick habits. Care some do care and to me the some counts because even though I was deprived their love shines deep inside.

This here goes out to all the homeboys and homegirls as well as my family that was here for me during my hard times for keeping my head up so I could shine like the brighter star I am. I'm grateful to have y'all in my life. And also to my sister ------, I mess you dearly and I'll always cherish the memories of me and you together. I luv you sis, for life!!

"I wanted and enjoyed being seen as an animal."

Because of the way I and my peers saw ourselves, I didn't care about what happened to others, I wanted and enjoyed being seen as an animal. I t gave me an edge and power that I had not know before. My relationship with women varied depending upon how I meet her and who she was. Because of my activities I scared a lot of women away and the other that did stay wanted and enjoyed the way I was. They wanted to be with someone they thought people knew as hard or crazy. So they were there for nothing but sex and recognition. But because of my activities I hurt my mother and my family and I even drove some of their friends away and hurt myself in doing so.

"8-Day's of Stress"

I've got eight days left to this place they call CYA. But instead they should call it "the house of jokes", because that's what it really is. Right now I'm stuck on a lifetime decision that will mold my future one way or the other. One way I could go is, go get high, start selling that drug I love so much, that good old methlcrank. I have learned more scams to breaking the law then I wish to admit. From white collar crime to credit card and check fraud, from internet hack sites to cooking almost every drug there is. If I take the route I'm not going to nickel or dime I'm going to sell hundreds of pounds I will become a cartel, a known drug lord, I probably won't even live in the U.S. and if my day comes when the law says no more, no more drugs into the country, no more illegal weapons, that is the day that law will have to take a human life, my life, because I will be ready to take their life or anyone at that matter who tries to stop me, because I refuse to go back to a jail setting. I rather die then go back. The other way I could go is get out and have a simple life. Let me explain, I want to get out and get into weight lifting and mountain biking. I want to be a healthy eater, get into boxing and learn how to salsa dance and learn to do the tango and other dances. I want to support my own self to be my own man. So like I said, I have two choices, live a simple life or become a millionaire cartelling over night or die trying. I've got eight days left.....

<u>The Mission</u>
Conclusion

I pray that those who have read this book have internalized and developed the skills of the four principles I discussed in the introduction: Awareness- how to identify thug mentality; Knowledge- to gain a deep understanding of it; Wisdom- and how to apply the knowledge; and a desired Mission- to enlighten the growing multitudes lost in the spiritual darkness of the thug culture with the previous three principles.

I want to take some time to clarify the purpose and mission of this book. I didn't write this book just for it to be a "good read." The interviews I conducted with the wards that are contained in this book are not to sensationalize but to bring clarity (clearing up the misconceptions) and to validate the information presented. Also the interviews were placed here for other gang members to see their rivals, just not as rivals but as individuals with real emotions, dreams, heartaches like themselves. Gang members have conveyed to me the idea that it's a lot easier to kill a rival – when they're viewed as just a rival – but it's a lot harder to pull the trigger when they see their rival as a real person who might have gone through or come from a similar life experience. After reading some of the stories from his peers in the book, a ward told me the other day that he looks at his rivals in a whole different way now. He was surprised to find out that behind some of those tough masks lay the many insecurities and emotional pains that led him into the thug culture. Many of the wards that I have let read these stories have said similar things. This is part of the mission: to reduce violence by letting gang members see their rivals not as just rivals, but as real individuals as themselves, with families who care for and love them.

The core Mission of this book is to expose the lies of the glitz and glamour of thug mentality, by teaching the four principles in this book: awareness, knowledge, wisdom and mission. Throughout my 16 years of counseling in group homes and correctional facilities, I have discovered that when you teach these principles with the right heart, it will awaken the conscience of an individual and prep their heart for change.

Once the conscience (heart) is awakened, this is when the battle begins within the person's soul. This process can begin a tidal wave of emotions that many feel are too unbearable to deal with (feelings from past sins and painful memories such as abuse from their childhood). Gang members have explained to me that these feelings of overwhelming guilt, shame and emotional pain can be more excruciating than physical pain. So many I talk to have lived a lifestyle inflicting violent crimes on the innocent, some have committed multiple murders for which they were never caught and don't care to remember, due to the nightmare of guilt which is associated with them. They believe that formulating a numb and heartless mindset protects them from experiencing these emotions. They live their lives strategically avoiding and running from God and morality, because just the mere presence of Godliness convicts their conscience. This is why many dive head-on into these evil and rebellious cultures, and are boastful about representing immorality by their foul language, obscene tattoos, substance abuse, etc. This is why "gangsta" music is so embraced, because it condones and praises evil behavior, and is a quick fix for their ailing conscience. So instead of the individual feeling the overwhelming feelings of guilt for their sins (which can lead to repentance), they replace it with a feeling of pride. This is the lie of thug mentality.

The thug mentality mind-set says, "I don't care," as I stated earlier in the book, a famous cliché is "I don't give a f%*@." But the truth be told, they're too afraid to care, because caring means feeling. That's why evil is stylized and embraced within the thug mentality cultures, because the more evil the presence, the further away they feel from guilt-filled memories and feelings. This is why so many are reluctant to give their life to God. The process of repenting and forgiving brings forth emotions that many feel they can't handle. So instead of receiving the awesome love and peace from God through forgiveness and Salvation, they search for peace elsewhere, in substance abuse, sexual perversion and other reckless, thrill-seeking behaviors which only bring forth more guilt once the high is gone.

Yet, thank God there are some willing to take that brave, painful journey to deliverance through Jesus Christ. However, once they arrive there, it is vital for them to connect with a Godly culture that will support them. In world full of cultures which condone sin, where are youth to go for support? This is why many turn back to the immoral cultures from which they came, even though they don't want to, because after they received Salvation, there was no Godly culture in place to take them in.

This is where the church, non-profit organizations and individuals in the community must come into the picture. If this Godly culture is not in place, many will go right back into the thug culture. Yet getting them to accept this culture is easier said than done. As we all know, if a culture is not interesting or exciting, the youth won't embrace it. Earlier I told how I made my transition from an immoral culture into a moral culture as a youth. The culture cultivated by a church youth group had created an exciting atmosphere of love, peace, friendship, music, entertainment, recreation, education and outreach which all pointed back to the Savior, Jesus Christ. Every week I looked forward to the fellowship within that youth group, and some of those friendships are still strong and are a blessing even up until today.

I know from my school-age years, that it's natural for youth to desire to be cool, but the definition of "cool" from the past, which was: smooth, laid back, calm under pressure, stylish has been redefined –with the help of the entertainment industry – into a word synonymous with prideful and evil behavior. Many of these popular cultures now define "cool" as being thuggish, "gangsta," eccentric, conceited and sexually promiscuous. My mission is to assist in re-creating and promoting cultures that will re-define "cool" as being morally good, fun, exciting, loving and stylish (however not in a prideful way). Why can't cool be staying true to your God-given conscience through living a life of integrity, and a willingness to deny selfishness to help a neighbor in need? The problem I see in some non-profit organizations and even churches, is that in a desperate plea to save the youth, many of them have attempted to blend in elements of the immoral cultures into their programs. Believing this to be a good marketing technique for their organization, they have in essence tainted it with not only immorality, but also contradictions.

For example, I have seen well-intentioned organizations put on an after-school dance, in order for it to be supervised closely by adults, assuring there would be no alcohol, drugs, gang activity and sexually promiscuous behavior. But during the party they allow the DJ to play music that promotes sexual promiscuity, drugs, alcohol and violence. Then the following week the organization holds an anti-gang and drugs workshop. I remember a time I went to speak at a Christian high school, and a faculty member – in an attempt to get the students' attention – got up during the assembly and asked for a volunteer to get up on the stage and sing their favorite rap song. An eager youth dressed in gang member attire hopped on the stage, grabbed the microphone out of the faculty members hand and begin to rap a Snoop Dogg song, which was about "slangin" (selling) dope in Long Beach. I couldn't believe that after the staff member had listened to the words that he actually encouraged the rowdy assembly to rap and dance along with the youth, which they did ecstatically.

Sadly it appears to be a growing trend with some churches that as certain types of immoral behaviors or cultures become popular or accepted by mainstream society they jump on the bandwagon. They then attempt to integrate and modify it – or should I say counterfeit it – into the church culture to make church more appealing to the public. Just the other day I was looking at a local church's website that was advertising that they play secular (worldly) music in their church service. The problem with these tactics is that once the world sees the church begin to compromise, the church begins to lose respect and credibility in the eyes of those in the world that are desperately seeking truth. This trend is a great tragedy and a violation of God's law. Let's look at what God told Israel, after he pulled them out of captivity from Egypt. During the time of their captivity many of the Israelites had turned from God to embrace the pagan lifestyle of the Egyptians, but God corrected them, saying:

30 Keep my requirements and do not follow any of the detestable customs that were practiced before you came and do not defile yourselves with them. I am the LORD your God.
Leviticus 18:30

So how do you replace an immoral culture with a positive one?

First, it will take a team effort from individuals with the right heart willing to pull together all their talents and resources. But there is no reason for you to wait to join or assemble a team. Remember that a component of the mission is to "teach-one to teach-one," so start where you are. We all know someone who is being held captive to thug mentality.

It is important to spend time in prayer, in order to obtain a clear direction for your mission. Here are some ideas I believe God put in my heart regarding methods for promoting a revolution for an exciting and Godly culture that youth will be drawn to embrace through the Holy Spirit.

Create Public Service Announcements: make them interesting, funny, scary (example: dangers of drugs and gangs) and cool. What can be used as a PSA? Posters, commercials, plays, movies (short films to be broadcast on websites like YouTube.Com), websites, and podcasts. What's so great about the Internet is that you can take this message in these formats worldwide in a matter of minutes. Other effective methods are clothing (with positive mission statements), art, music, dance (praise dance), sports camps, community functions and workshops.

In the facility where I work, the wards and I just completed a short film in honor of Victims Week. We all had a lot of fun putting the project together. At the same time, some marketable job skills were taught to them, such as script writing, digital editing, music, videography, computer graphics and theatre. However, most important was the gratifying feeling we all had in putting out a powerful message against gang violence. If I get permission from my institution, I will place the movie in front of a worldwide audience on YouTube.Com.

Who must get involved? Community and religious leaders, teachers, mentors, organizations, businesses, schools, churches, students, law enforcement, athletic coaches, etc. I encourage more non-profit organizations (churches, job placement agencies, living assistance programs, vocational schools) aimed at reducing crime to get more aggressive against this thug mentality. For example, we need more volunteers and mentors going into the prisons, juvenile halls and group homes. Many assume that once inmates or those in youth or rehab placements come to the end of their stay, they're just going to walk through the door of these non-profit agencies. Most of the individuals don't know about these organizations, and if they do, the "streets" often sidetrack them before they reach the door. That's why it's important for organizations to make their presence known and become a part of the planning stage of these individuals' transition back into the community.

I think about the multitude of non-profit and religious organizations out in the community, the majority of which are rarely or never seen within the correctional facilities. Visiting those in prison is one of the commandments in the Bible.

34"Then the King will say to those on his right, 'Come, you who are blessed by my Father; take your inheritance, the kingdom prepared for you since the creation of the world. 35For I was hungry and you gave me something to eat, I was thirsty and you gave me something to drink, I was a stranger and you invited me in, 36I needed clothes and you clothed me, I was sick and you looked after me, I was in prison and you came to visit me.'

37"Then the righteous will answer him, 'Lord, when did we see you hungry and feed you, or thirsty and give you something to drink? 38When did we see you a stranger and invite you in, or needing clothes and clothe you? 39When did we see you sick or in prison and go to visit you?'

40"The King will reply, 'I tell you the truth, whatever you did for one of the least of these brothers of mine, you did for me.'

41"Then he will say to those on his left, 'Depart from me, you who are cursed, into the eternal fire prepared for the devil and his angels. 42For I was hungry and you gave me nothing to eat, I was thirsty and you gave me nothing to drink, 43I was a stranger and you did not invite me in, I needed clothes and you did not clothe me, I was sick and in prison and you did not look after me.'

44"They also will answer, 'Lord, when did we see you hungry or thirsty or a stranger or needing clothes or sick or in prison, and did not help you?'

*45"He will reply, 'I tell you the truth, whatever you did not do for
one of the least of these, you did not do for me.'
46"Then they will go away to eternal punishment, but the righteous
to eternal life."*
Matthew 25:34-46

I challenge not only on the non-profit organizations, but also you
and the individuals within the community to act on this mandate:
those who worry and complain about the rebellious youth and crime
after reading the newspaper or watching the news, but never take
action. As they say, "If you're not part of the solution, you're part of
the problem," and the problem truly is when those in society sit back
and watch and hear about all the crime, yet decide to do nothing. A
good illustration was in the movie Spider Man, when Peter Parker
(Spiderman) knowingly allowed a criminal to go free for selfish
reasons. Unbeknownst to him, that same night the criminal he didn't
apprehend would kill his Uncle Ben during a carjacking. Parker,
tormented with the memory of this guilt, vowed to make amends
for his irresponsible and reckless decision that night by becoming a
crime-fighter for all humanity.

All of us are capable of doing something against the epidemic
of thug mentality (especially now that you have learned the four
principles). To continue do nothing is to commit the same travesty
Peter Parker did.

I pray that those with the love and courage to take on this mission
will have the mind-set to take the four principles in this book, to
"teach-one to teach-one." This will keep this curative cycle alive,
creating a new cultural foundation of divine truth and salvation
through Jesus Christ, which in turn will give birth to peace, love,
hope, purpose and joy in the lives of many.

God bless you,

Rayford L. Johnson

If this book has been a blessing to you, your feedback and testimonies would be greatly appreciated.

Email: info@thugexposed.com

Book Notes, Photo Gallery, Resources and more...
Go On-line at:
www.thugexposed.com